The Making of the Middle Ages
Liverpool Essays

The Making of the Middle Ages
Liverpool Essays

edited by

Marios Costambeys, Andrew Hamer and Martin Heale

LIVERPOOL UNIVERSITY PRESS

First published in 2007 by
Liverpool University Press
4 Cambridge Street
Liverpool L69 7ZU

British Library Cataloguing-in-Publication data
A British Library CIP record is available

ISBN 978-1-84631-068-3

Typeset in Sabon by XL Publishing Services, Tiverton
Printed and bound in the European Union by Bell and Bain Ltd Glasgow

Contents

Preface

This volume arises from a series of lectures organized by the Liverpool Centre for Medieval Studies and sponsored by the University of Liverpool. Both that series and this book were conscious responses to the approach of the 800th anniversary of the traditional foundation date of the city of Liverpool. The theme was chosen to reflect this commemoration of a medieval event. Liverpool is not a medieval city, but it is a city in which the study and influence of the middle ages has often flourished, and it was this aspect of the city's culture, as well as its thirteenth-century origins, that we wished to bring out.

It is a ripe time to do so. As several of the contributors to this book point out, medievalism has until recently been one element in a view of the past based on a simple dichotomy of the universal versus the national. To 'universal' have been attached adjectives such as 'imperial', 'patristic', 'classical', while with 'national' have been put 'royal', 'catholic' and 'medieval'. It is only now that the study of medievalism is moving on from these simple oppositions, beyond the notion that to recall the middle ages was to react against the values associated with classicism.

Assessing medievalism on the regional level is valuable precisely because it reveals how it blended with other cultural influences under those particular conditions. As is obvious to every visitor, the classical and the medieval co-exist in Liverpool. Harvey Lonsdale Elmes designed both St George's Hall ('the freest neo-Grecian building in England and one of the finest in the world', according to Pevsner), and the grandly Gothic Collegiate Institution in Shaw Street.[1] These styles exist, moreover, in a different balance from, for instance, the more obviously Gothic Manchester. To take another example, Alfred Waterhouse, that most eclectic of Victorian architects, was born in Liverpool and worked in Manchester, and contributed buildings to both; he was responsible, indeed, for the core university buildings in both cities (both Gothic, and both named after the then queen). How did a figure like Waterhouse, who at one time or another used Classical, Romanesque, Gothic and Italianate styles in his designs, conceive of the middle ages? There is a problem here of periodization, one which will be clear to anyone whose eyebrow raised at the sight of William Roscoe, biographer of Lorenzo de'Medici, in a book on the making of the middle ages. Another Victorian gentleman epitomizes the dilemma. Thomas Hodgkin's first response, as an enthusiastic historian ('amateur' only in the literal sense), to his first sojourn in Italy in 1868 was a series of lectures on Renaissance Italy. The book that followed, however, the still valuable *Italy and Her Invaders*, treated the 'other end' of the middle ages: the fate of this central province of the former Roman empire from the fifth to the ninth centuries.[2] Hodgkin's middle ages, like those of these other figures, were ambiguous, still in a state of formation.

It is these multiple middle ages, their construction and influence, that this book seeks to explore. The original lecture series on which the book is based included contributions too from David Bates and Peter Linehan, and a different offering from Pauline Stafford. These are not here included since they have all appeared in one form or another elsewhere.[3] But we thank warmly not only these but all our lecturers for their contributions to an absorbing and successful series. Issues were raised during its course that led us to invite contributions in addition to the original lectures. Our gratitude is equally great, therefore, to Arline Wilson, Edward Morris and Joseph Sharples, who all agreed to give to this volume the benefit of their particular expertise. Our thanks go also to the Faculty of Arts of the University of Liverpool for its help in covering the costs of the lecture series, to Robin Bloxsidge, Andrew Kirk and all at Liverpool University Press for expediting the book in time for the 2007 celebration, to those archives which kindly allowed permission to reproduce images in their possession, and to all the members of the Liverpool Centre for Medieval Studies for their steadfast support.

Marios Costambeys, Martin Heale and Andrew Hamer

Notes

1 Sir Nikolaus Pevsner cited in J. Sharples, *Liverpool* (New Haven and London, 2004), p. 13. See also Sharples in this volume.
2 T. Hodgkin, *Italy and Her Invaders*, first four volumes published 1880–85; revised eight-volume edition published by Oxford (Clarendon Press), 1892–99.
3 D. Bates, '1066: does the debate still matter?', *Historical Research*, 78 (2005), pp. 443–64; Pauline Stafford's lecture 'Women in the early middle ages: the making and remaking of a Golden Age' was a development of the first section of her 'Women and the Norman Conquest', *Transactions of Royal Historical Society*, 6th ser., 4 (1994), pp. 221–49.

List of Contributors

Pauline Stafford is Professor of Medieval History at the University of Liverpool, and the author of (most recently) *Queen Emma and Queen Edith* (Blackwell, 1997).

T. M. Charles-Edwards is Jesus Professor of Celtic in the University of Oxford and the author of, inter multa alia, *Early Christian Ireland* (Oxford, 2000).

Ian Wood is Professor of Medieval History at the University of Leeds, and author of *The Missionary Life* (London, 2001).

David Matthews is Senior Lecturer in English at the University of Manchester, and author of *The Making of Middle English, 1765–1910* (Minneapolis, 1999).

Helen Phillips is Senior Lecturer in English at the University of Cardiff and the author of *An Introduction to the Canterbury Tales* (Macmillan, 2000).

John Marshall was, until recently, Senior Lecturer in Drama at the University of Bristol and is the author of numerous publications on modern productions of medieval plays.

David Mills is Emeritus Professor of English in the University of Liverpool, and the author of *Recycling the cycle: the city of Chester and its Whitsun plays* (Toronto, 1998).

Andrew Wawn is Professor of Anglo-Icelandic Literature in the University of Leeds, and the author of *The Vikings and the Victorians: Inventing the Old North in Victorian Britain* (Cambridge, 2000).

Edward Morris was, until his retirement, curator at the Walker Art Gallery, Liverpool, and is the author of, most recently, *Public art collections in north-west England: a history and guide* (Liverpool, 2001).

The Making of the Middle Ages

Arline Wilson is Lecturer in History at the University of Liverpool.

Joseph Sharples is a Research Fellow in the School of History, University of Liverpool, and the author of the Pevsner Architectural Guide to Liverpool (Yale UP, 2004).

Editors

Martin Heale is Lecturer in Medieval History at the University of Liverpool, and the author of *The Dependent Priories of Medieval English Monasteries* (Woodbridge, 2004).

Andrew Hamer is Lecturer in English at the University of Liverpool, and the co-editor of *Wulfstan's Canon Law Collection* (Rochester NY, 1999).

Marios Costambeys is Lecturer in Medieval History at the University of Liverpool, and the author of *Power and Patronage in Early Medieval Italy* (Cambridge, 2007).

Introduction

PAULINE STAFFORD

Medievalism is currently defined as the use of and responses to the medieval past, 'at all periods since the sense of the medieval began to develop',[1] and the scholarly study of these responses. It is a topic of considerable contemporary academic interest. In 2004–05 the Liverpool Centre for Medieval Studies organized a series of lectures on this theme, under the general heading of 'The Making of the Middle Ages'. This volume is the result. The original series included lectures considering the making of the middle ages on Merseyside (Wawn and Mills). This theme has been reinforced by three essays specially commissioned for this volume (Wilson, Morris and Sharples). The result is a collection which contributes to the study of medievalism in general, and one which provides a particular, and more unusual, focus on its local and regional dimensions.

Medievalism, as a term, is not new. It was in use in the second half of the nineteenth century, as the first edition of the *Oxford English Dictionary* makes clear.[2] The dictionary defines 'mediœvalism' [sic] as both the 'system of beliefs and practice characteristic of the Middle Ages' and 'the adoption of or devotion to mediœval [sic] ideas or usages', i.e. the middle ages as they were, and the middle ages as utilized by later ages. The dictionary drew its examples from the nineteenth century, a heyday of enthusiasm for the middle ages. At that date the term was used in both senses, as the dictionary's examples indicate; and, as its definitions make clear, medievalism often meant not only a response to the medieval past, but a very positive one.

John Ruskin, for example, in his *Lectures on Architecture and Painting* (1853), saw medievalism as a period in the history of art: 'You have then three periods: Classicism, extending to the fall of the Roman Empire; Mediœvalism, extending from that fall to the close of the fifteenth century; and Modernism'. In 1873 John Addington Symonds referred to Renan's view that 'a sentiment of the infinite' was the chief legacy of medievalism to modern civilization. For Ruskin, Symonds – and Renan – medievalism not only had a chronological signification, but was associated with the aesthetic, spiritual and cultural aspects of a historical period, associations which have persisted. All flagged the middle ages as significant in the development of art, feeling and modes of being and explicitly separated them from the 'modern', and, in Ruskin's case, from 'classicism'. For Ruskin medievalism, the middle ages and their characteristic expressions had a prime place in developments in these areas. The middle ages and medievalism were also implicitly Western. Lord Acton, not among those quoted in the *OED*, echoed Ruskin in seeing the middle ages alongside Antiquity as one of the

> two great principles [which] divide the world and contend for mastery ... the two civilisations that have preceded us, the two elements of which ours is composed. All political as well as religious questions reduce themselves practically to this. This is the great dualism which runs through our society.[3]

Acton did not use the term 'medievalism' but for him, again, the middle ages was characterized by a mind-set and world-view. And it was here a more explicitly Western mind-set and world-view: the middle ages were seen as the source of 'us' (which slips easily into 'the world'), as 'our' origin. That origin was already laden with value, as were other nineteenth-century usages of the term medievalism, though not always so positively. 'It is a pity to have our language interlarded with Orientalisms and Mediœvalisms' wrote a contributor to *The Nineteenth Century* in 1886, associating Orientalism and medievalism in a common condemnation. Such negative views of the middle ages, labelled again as medievalism, exasperated the great English medieval historian, William Stubbs, 'I am sick of hearing about sacerdotalism and mediœvalism from men who scarcely know how to spell the words'.

It was from such references (without Acton) that the *Oxford English Dictionary* derived its meanings of medievalism at the date of that term's initial coinage and popularity. To an eye influenced by modern studies of medievalism and, loosely speaking, by the postmodernism which has informed them, it is remarkable how many of the modern connotations of the word were already present, how many of the themes of recent work were already flagged. The significance of the middle ages in a search for origins is clear. There is a view of the middle ages as 'our' origins, in a way which defines 'us' as much as it does 'the Middle Ages': the study of, or use of, or reference to the middle ages is already implicated in the issue of identity. The middle ages are both positive, the source of much that is best in 'us', and negative, as much an 'other' as the Oriental[4] or the sacerdotal (to which supply, in English context, 'papist'). The middle ages are both what has shaped 'us', by virtue of their place at 'our' roots and origins, and the alien and 'other' against which 'we' are defined. They take their place in a procession of periods of Western civilization and culture alongside, but in distinction from, classical antiquity and modernism. They are viewed, commented on or casually used by a spectrum of people of which the professional historian forms but a part (and the exasperation of their professional ancestor, Stubbs, vis-à-vis the, in his view, uninformed general public strikes a familiar note for early twenty-first-century historians). But whoever viewed or commented on them, the use of the middle ages was never value-free or value-neutral. What characterizes all these uses of the middle ages is the judgement involved, the value whether positive or negative which the middle ages carried. The study of all this is what is now meant by 'medievalism'.

The quotations chosen by the compilers of the *Oxford English Dictionary* linked medievalism especially with the cultural and the religious, with art, language and literature. The bulk of recent study of medievalism, consciously so defined, has continued to be concerned with these latter areas. In the Anglophone world it has become an '-ism' in its own right, allowing medievalism to claim the place in the academic sun which such status accords. Many scholars have been involved in this enterprise, including several of those published in this volume. Leslie Workman, however, has been a driving force. Workman, although a professional scholar by training, developed his interests in this area after the end of his formal professional life;[5] a nice irony given medievalism's constant straddling of the amateur and professional, popular and academic divides. He was the founder of a series of conferences and of the resulting journal, *Studies in Medievalism*, which has appeared annually since 1979. They, in their turn, have led to the production of the bibliography, *The Year's Work in Medievalism*, and, more recently, the Brepols series, *Making of the Middle Ages*. A glance at any of these works reveals the vigour of academic study of this field.

An early concern of that study, and of the journal, was to establish and vindicate 'Medievalism' against, in distinction from and on an equal footing with 'Romanticism' and 'Victorianism'. This underlines how far significant strands of recent work on responses to the middle ages were born in academic cultural and especially literary studies.[6] That location

3

has remained important. It characterizes much of the work in this field, including that by scholars outside the group associated with this influential journal.[7] These disciplinary homebases have ensured that the study of medievalism has been much affected by modern literary and cultural theory. Several of the authors in this volume write from a standpoint informed by – or at least affected by – such approaches (Matthews, Phillips, Mills, Marshall and Wawn). These theoretical standpoints share a common emphasis on constant construction and reconstruction through language and text. They have proved both relevant and fruitful in the study of such a reflexive phenomenon as medievalism.

At their extreme such approaches raise an important epistemological question – what can we really know about the middle ages – a question with important implications for the distinction between medieval studies and medievalism. The earliest answers to it, or rather the disciplinary developments which provided those answers, created a divide which separated the amateur and professional, medievalism and medieval studies. These developments in the study of the middle ages were occurring from the seventeenth century onwards, and especially from the later eighteenth century. The technical, scientific disciplines of, for example, philology, archaeology and history, growing now, were seen to provide routes to greater certainty through their rigorous methods. Their development has been identified as separating the amateur from the professional, the antiquarian from the trained historian, philologist or archaeologist. The process had significant long-term results for disciplinary divides and thus for the specialization whose baleful results Andrew Wawn reflects upon in this volume. Recent work on the antiquarians has questioned the earlier devaluation of them and their activities, largely by making claims about where this group stands in relation to this division.[8] Postmodernist study, however, has questioned the divide itself, and with it the distinction between the detached, objective, scientific professional of medieval studies and the immersed, engaged, unreflective amateur of medievalism. And Kathleen Biddick saw the birth of medievalism, in its pejorative, devalued sense, as a result of the strategies of nineteenth-century academic medievalists, who drew the distinction between amateur and professionalism in their own interests, separating the popular and the academic and labelling the non-scientific as medievalism.[9] Indeed to the radical postmodernist the answer to the question 'what can we know' would be that this is *une question mal posée*, since all accounts of the middle ages are necessarily representations, not reflections of reality.

Given the loosely postmodernist nature of much of the study of medievalism, it is thus no surprise to find that its meaning has recently been enlarged, at the expense of medieval studies. The editorials of the journal *Studies in Medievalism* began with a clear distinction between the academic, scientific nature of 'medieval studies' and 'medievalism', between an academic and, broadly speaking, a popular reception of the middle ages which would have commanded the approval of Bishop Stubbs.[10] But by 1995 its editorial claimed that medievalism included medieval studies.[11] The journal has not been a lone traveller on this path. In 1991 Norman Cantor, a trained professional historian, implicated his fellow medieval historians in the subjective invention of the middle ages.[12] These are questions not merely about what we can know, but also about the classification of knowledge, including classifications which establish hierarchies and canons, and function as part of strategies of power. They have been a central concern of postmodernism since the work of Foucault.[13]

At least one essay in this volume is explicitly concerned with these processes, this 're-organization of knowledge', seen as at work already in the later eighteenth century (Matthews). More generally, the distinction of amateur and professional, the methods and structures within which the latter work, and questions about the results and desirability of such divisions are themes which run through many of these papers (Charles-Edwards, Wood, Mills, Wawn). Few authors in this volume appear to espouse a full-blown postmodernist critique of that division. Few, at least here, confound medievalism and medieval studies or advocate the replacement of questions about what we know with those about the organization and classification of knowledge. But these essays provide a thoughtful consideration of the losses as well as gains of professionalism and its attendant modern academic structures, as well as some rehabilitation of those who have fallen on the wrong side of this divide. They give food for thought on how and when the scientific study of the middle ages has had an impact on more popular perceptions.

If medievalism is 'the study of the responses to the Middle Ages at all periods', that study has not been confined to literary and cultural disciplines, nor to the Anglophone world. 'Mittelalter-Rezeption' is an established interest of modern German scholarship.[14] And, as Wood and Charles-Edwards make clear, Scandinavian, Italian, French, Irish and Welsh scholars – to name only those geographical areas covered by these two essays – have all been active in the field. Nor was such interest born in the last, theoretically driven, decades of the twentieth century. Work, for example, on the use and study of the English middle ages in later periods was well established in the 1950s, 60s and 70s.[15] And such work was far from being confined to the study of England and English responses,[16] or to those concerned with medieval literary and artistic culture. The essays in this volume are not unusual in including the work of historians and historian-philologists alongside that of students of art, architecture and literature.

Medievalism is obviously a part of the general 'use of the past', a phenomenon of whose ubiquity historians are well aware. Medievalism per se, however, cannot exist without the notion of the middle ages. It is dependent on the periodization which distinguishes the middle ages. If the later eighteenth and early nineteenth centuries were important in the separation of amateur and professional, the definition of the middle ages has a much longer history. The creators of medievalism, as of the middle ages, are to be sought in the Renaissance. Renaissance writers defined the middle ages, and did not flatter them in the definition. They saw the middle ages as a dark period lying between the classical age and their own revival of it. Liverpool's William Roscoe commenting on the 'sleep of the human intellect' during the middle ages revealed a typical Renaissance disdain (Wilson). Such definition is a reminder of the other strand of thinking about and periodization of the European past, namely classical antiquity, and how far the middle ages were, from their first definition, seen in contrast with that. A strong current in Western thinking has long seen classical antiquity as at least one of the origins of Western civilization. For Acton, as for many others educated within the Western tradition, European origins lay as much in the classical world as in the middle ages, and the lure of the classical past was very apparent during the middle ages themselves. Later valuations of the medieval have often faced the tension between classical and medieval which derives from these periodizations. And revaluations may take the form of seeing the middle ages as continuations of the classical past or of seeking common origins for both (Wood, Charles-Edwards).

'Origins' is the key notion here, and a complex one. It may denote a stage of development, a 'childhood', with all childhood's contradictory meanings;[17] 'us' in all our potential and/or innocence (Phillips), yet also that stage of crude even primitive beginnings which the adult 'we' leave behind. Origins are where 'we' came from, what we 'first were', offering particularly convincing answers to deeper questions about who 'we' are and what we should be. The past is a source of identity and legitimation, most powerfully of both combined: that power is never felt so strongly as when the past in which both identity and legitimation are sought is seen as 'origins'. But where are origins to be located? They speak deeply to the sense of the natural – what we first were, what we truly are – and therein lies much of their seduction. Yet they are no more natural and obvious than any other division of the past. Origins are themselves chosen, constructed and contested. Arguably, they are to be sought as early as possible: the earlier the better; the older the more venerable, the more powerful. But lines are always drawn, and specific origins defined. In this use of the past as in all uses of the past, the origins which define us are themselves defined by us.

A Renaissance, self-definedly republican, Italian city such as Florence found its own 'original' past in classical, republican antiquity. German humanists imbued with the same Renaissance love of history, sought theirs elsewhere – in Tacitus' *Germania*.[18] In each case fifteenth- and sixteenth-century self-perceptions were critical. Who is searching, and when and why, always play a part in defining the past which is found and used. Crudely speaking, for a Europe of peoples, nations and eventually nation-states, and from at least the sixteenth century if not before, the unity of the Roman Empire, and thus classical antiquity, offered a less usable past than the diversity which was perceived to have succeeded it. It was here that the foundation of a more varied range of political units could be seen. Some thinkers in Renaissance Italy might be defining the middle ages, and negatively. But other uses of the past were valuing them, or at least parts of them. This applied especially to what we would now term the early middle ages, which saw the arrival of groups who came to be seen as both the death knell of Roman unity and the founders of modern peoples. Origins were thus to be found in the forests of Germany as well as on the sun-drenched shores of the Mediterranean, in a post-Roman, or medieval, as much as in a classical world. The definition of these dual Western origins – classical and medieval – have left their mark. The middle ages are usable both in distinction from classical antiquity, and as its continuation. Teasing out the reasons for such choices and interpretation of them have much to tell us (Wood). The implication of the middle ages in definitions of national identity was to have a sadder legacy.

The term middle ages was coined by Renaissance scholars. But a very similar chronological period was also defined in parts of Europe by another phenomenon of the sixteenth century, namely the Reformation. Not necessarily initially labelled as 'the middle ages', the pre-Reformation centuries were nonetheless separated from and characterized by contrast with the reformed, Protestant present. This was the middle ages as the Catholic past, with varying supplementary meanings as papal, sacerdotal, ritualist, superstitious or idolatrous, depending on the Protestant temper of the beholders. There was, however, a paradox. The middle ages, or at least the post-Roman centuries, were seen as a significant point of national origins for many; yet the Reformation, itself implicated in processes of national definition, threatened to blacken them in Protestant Europe. England provides an example both of the conundrum, and of one particular resolution of it. In England the middle ages and medieval could simultaneously carry Catholic, papist and thus un-English meanings, yet also be seen as identifying, if not legitimating, national origins. This unarticulated conundrum was resolved to some extent by a significant division within the English middle ages, between the period before and after the Norman Conquest of 1066. This 'French' conquest conveniently separated a native, 'pure', vernacular – and thus fully, and usably, English – early middle ages (here labelled Anglo-Saxon) from an adulterated, monkish if not papist, Latin, or even French high middle ages. Anglo-Saxon England was thus available for definition as proto-Protestant, as proto-constitutional, even as proto-feminist – depending on the perspective of the viewer – while the high middle ages in England, at least, carried a more potentially tainted legacy. This English example is a warning not to assume that the 'middle ages' and thus 'medieval' will always be interpreted as a unity.

As with the medieval/classical antithesis, the divisions between a Catholic middle ages and its Protestant successor were far from simple – and many of the essays in this volume show how far the negative meanings of a Catholic middle ages in Protestant England could be happily ignored. But the confessional changes of the sixteenth and seventeenth centuries defined the middle ages in general as 'Catholic', and this persisted and long continued to have an impact on their potential meanings. For the patrons of late eighteenth- and early nineteenth-century Merseyside, this Catholic, confessional meaning still attached to styles and objects identified as medieval (Wilson, Morris, Sharples). The tale of the Chester Plays' date and origin and the construction of their medievalness, so skilfully traced by David Mills, started with the defensive pronouncements of their sixteenth-century revivers addressing a Protestant critique.

To understand the meanings of 'medieval' and its first uses, it is necessary to go back at least to the Renaissance. But, with one or two exceptions which reach back to that date, the essays in this volume are largely concerned with the period from the eighteenth century onwards. That is no accident. The eighteenth century was a great age of interest in the middle ages. Antiquarian and popular interest flourished. In the 1750s

P.-H. Mallet's influential *Histoire du Danemarck* was published in French. This picture of the early medieval North was translated into English in 1774 by T. Percy as *Northern Antiquities*. Percy's own *Reliques of Ancient English Poetry* had already appeared in 1765. Macpherson's *Ossianic fragments*, the manufactured Celtic early medieval epic published in 1760, took Europe by storm. These works, and their publication successes, are one indication of the appetite for things medieval in the eighteenth century. That enthusiasm was widely shared and at a popular level (Matthews). Enlightenment philosophical history gave its own boost to the study of the middle ages. In its search for a connected account of the evolution of humanity, the medieval period inevitably had its place. This interest reached new heights in the first decades of the nineteenth century. The significance of Walter Scott's novels in Britain, the development of comparative philology, especially in Germany, and the work of the brothers Grimm ushered in the great age of medievalism.

If legitimation and identification are abiding themes in the uses of the middle ages, this eighteenth- and nineteenth-century interest highlights another – nostalgia. Nostalgia encompasses a spectrum of meanings of the past, from the Golden Age, via the World We Have Lost to the Good Old Days.[19] They are united by a common construction of the past – or part of it – as an ideal and idealized place, where all the deficiencies of the present are absent, where all that is desired now is to be found. Among the technical meanings of nostalgia, a longing for home is central. The past becomes the home which has been lost, is sought and which may be recovered. It can be an intensely conservative notion – the past as tradition, a time when all knew their place, of duty and respect.[20] But it also has radical potential, an imagined past in which the equality and justice sought now existed, giving hope and legitimation to those who thus desire merely to restore. As such uses indicate, nostalgia is not separate from legitimation or identity; most uses of the past draw strength of meaning from a broad matrix. But nostalgia was prominent in the medievalism of the late eighteenth century onwards, for a world different from the alienated present of commercial and industrial society.[21] Merrie England was one of the results (Phillips, Marshall).

Among the technical developments in scholarship that characterized the eighteenth- and early nineteenth-century interest in the middle ages, philology must have a central place. Early nineteenth-century advances in the study of language, and especially in comparative philology, are rightly emphasized (Charles-Edwards). German scholarship, exemplified by the brothers Grimm, dominated this field, and the vernacular languages were studied with as much rigour as the classical. Interest in the vernacular was not an entirely new departure. The Reformation had emphasized biblical translation if not rejected Papist Latin. Protestant clerics in England were among the first collectors of vernacular Anglo-Saxon manuscripts. Interest in the vernacular readily combined with interest in peoples, if not nations, and their history; the brothers Grimm collected folk tales as part of their study of the German language. The *Oxford English Dictionary* was a product of the high value placed on the tongue of the people in the nineteenth century.[22] The vernacular and its study was a route back to the origins of peoples (Charles-Edwards, Wood), or to the 'people' unsullied by monkish, Latin (papist) culture (Wawn). The 'people' and their vernacular are not, however, always simply synonymous with the nation. The vernacular could be the tongue of the 'common' people, and share their status: for worse (Mills, Matthews), but also for better (Wawn, Mills).

The fundamental results of the study of philology are still among the most enduring legacies of nineteenth-century medieval scholarship. Philology sought the origins of languages. In doing so it produced affiliations and families, inclusions and exclusions that resonated with nineteenth- and twentieth-century nations and their politics (Charles-Edwards, Wawn, Wood). The history of vernaculars looked back to the medieval past as a critical period in their development. Another link was forged in the chain which could bind the middle ages to national origins and identity, and to the racist ideologies of the nineteenth and early twentieth centuries. The sad history of the twentieth century revealed the dangers of these uses of the past, and produced a historiographical reaction (Wood). The First and Second World Wars proved watersheds in medieval studies, if not in historiography more generally. 'Ethnicity', with its emphasis on the constructed and the subjective, has replaced biological 'race' in the historical lexicon. Nations and national identity are now lively subjects of historical enquiry rather than the unexamined contexts of it. The study of the study of the middle ages has not been immune.[23]

The middle ages have been constantly used and redefined from and in terms of the present – and thus by a series of past 'presents' into which those definitions and uses offer insight. The critical questions here, as in all aspects of the use of the past, are not only 'which present' but also 'whose present'? These are questions of authorship and of authorization, and of audience and reception. They are ones on which modern theoretical studies have thrown considerable light. But the answers also involve money. Who gets to see what past is a question of politics and economics, whether it is a case of the production of nineteenth-century pageants

(Matthews) or late twentieth-century exhibitions (Wood). Large-scale, public recreations of the past must be sponsored and patronized. Who is paying at this level of publication, construction and reception has a significant bearing on which past can be seen. The structures of academic life also come at a price, and are often accessed for payment. Such costs need to be counted (Charles-Edwards), and postmodernist insight into representations and reconstructions must not preclude this more traditional line of enquiry.

These essays were either written or delivered (or both) in Liverpool. Some were commissioned to consider how the Making of the Middle Ages appears when the focus is a region, in this case Merseyside. As Wawn asserts, localism needs no justification. The inclusion of local essays does, however, prompt the question – was there a regional dimension to medievalism, a peculiarly or appropriately Merseyside medievalism? To the sixteenth-century defenders of Chester's plays, their own local past was important, and could be mobilized as a peculiarly strong defence. A local response to a centralizing Reformation is also discernible, albeit in neither case a specific evocation of 'the medieval' (Mills). Some of these essays suggest how far religion played a role in local identity, with the strength of recusant Catholicism of special significance for medievalism (Morris, Sharples). The Irish Sea situation of Liverpool and Merseyside has always shaped its past, and not least its early medieval one when Viking activity was prominent. It is thus no surprise to find an Icelandic scholar calling in on late nineteenth-century Liverpool en route to the Isle of Man (Wawn). And the city's mercantile links may explain some of the interest in the medieval North that Wawn discusses. Wawn sets out to trace an 'emerging medieval consciousness on Merseyside', and, in spite of Vigfusson's obvious doubts, it was certainly there.

Yet in many respects, medievalism appears to have had a faltering and limited history on Merseyside. Architecturally, commercial Liverpool easily appears as a classical, Greek Revival city, with the Gothic appealing rather to manufacturing Manchester, Manchester here as 'Coketown', that symbol of alienated labour that inspired so much Victorian medievalism and related rural – and medieval – nostalgia. Certainly at the beginning of the nineteenth century Roscoe found the model for the Liverpool commercial gentleman in Renaissance Florence, not in the middle ages – though his appeal to the Liverpool merchants to 'protect the arts, [and] the arts will and ought to remunerate you' might have served as an appropriate defence of the middle ages to a recent Education Secretary.[24] Studies of medievalism must take account of absence as well as presence.

There was, however, interest in the middle ages on Merseyside, and tracing it has much to tell us, including, perhaps, something about identity. The male (and they are here all male) elite, merchants and landowners, of late eighteenth- and nineteenth-century Merseyside and Liverpool appear as collectors (Morris), as commissioners of buildings, public and private (Sharples), as antiquaries, amateur and professional scholars (Wawn). What did the middle ages mean to them? What meanings did they draw from that great cultural ragbag? What can their interest in the middle ages tell us about them? Certainly the Catholicism of the north-west found an expression in medievalism. The Catholic Henry Sharples had Pugin build the Gothic Oswaldcroft (Sharples). And Charles Blundell's collection of medieval manuscripts, like his neighbour Scarisbrick's interest in late medieval sculpture and painting, is clearly related to the Catholic meanings of the middle ages in a Protestant England (Morris). Yet the High Anglican Tobin also made one of the greatest of early nineteenth-century private collections of medieval manuscripts, and Blundell's father was one of the most prominent collectors of classical statuary of his age – albeit using papal connections to facilitate the movement of his acquisitions.

The interpretation of such evidence must be handled with extreme caution. How easily can we read 'taste' let alone identity from, for example, choice of architectural style, especially given ideas about the appropriateness of styles for particular types of building, questions of cost and considerations of function and utility (Sharples)? If identity is to be read from such activity, it must be carefully done. Yet the patronage of Heywood seems to shows a complex identity, shifting and developing over his lifetime, revealing different faces to its different audiences, including those of the private and public man. These questions are fraught with problems, not least the danger of over-reading and of ignoring fundamental issues of cost and access, and the essays here rightly offer no easy answers. But one of the many exciting aspects of recent study of medievalism is the insight it offers into identities, not just group identities but individual ones. It has a part to play in the growing interest in the history of the self. The case studies of individual scholars, merchants and collectors present not only additional information on the reception of the middle ages, but tantalizing possibilities for the exploration of identity and its construction and expression.

The middle ages have had many meanings, and have been studied, co-opted and appropriated for many purposes, in many contexts and from many stances – as these essays show. One thing is, however, clear. Whether theoretically inspired or informedly populist (Wawn) medievalism and medieval studies are vigorous. These essays are testimony to that fact.

Notes

1 T. Shippey, in the prospectus to the series *Studies in Medievalism*: www.medievalism.net

2 J. A. H. Murray et al., eds, *The Oxford English Dictionary* (Oxford, repr. 1933), Historical Introduction, Sect. IV, p. viii. The dictionary as a whole appeared between 1884 and 1928. 'M' was published 1904–08.

3 Quoted from an unpublished paper delivered in 1859 by H. Butterfield, *Man on His Past* (Cambridge, 1955), p. 212. The quotation was chosen as a motto by the Conference and Studies in Medievalism, see below.

4 On which, as one of the archetypal 'others' of Western civilization, see E. Said, *Orientalism, Western Conceptions of the Orient* (London, 1979). For Freud's explanation of fear and dislike of the 'other' who is similar to us but in some ways different, see S. Freud, *On Narcissism, An Introduction*, Standard Edition, 14 (1914).

5 R. Utz and T. Shippey, eds, *Medievalism in the Modern World, Essays in Honour of Leslie J. Workman* (Turnhout, 1998), p. 2 and interview with Workman, ibid, p. 441.

6 Ibid., p. 4 and L. Workman, 'Medievalism and Romanticism', *Poetica*, 39/40 (1994), pp. 1–44.

7 See e.g. R. Howard Bloch and S. G. Nichols, eds, *Medievalism and the Modernist Temper* (Baltimore, MD, 1996).

8 R. Sweet, *Antiquaries, The Discovery of the Past in Eighteenth-Century Britain* (London and New York, 2004).

9 K. Biddick, *The Shock of Medievalism* (Durham, NC, 1998), pp. 1–2. On the skills of traditional scholarship, their defence, but also on the need to examine and place them historically, compare A. J. Frantzen, 'Prologue: Documents and Monuments: Difference and Interdisciplinarity in the Study of Medieval Culture', in A. J. Frantzen, ed., *Speaking Two Languages: Traditional Disciplines and Contemporary Theory in Medieval Studies* (Albany, NY, 1991), pp. 32–33.

10 *Studies in Medievalism*, 1.2 (Spring 1982), p. 4.

11 *Studies in Medievalism*, 8 (1995), p. 2 – and cf. 9.1, *Medievalism and the Academy* (1997), p. 2, where the editorial asked rhetorically whether medievalism was the 'poor and somewhat whimsical relation of medieval studies', or whether medieval studies was a facet of medievalism. The answer, by implication, was the latter.

12 N. Cantor, *Inventing the Middle Ages* (New York, 1991).

13 *Power: The Essential Works of Michel Foucault*, ed. J. D. Fabion (Harmondsworth, 2002).

14 See e.g. Joachim Heinzle, *Modernes Mittelalter. Neue Bilder einer populären Epoche* (Frankfurt am Main, 1994), and F. G. Gentry and U. Müller, 'The Reception of the Middle Ages in Germany: An Overview', *Studies in Medievalism*, 3.4 (1991).

15 See e.g. M. McKisack, *Medieval History in the Tudor Age* (London, 1971); C. Hill, 'The Norman Yoke', in C. Hill, *Puritanism and Revolution* (London, 1958), pp. 46–111; A. Briggs, *Saxons, Normans and Victorians*, Historical Association, Hastings and Bexhill Branch, 1966, reprinted in *The Collected Essays of Asa Briggs* (Brighton, 1985–91), II, pp. 215–35.

16 L. Gossman, *Medievalism and the Ideologies of the Enlightenment: The world and work of La Curne de Sainte-Palaye* (Baltimore, MD, 1968); N. Edelman, *Attitudes of seventeenth-century France towards the Middle Ages* (New York, 1946).

17 For some introduction to these see e.g. S. Shahar, *Childhood in the Middle Ages* (London, 1990).

18 J. Ridé, *L'Image du Germain dans la pensée et la littérature allemandes, de la redé-couverte de Tacite à la fin du XVIe siècle* (Paris, 1977); idem, 'Un grand projet patriotique: *Germania Illustrata*', *L'humanisme allemand (1480–1540)*, XVIIIe colloque international de Tours (Munich, 1979), pp. 99–111; L. Krapf, *Germanenmythos und Reichsideologie. Frühhumanistische Receptionsweisen der taciteischen "Germania"* (Tubingen, 1979).

19 C. Shaw and M. Chase, eds, *The Imagined Past: History and Nostalgia* (Manchester, 1989), especially Introduction.

20 See R. Williams, *Keywords* (London, 1976), p. 269.

21 See esp. W. Stafford, '"This once happy country": nostalgia for pre-modern society', in C. Shaw and M. Chase, eds, *The Imagined Past*, pp. 33–46 – quoting William Cobbett in the title.

22 See e.g. the biography of its first editor, James Murray: K. M. Elisabeth Murray, *Caught in the Web of Words, James A. H. Murray and the Oxford English Dictionary* (Yale, 1977, Oxford, 1979), pp. 87–100; and note the insight here into the 'fervent patriotism and zeal for popular education' of the founder of the Early English Texts' Society, Frederick Furnivall.

23 See e.g. S. Berger, M. Donovan and K. Passmore, eds, *Writing National Histories, Western Europe since 1800* (London, 1999); M. Oergel, 'The redeeming Teuton: Nineteenth-century notions of the "Germanic" in England and Germany', in G. Cubitt, ed., *Imagining Nations* (Manchester, 1998), pp. 75–91. For a medievalist's view, see P. Geary, *The Myth of Nations: The Medieval Origins of Europe* (Princeton, NJ, 2002).

24 Alleged remarks of the then Secretary of State for Education, Charles Clarke, in 2003 ('I don't mind there being some medievalists around for ornamental purposes, but there is no reason for the state to pay for them.') acted as grit to Ian Wood's oyster in his own study of the uses of the Middle Ages, of which first fruits appear in this volume.

The Lure of Celtic Languages, 1850–1914

T. M. CHARLES-EDWARDS

In 1853 Johann Caspar Zeuss, from Oberfranken in the kingdom of Bavaria, published in Latin a work of 1163 pages entitled *Grammatica Celtica*; in 1913 a Danish linguist, Holger Pedersen, completed the second and final volume of his *Vergleichende Grammatik der keltischen Sprachen*.[1] These two books were the beginning and the end of the period in which Celtic linguistic scholarship flourished most vigorously outside the Celtic- or recently Celtic-speaking countries; they form the end-points of my essay.[2] About the principal scholars of the period I shall ask two questions: what drew them to work on Celtic and what, more importantly, kept them working in this field even after, very often, their initial concerns had been satisfied.

Celtic came late and hesitantly to the philological feast. In the decade after the Battle of Waterloo the discipline of Indo-European comparative philology was established on the lines which would, with appropriate development, be followed until the present day.[3] The crucial argument was that comparison between languages could lead to proof that they were genetically related provided that, first, isolated comparisons between words were avoided and, secondly, attention was focused on some of the central and relatively conservative parts of a language, such as its pronouns or numerals or kinship terms. If systematic equivalences could be demonstrated in such areas, such as that between English *f* and *th* as against Latin *p* and *t* in, say, *father*: *pater*, then one had secure evidence on which to posit that both descended from a third language. A further crucial weapon in the armoury was to distinguish between inherited elements of the language and borrowings from one language into another; for example, *fame* in English does not have a Latin counterpart beginning with *p*; instead it is derived, *via* French, from Latin *fama*. To confirm equivalences of the *father*: *pater* type, one had to exclude the quite different relationship seen in *fame* and *fama*. Three steps then led to Indo-European, namely to the positing of a language which had once existed in remote prehistory, but which had split up into numerous daughter-languages, just as Latin gave rise not just to Italian but to French, Spanish and the other Romance languages. First, it was shown that the relatively obvious Germanic family was related to Latin and Greek as sister, not as daughter. Secondly, Sanskrit, the ancient sacred language of Hinduism, was shown to be related to the principal European languages or language-families, Greek, Latin, Germanic, and then Slavic. At first it was often claimed that Sanskrit might itself be the ancestor language of Greek, Latin and the rest, but eventually the view prevailed that they were all derived from another, still more ancient language, namely Indo-European, so called because its daughter languages extended from India to western Europe.

In the early nineteenth century this issue of discriminating between native and borrowed elements in a language was what made life difficult for Celtic. No one denied that the Celtic languages were related one to another – that had been established in some detail by Edward Lhuyd in 1707 – or that there were resemblances between Celtic languages and those others which were admitted by competent scholars to belong to the one Indo-European family.[4] Yet the resemblances might be due to borrowing, not to a common inheritance. And one property of the Celtic languages known at that date suggested that they were outside the Indo-European family. Ancient Indo-European languages vary the ends of words, as in Latin *amo, amas, amat*, 'I love', 'you love', 'he loves'. As is evident, modern English is by this standard far removed from the Indo-European type: the independent pronouns, *I, you* (or in parts of the north of England forms of the ancient *thou*) and *he* count for more than the difference between *love* and *loves*. Yet as soon as one goes back to Old English it becomes clear that the language was once highly inflected like Sanskrit, Latin and Greek.

The problem with Celtic at this point was quite simple: in both Irish and the Brittonic languages, Welsh, Cornish and Breton, certain classes of word in particular positions vary at the beginning as well as at the end. The Welsh word *geneth* 'girl' has a plural ending *-od*, as in *genethod*, but when the singular feminine *geneth* is followed by an adjective, the latter changes from its base form at the beginning, not at the end, as in *geneth brydferth* 'beautiful girl', where the initial *p* of *prydferth* is 'lenited' to *b*. This appeared to some to be so fundamental a typological difference that there could be no genetic relationship. On the other hand, James Cowley, a Bristol physician, published a book in 1831 on *The Eastern Origins of the Celtic Nations*, in which he provided solid arguments that Celtic was a branch of Indo-European along with Sanskrit, Germanic, Latin, Greek and Slavic.[5] Cowley's case was rejected by one of the principal German philologists, Schlegel, but was further reinforced by Adolphe Pictet's *De l'affinité des langues celtiques avec le Sanscrit*, published in 1837.[6] At this stage, then, scholarship was in an impasse, with good evidence pointing in two incompatible directions.

The solution came with a work published in 1838 by one of the principal German philologists, Franz Bopp, responding to, and carrying further, Pictet's argument: he showed that lost endings in the immediately preceding word had played a crucial role in causing the puzzling initial changes in Celtic.[7] To take Welsh *geneth* again as our example, the corresponding Gaulish form is attested, although it was not known to scholars of Bopp's generation: *genetta*. An adjective following a feminine singular noun was liable to initial lenition because the most common feminine nominative singular ending had been *-a* and a single consonant between vowels was regularly lenited in both Irish and the Brittonic languages. To an attested Gaulish *genetta daga* (good girl), corresponded Welsh *geneth dda*, where *dd-* stands for a voiced *th* as in English *this*.[8] The very feature which had seemed to put typological distance between Celtic and the Indo-European family now testified to former endings characteristic of Indo-European. This solution of the Celtic problem demonstrated the power of the combined comparative and historical method: by comparing Celtic with hypothetically related languages and by following the historical evolution of the Celtic languages themselves fundamental results were obtained which typological comparison alone could not yield. Moreover, the testimony of the ancient Continental Celtic languages, such as Gaulish, amply bore out the results first obtained by comparison. What is remarkable about Bopp's work is that he was able to find his way to this solution even though he was working from relatively modern forms of Irish, Scottish Gaelic, Welsh and Breton. Even in these, however, the pronouns – a relatively stable part of the vocabulary – seemed fairly obviously Indo-European.

Now, all this, you might think, might well be fun for the philologists but what might it signify for the understanding of human history as a whole? The answer in the middle third of the nineteenth century was that it meant a very great deal: for one thing, ethnology and linguistics went hand in hand, as one can already see in the full title of Prichard's great work of 1831, *On the Eastern Origins of the Celtic Nations proved by a Comparison of Their Dialects with the Sanskrit, Greek, Latin, and Teutonic Languages: Forming a Supplement to Researches into the Physical History of Mankind*. Prichard later published a major work on

The Natural History of Man, in which he argued that the whole of humanity constituted a single species. The new comparative and historical linguistics offered a tool by which a scholar might identify and classify peoples. This was the path along which our first great Celtic scholar of the nineteenth century came to the subject. Johann Caspar Zeuss only achieved a university post towards the end of his career when it was about to be cut short by ill health.[9] When he was still a teacher in what may roughly be compared to a seminary or college of further education he published a major work entitled *Die Deutschen und die Nachbarstämme* (*The Germans and the Neighbouring Peoples*). For him the Germans, the Slavs (or Wends) and the Celts were 'the three great linguistic groups (*Sprachstämme*) in Central Europe'. In the term *Sprachstamm* he combined together the concepts of language (*Sprache*) and ethnicity (*Stamm*, 'tribe' or 'people' conceived as an organic growth). We can now see that this had serious dangers: a shared language and a shared literary culture in that language might indeed be of central importance for nineteenth-century Germans, but it was not of equal importance for all nations. One only had to look a little further south and west, to Switzerland, to see something different; and yet, for men such as Zeuss, Switzerland, as a relatively recent creation, did not have the same significance as the nations of Antiquity, Germans among them. Moreover, Zeuss's methods were, within limits, entirely valid: he could show, for example, that southern Germany was an area in which Celtic- and Germanic-speaking peoples had met and, to some extent, mixed. It was not true to say that where German now ruled, German had always ruled. On the other hand, he could also refute the claims of the so-called Celtomaniacs, who exaggerated greatly the extent of everything Celtic, including settlement. For Zeuss, sound philology provided a rational guide to enable one to steer a course between the Scylla of Celtomania and the Charybdis of Celto-scepticism.[10] To my mind it still does, which is important, since the same tendencies, though in different forms, are all too alive and well.[11]

A further element in the intellectual climate also told in favour of Celtic. This was a period of grand intellectual constructions, including theories about the development of human society as a whole. Since language is central to human culture, no one who wished to trace the development of humanity could hope to succeed without the best linguistic methods. Moreover, since scholars hoped to understand the broad sweep of human history over a long period, comparative Indo-European linguistics in particular, together with its Semitic counterpart, offered one tool which could take one back far into prehistory. It was now evident, for example, that an understanding of the Old Testament would be radically transformed by comparative Semitic linguistics; and that was a matter which concerned not just scholars but all Jews and Christians. So it was that such figures as Marx and Engels and Sir Henry Maine naturally included Celts in their studies, which one quotation from a letter of Marx to Engels about Maurer will sufficiently illustrate:[12]

> I was extremely struck by the fact that Maurer, though often referring to Africa, Mexico, etc., for purposes of illustration, knows absolutely nothing about the Celts, and therefore ascribes the development of landed property in France entirely to the German conquerors. 'As though'—as Herr Bruno would say—'as though' we did not possess a Celtic (Welsh) book of laws from the eleventh century which is entirely communist.

Marx's view on the importance of language is equally forthright: 'Language itself is just as much the product of a community, as in another respect it is the existence of the community: it is, as it were, the communal being speaking for itself.'[13]

Celts had another advantage: they were indisputably one of the great peoples of Antiquity. When the ancient curriculum of Greek and Latin broadened out, looking not just to the east to the Semitic languages or to the Hindu civilization whose sacred language was Sanskrit, but north into Europe, Celts were inescapable. True, they did not always appear in a flattering guise. One only has to think of Aristotle's thoughts on climate and culture: Asiatics, who lived in a hot climate, might be cultivated and clever but they lacked energy; the peoples of Europe living in the cold lands to the north of the Greeks, Celts among them, were, on the other hand, startlingly brave, but they were also somewhat dim; the Greeks in the middle were just perfect.[14] Still, in spite of Aristotle, Classical philology bestowed great benefits on its Celtic counterpart. In this tradition, the study of languages went hand in hand with the study of texts – and, what is more, a wide range of texts from epic to inscription. Literary works needed to be edited by scholars competent in the language as well as in assessing the testimony of the manuscripts; and, on the other hand, the linguist needed good editions with which to work. In alliance with comparative and historical linguistics, this scholarly tradition could be carried over into other languages and other cultures. In the nineteenth and early twentieth century there was a scholarly continuum between linguistic, literary and historical research on the Celtic peoples. It was obvious that all these studies were essentially historical in nature and that they all needed to advance together. Interdependence created a consensus that, if the individual scholar was specialized, the subject was not.

The Celtic languages were a splendid field for such an allied investigation. In much of Europe, because of the cultural domination of Latin in the west and Greek in the east, there is little vernacular literature before the late eleventh century or even later; but Irish, and to a lesser extent also Welsh, have rich literatures beginning in the late sixth century. There was plenty of material with which to work. Moreover, because their literatures began unusually early, the gap between the Insular Celts of the British Isles and the Continental Celts of Antiquity did not seem unbridgeably wide. As we have seen, for some scholars, especially from France and Germany, these ancient Continental Celts were the ones who really mattered, the ones closer to home. Their languages could be studied in a small number of inscriptions (in the twentieth century considerably augmented by new discoveries) and also in names preserved by classical writers.[15] Zeuss's pupil, Glück, produced a scholarly study of the Celtic names in Caesar's Gallic Wars;[16] hence, even if there was no surviving Celtic literature from the Continent, the ancient Celtic languages were open to investigation, provided that one employed the evidence of the Insular Celtic languages according to the rules of comparison.

By the middle of the nineteenth century, therefore, it was evident that the Celtic languages formed part of the great Indo-European family, and that they could be investigated both on the Continent and in the British Isles. Yet there was no work which came near to offering a guide across this wide territory. For Welsh there had been an excellent grammar of the early modern literary language ever since 1621, when a Welsh humanist scholar, John Davies of Mallwyd, completed and improved the work of his predecessors.[17] There was a good grammar of Modern Irish by John O'Donovan; and Edward Lhuyd's *Archaeologia Britannica* of 1707 offered a comparative account of the Celtic languages. This was, however, largely based on modern materials. The person who supplied the comparative linguistic map for Celtic was Zeuss, who published his *Grammatica Celtica* in 1853.[18] This two-volume work was written in Latin and was thus equally accessible to the scholars of all Europe. More importantly, Zeuss had sought out the earliest remains of Irish, Welsh, Cornish and Breton in libraries both on the Continent and in the British Isles. When he was doing the preparatory work, Zeuss was teaching at a Lyceum in Speyer. Fortunately for him, perhaps the most important source of all for the investigation of Old Irish lay not far away at Würzburg – a manuscript of the Pauline Epistles with extensive glosses, in Latin and Irish – but Zeuss also went to Milan, Turin, St Gallen, London and Oxford in pursuit of similar materials.

The reason why all this was critical for the progress of Celtic linguistic studies was a central feature of the transmission of Irish texts to the modern world. Early medieval Irish manuscripts survived, in general, only if they were taken from Ireland to the Continent before *c*.900. Those critical for the study of Old Irish were teachers' books, copies of useful Latin texts glossed in Irish for the purposes of instructing pupils. Three such manuscripts were especially heavily glossed: the Würzburg Pauline Epistles, a copy of a commentary on the Psalms attributed to Julian of Eclanum, preserved in Milan, and a text of Priscian's Latin grammar in the monastery of St Gall in Switzerland.[19] From later Irish manuscripts one could gather a much larger body of early Irish texts, but in these later copies the language had been more or less modernized, usually inconsistently and thus preserving old forms alongside later ones. A similar feature was crucial in the preservation of the earliest Welsh manuscripts. They survived if they found their way to England in the tenth century: a splendid example is the so-called 'St Dunstan's Classbook', in the Bodleian Library at Oxford, a volume that once belonged to the tenth-century archbishop of Canterbury; it is of heterogeneous origins including glossed quires from Brittany (the Latin Grammar of Eutyches), a miscellany from Wales written about 820, and a later and much more luxurious copy, also from Wales, and also glossed, of Book I of Ovid's *Art of Love*.[20] Again there was considerably more early material from thirteenth- and fourteenth-century manuscripts in Wales, but these contained texts that had been considerably modernized and were difficult to date at all closely.

The early manuscripts from the Continent and from England were critical for the success of Zeuss's enterprise because of a central principle of comparative linguistics as it had developed in the early nineteenth century: it was both comparative and historical. That is to say, the history of any particular language in the Indo-European group had to be investigated first in order to establish what was the earliest stage of the language that had been preserved. This earliest stage was then compared with similar early stages of related languages. Only by following this principle could one avoid, so far as possible, the danger of attributing a quite false significance to forms of words or phrases or sentences which had arisen only at a relatively late stage. (Bopp, for example, working from relatively modern Celtic forms, often made wrong inferences.) The eighth-century

Würzburg glosses on St Paul's Epistles were the earliest extensive body of material in any Celtic language, extensive enough to provide the basis for a reasonably full grammar of the language. The key to Old Irish was thus continental even though the entertaining literature in the language was preserved in later manuscripts in Ireland itself.

Zeuss's *Grammatica Celtica* gathered together much of this early material and described it according to the best current linguistic practice. It offered both a collection of the sources and an analysis of the languages. In one way, its approach was narrower than Holger Pedersen's *Comparative Celtic Grammar* at the end of my period. Pedersen's interest was primarily in Indo-European: even while he was working on his Celtic grammar, he was also publishing articles on Armenian and Slavic; and he would later do major work on those Indo-European languages newly discovered in the early twentieth century, Hittite from ancient Anatolia and Tocharian from central Asia. Zeuss, however, largely confined himself in the *Grammatica Celtica* to the Celtic languages themselves. His purpose was more to sort out one branch of the Indo-European family, Celtic, than to cast light on Indo-European itself. As a consequence, the Celtic evidence presented by Zeuss was often richer than that adduced by Pedersen. It is still sometimes the case that the best guide on a particular issue continues to be Zeuss, not so much for his own views but because he presents the relevant evidence in such abundance. This is in spite of the subsequent appearance of the major works by Pedersen and Thurneysen, and even in spite of the dictionary of Old and Middle Irish finally completed thirty years ago. This helps to explain why Zeuss transformed the study of the Celtic languages: his map of Celtic was sometimes wrong and often sketchy, but it demonstrated the material which any further map-maker ought to use and offered a noble example of linguistic scholarship which they might seek to emulate if they dared.

What Pedersen's work offered in addition was not only a broad Indo-European perspective on Celtic; he had also acquired a good knowledge of the modern Irish spoken on the Aran Islands.[21] His form of linguistics extended the history of Celtic from remote prehistory to the end of the nineteenth century; and his interest in the phonology of Modern Irish looked forward to the central concerns of linguistics in the first half of the twentieth century. His contribution can thus be seen by comparing his work with that of Bopp, Prichard and Zeuss. In the early part of the nineteenth century, the central concern had been with the prehistory of Celtic and its relationship to Sanskrit and the other Indo-European languages. The particular issue of Celtic's relationship to Indo-European had been settled even though reliance was placed on relatively modern forms of the Celtic languages. Zeuss offered the first comprehensive map of Celtic that concentrated on the earliest surviving records and thus offered the surest basis for a backwards look towards Indo-European. In this phase, therefore, the movement of scholarship was essentially backwards. But there was the other aspect, namely the history of the Celtic languages from their earliest records down to the present day: if one takes one's stand where Zeuss took his – in the early middle ages – this can be seen as the forward look. The detailed history of the Celtic languages was in its infancy in the second half of the nineteenth century, but Pedersen's interest in Modern Irish, and also in Modern Breton, represented the first crucial step, namely to analyse the modern state of a language as scientifically as the earliest records.

In Zeuss's Celtic – and, indeed, ever since – Old Irish played a central role. This is not just because it offers earlier extensive material in contemporary or near-contemporary manuscripts than any other Celtic language. Old Irish is an ancient language in a medieval disguise; but Old Welsh and Old Breton were, by and large, languages of the normal western medieval type, heavily influenced by Latin during Roman imperial rule in Britain. To appreciate this difference we need to grasp two contrasts; first between the linguistic history of eastern as opposed to western Europe and secondly between the type of language prevalent in Europe in antiquity and that prevalent in western Europe in the middle ages. Some of what I shall now argue is, I should warn you, broad-brush and even speculative, but I think it stands a very good chance of being true. In their grammar, the main Indo-European languages of eastern Europe, both the Slavonic group, such as Russian or Polish, and the Baltic group, such as Lithuanian, often remain relatively close to Indo-European. Lithuanian, attested only from the early modern period, is more conservative than any of the Germanic languages, even though one Germanic language, Gothic, is attested from the fourth century AD. By contrast, the Romance languages, such as Rumanian, French and Spanish, the Celtic and Germanic languages have grammars very different from Indo-European. This process has significantly gone furthest in Welsh, in the Romance languages, and in some Germanic languages; it has not gone so far in modern High German as in English or Welsh.

Sometimes English-speakers talk as if what distinguishes English from the languages of European antiquity were part of some inevitable march of progress towards modernity. But that is insular-minded rubbish. It probably has a much more specific starting-point, namely in the demotic

Latin of the north-western provinces of the Roman Empire, Britain and northern Gaul. British – that is to say the ancestor of Welsh, Cornish and Breton – shared in most of the developments in this demotic Latin, to such an extent that it is almost true to say that, whereas, as I have said, Old Irish is an ancient language in medieval disguise, Welsh and Breton are Celtic languages dressed up in the latest French fashion. We saw earlier that Indo-European words varied at the end, while modern Celtic languages also vary at the beginning; and we saw that Franz Bopp showed in 1838 that this difference was late – that the reason why the Celtic languages varied at the beginning was the way they had earlier varied at the end. Hence they were not so un-Indo-European in their origins as they seemed. This variation at the end, usually called inflexion, was characteristic of the Indo-European verb, noun, adjective and pronoun. In the Romance languages, however, it is characteristic to a vastly reduced extent of noun, adjective and pronoun: whereas the verb remains quite highly inflected, the noun, adjective and pronoun only vary for gender (masculine and feminine) and number (singular and plural). This broad description of how the Romance languages have changed from their Latin parent will do, word for word, for how Welsh and Breton have changed from Celtic. It establishes Welsh and Breton as reasonably typical modern western European languages. In the British Isles of the early post-Roman centuries we can see how these fundamental changes were common to the Latin at that time still spoken in Britain and to British, but not to either Old Irish or Old English: they were common, that is, to those the Franks and the English called Welsh, their Gallo-Roman and British neighbours.

A century or two later than these developments in north-western demotic Latin and British came a further set of changes, which also helped to separate western from eastern Europe. These set in about the time when the western Roman Empire ended; the domain of these changes partially overlapped with the earlier set: the Romance of northern Gaul (ancestor of modern French) and British (ancestor of Welsh, Cornish and Breton) were subject to these changes too, but they also affected Irish, English and the languages around the North Sea, from Frisia to Scandinavia. They did not affect the southern Romance languages, those of the Mediterranean. The northern languages got rid of most final syllables (except, of course, in monosyllabic words) and, at the same time, shifted distinctive features further back in the word. We tend to think that it was this loss of final endings which caused the loss of inflexion in the noun, adjective and pronoun of western European languages, but that cannot be true: Italian, to take one example, lost nominal inflexion for case but did not lose most final syllables; and, on the other side, Old Irish lost final syllables but did not lose inflexion.

It is at this point that we reach a fundamental reason why Old Irish was such fun for nineteenth-century linguists. It had a complex inflexion in both the nominal system – noun, adjective and pronoun – and the verb, even though the final syllables which had once expressed that inflexion were mostly gone. The reason was that it found new means to play old games. One such device we also find in English, as in *men* the plural of *man*, that is, varying a vowel in the middle of a word (this new variation is, historically, also caused by the lost endings); but another is not found in any other western European language, the distinction between palatal and neutral consonants. In English the pronunciation of the /k/ in *key* and in *car* is different, but it is not significantly different because it is entirely determined by the following vowel. In Irish the same difference is not determined by the following vowel and thus it is significant. In this respect, Irish had been like English roughly up to the end of the Roman Empire. What happened was this: the vowels of the final syllables that were lost *c.* 500 had previously determined the pronunciation of the preceding consonants, but the effect of those vowels on the consonants remained when the vowels themselves had disappeared. The effect thus became significant; and the significance then extended to consonants followed by surviving vowels. What it did was to double the number of consonants at a stroke. To a large extent, it was the same process as that observed by Bopp: an apparent medieval novelty went back to something in the language in its earlier, ancient, phase. Both the initial mutations studied by Bopp and palatalization acted as substitute devices used by an old inflexional system: an ancient chrysalis had yielded up a rare medieval butterfly; but, also, by studying the butterfly one could reconstruct the chrysalis.

All this helps to explain why scholars who had once got into Celtic often stayed there and why Zeuss's *Grammatica Celtica* had such an effect. Zeuss's work was the very reverse of Romantic burbling in the Celtic twilight: it was an immensely painstaking and logical construction according to the best standards of historical and linguistic scholarship. To illustrate its effect I shall give an example from a letter from the eighth Viscount Strangford to E. A. Freeman, the well-known English historian. Lord Strangford had been Oriental Secretary in the British Embassy in Constantinople at the time of the Crimean War, a post of considerable importance close to the eye of the contemporary storm in European affairs. He held this post because of his knowledge of Greek, Turkish,

Persian and Arabic. He came of a northern Irish family and his title was of the Irish peerage. Through his knowledge of languages he came to be deeply interested in the comparative linguistics of his time; an interest which can be seen in the notes he contributed to Matthew Arnold's *Study of Celtic Literature*. Here, then, is Strangford writing to Freeman in November 1863:[22]

> The common-sense man chatters and grins like a monkey over the absurdity of Ogham inscriptions, and treating accidental or meaningless scratches as actual alphabets. Well, Dr. Graves claims to interpret these scratches by means of the old Irish language, existing in remains fairly well known and investigated. Meanwhile an Ogham and Latin bilingual is found at St. Dogmael's in Merionethshire. It can hardly, therefore, be accidental. The Latin is *Sacrani Fili Cunotami*. But the application of Dr. Graves's method gives the same with *maqi* for *fili*. So you get at once the proof of Graves's system and an older stage of a Celtic genitive, identical with the Latin and that of the old Gaulish inscriptions. When will people read Zeuss?

To have any scholarly authority over the whole range of languages in the British Isles, one now had to know one's Zeuss.

Mere delight in the linguistic riches displayed in the 1247 pages of Zeuss (in the second edition) was not, however, what explained why scholars took up the study of Celtic in the second half of the nineteenth century. We began with two questions: what drew scholars to Celtic and what kept them there? I have now given some reasons which kept them there, but before we look at some more, we need to consider why they got into the business in the first place. Two examples will be enough to illustrate the variety of paths to this particular destination. In the second half of the nineteenth century the premier German university for linguistic studies, and therefore the premier university in the world, was Leipzig. There from 1871 Ernst Windisch was Professor of Sanskrit, to which he then added Celtic. He had three outstanding Celtic pupils, Heinrich Zimmer, who later turned against his old teacher, Kuno Meyer and Rudolf Thurneysen, from Basel in the German-speaking part of Switzerland, the greatest Celtic scholar of all time.[23] Windisch explained how he got into Celtic in the preface to the first volume of his *Irische Texte*.[24] He was working in England for two years cataloguing Sanskrit manuscripts for the India Office and his professor of Sanskrit, Herrmann Brockhaus, told him to find out precisely what lay behind MacPherson's *Ossian*. Could a work of literature that had taken Europe by storm be a mere fake? The answer was not easy, since, although it was certainly a fake, it was not a mere fake, just as neither his Welsh contemporary Iolo Morgannwg nor, much earlier, Geoffrey of Monmouth, were mere fakes. However, in order to know quite what might lie behind *Ossian* one had to get a grip on early Irish literature; and, in order to do that, one needed some scholarly editions of texts. Providing such editions was what Windisch proceeded to do, when he was not writing his history of Sanskrit literature or trying to recover his balance after yet another poisonous attack by his old pupil Zimmer.

Thurneysen's path into Celtic was quite different – and here one can rely on his own account:[25]

> When still a schoolboy I heard (from whom I cannot now recollect) that the French language, familiar to every Swiss from childhood, was a mixture of Latin and Gaulish. When later I made up my mind to study philology I had this problem of the origin of French before my eyes. I studied on the one hand Romance philology, on the other hand Latin, comparative philology, and so on.

That sentence of Thurneysen's 'I studied on the one hand Romance philology, on the other hand Latin, comparative philology and so on' gives us something of the intellectual atmosphere of the best universities in the 1870s.

Another crucial point was clarified by Thurneysen in the same article. An immense advantage for minority subjects was the mobility of the German student. Thurneysen started his university studies at his home university of Basel, but when his interest was caught by Romance and comparative linguistics he could go to Leipzig, then the chief centre of the discipline. Having sat at the feet of Windisch, he could go on to Berlin and be taught by Zimmer, Windisch's former pupil and now academic rival. A subject such as Celtic is never likely to be taught in more than a handful of universities in any one country outside Ireland, Scotland, Wales and Brittany. Moreover, both Windisch and Zimmer taught Sanskrit quite as much or more than Celtic. A chair devoted to Celtic did not exist in Germany until 1901, when a chair of Celtic was created at Berlin for Zimmer; but German scholars had been at the forefront of the discipline for much of the previous century. Yet as the student was encouraged to try disciplines other than his first choice, so the university professor might cover more than one subject. There were as few obstacles as possible in the way of the student seeking out the teacher who could offer him instruction in a subject he would never have met at school and would never meet in most universities. One of the best things we could do with the universities of Europe today would be to create a similar flexibility and a similar encouragement to students to try out something new.

Britain and Ireland, in the mid-nineteenth century, offered less opportunity for Celtic scholars than did Germany or even France. The outstanding figure was Whitley Stokes (1830–1909), a member of a highly cultivated Dublin family, who was an early member of the council of the Philological Society. The Philological Society was the principal organization, and its *Transactions* the principal publication, for linguistic research in the British Isles. In the period after the *Transactions* first appeared in 1859 and up to the years before the First World War, it gave a platform for some of the best research on Celtic anywhere in the world. Many of Stokes's editions of Cornish, Irish and Welsh material appeared in its pages. Yet Stokes was not employed as a scholar. In spite of his huge output – in these unhappy days of the RAE universities would offer tidy sums to have a Stokes on their books – he earned his keep as a legal civil servant in India producing major codifications of Indian law and ending up as President of the Indian Law Commission. Some of his Celtic articles are given a date and place: Madras, 8 October 1864; Calcutta, 6 February 1867; screw-steamer *Surat* between Aden and Bombay, 4 March 1872.[26]

The *Transactions of the Philological Society* for 1865 included an article by John Rhŷs, a schoolteacher at Rhos-y-bol in the north of Anglesey.[27] The article, entitled 'The Passive Verbs of the Latin and the Keltic Languages', employed Celtic evidence to demonstrate the implausibility of a then-current explanation of the Latin passive. Rhŷs had been born in 1840 to a poor farm- and leadmine-worker on the slopes of Pumlumon to the east of Aberystwyth. He progressed from being a pupil at the local 'British School' at Ponterwyd to being a pupil-teacher at a school slightly further away, then to the teacher-training college at Bangor, and so to being a teacher in Anglesey. In the same year as his article appeared he entered Jesus College, Oxford, as a scholar. He was later enabled to go for a short period to Germany to pursue his linguistic interests. As a young Fellow of Merton College, he was invited to the newly established university college at Aberystwyth, near his birth-place, in order to give a course of lectures on Welsh philology. The resulting book was published just after he was appointed to the new Chair of Celtic at Oxford, founded principally at the expense of the Fellows of Jesus

College in response to Matthew Arnold's lectures on Celtic Literature. Rhŷs was perhaps too cheerful in speculation to make a first-rate philologist, but a deep interest in epigraphy already underpins this, his earliest book; and he was a better archaeologist than most philological epigraphers, ready to travel far in order to see an inscription himself and careful to record the physical condition as well as the original location of the stone. There is one, probably sixth-century, inscription from County Meath which is critical for early Irish history. For its dating it is essential to know whether the inscription is complete. One still has to go back behind the standard works to an article written by Rhŷs and an Irish antiquarian to get the crucial information.[28] Rhŷs, however, worked on folklore, history and literature as well as on linguistic topics. He was clearly Mr Celtic-for-all-purposes in late nineteenth-century Oxford.

Matthew Arnold's Oxford lectures on Celtic Literature, subsequently published as *The Study of Celtic Literature*, were not directly concerned with the Celtic languages as such. What is interesting for our purposes is, first, that they led to the appointment of a philologist as the first Professor of Celtic. Lectures on Celtic Literature would hardly lead to the appointment of a philologist today, but in the conditions of Celtic studies in the 1870s it made excellent sense. There was the simple point that, before one could say anything of secure value about literature in the Celtic languages, it would help to publish it in reliable editions. But there was much more to it than that, as we can see by returning to the Celtic career of Rudolf Thurneysen. This went through three main phases: first, there was the philological phase, which lasted right up to the publication of his grammar of Old Irish in 1909;[29] secondly, there was Thurneysen the student of Old and Middle Irish literature; and, thirdly, after his retirement in 1922 he took up a new career as editor and interpreter of early Irish law. The philological phase came first and lasted longest, partly because he was then employed as Professor of Comparative Linguistics at Freiburg-im-Breisgau and only occasionally taught Celtic. The second phase, with which I am now concerned, lies at the end of our period. Two crucial works appeared before the outbreak of war, but the most important was only published in 1921 with the financial support of the new Irish government.[30] Still, the enterprise began before the First World War, and I shall therefore take the liberty of considering it as a whole. It is perhaps the best example in our period of the rewards to be gained from uniting linguistic and textual scholarship. Thurneysen wrote briefly on the general history of early Irish literature, but his chief concern, as one can see as soon as one dips into his main publications, was to sort out texts in terms of their chronology and their relationships to each other. In his own words, he aimed 'to bring some order into the chaos prevailing in the world of Irish saga'.[31] Some of these sagas existed in more than one extant version; some were compilations from more than one Old or Middle Irish text; some clearly presupposed the existence of others. An essential tool in the task of bringing order into chaos was linguistic: the different texts and versions of texts had to be placed in a chronological sequence. Occasionally there might be a reference which would offer a clue, but mostly it depended on dating the form of Irish used in the text. Literary history depended on linguistic history.

In some respects the immense achievements of nineteenth-century Celtic scholarship were ill-fitted to supply this necessary tool. What Zeuss and his successors had aimed to achieve was a comparative description of the oldest recoverable form of each language; as we have seen, for Irish this essentially meant the language of the glosses preserved in eighth- and ninth-century manuscripts. That was what mattered for Indo-European comparative linguistics. Tracing the detailed history of Irish all the way from the eighth to the nineteenth century was a task for another day. The first major steps in this direction were taken by a Scot from Banff, John Strachan (1862–1907). His background was in the philology of the classical languages, especially Greek, and the job he held was as Professor of Greek in the newly founded Owen's College, the forerunner of the University of Manchester.[32] His work on Old Irish provided important material for use in Thurneysen's grammar of 1906, but what was new was his work on Middle Irish, the stage of the language which stretched roughly between 900 and 1200. The articles that he published in the *Transactions of the Philological Society* around 1900 made a major contribution to bring order into this particular chaos, and it is only a few years ago that the task was taken significantly further.[33] It was thanks to Strachan, therefore, that dating Middle Irish texts could be anything more than guesswork. Most unfortunately he died relatively young in 1907 from pneumonia.

A number of developments occurred in the years before the First World War, most of which were highly favourable. This was the period of greatest productivity of the last great scholar whom I wish to bring before you as an example of Celtic studies in the nineteenth century, namely Kuno Meyer (1858–1919), who began his career as a university teacher in 1884 as Lecturer in Teutonic Languages in Liverpool University.[34] His most fruitful years were spent in Liverpool; when he went to the chair of Celtic at Berlin in 1911 vacated by the death of Zimmer, there was only a short time remaining before the outbreak of war. After 1914, perhaps para-doxically because he had been so happy in England, but also because his influence over the Irish was highly rated by the German government, he allowed political conflict to invade scholarship.[35] As a scholar, Meyer was a man of many small contributions rather than the lengthy tome, but in total he made a major contribution especially to the study of early Irish poetry and lexicography.[36] Not only did he edit much of the corpus of early Irish poetry, but he also translated many poems into English; and his translations were both faithful to the original and calculated to delight English readers. Moreover he was gregarious and good fun; and, more important still for Celtic, he was prepared to use his gifts at getting on with people to promote Irish studies. The consequence of his ability to present Irish literature to a wider readership and his ability as fund-raiser and persuader was that he did more than almost anyone else to advance the cause of the discipline. This may be why, when Heinrich Zimmer died, Meyer was chosen to succeed him as Professor of Celtic in Berlin, ahead of Thurneysen and Pedersen. In terms of pure scholarship this was the wrong decision, but the appointing committee in Berlin may well have hoped that he might go on to achieve in the capital of the German Empire what he had already achieved in Liverpool and Dublin.

Dublin is here added to Liverpool principally because of Meyer's role in founding the School of Irish Learning there in 1903. It is a lovely example of what can be achieved if one seizes the right moment to start something new. The success of the Gaelic League over the previous decade and the renewed interest in Ireland in its native literature was a huge help. Another was the argument that Irish studies should be primarily pursued in Ireland – that the situation ever since Zeuss's *Grammatica Celtica*, when they had been carried forward mainly by German philologists, should not continue. That this appeal was not merely nicely attuned to Irish hearts but in some sense right was shown by the response. The first students at the summer school of 1903 numbered forty, from all the provinces of Ireland and also from England. They were not given an easy-going intro-duction: John Strachan gave the class, the text being Whitley Stokes's edition of the Würzburg glosses, to be studied with the aid of Windisch's Irish Grammar, but Strachan was a fine teacher and all seems to have gone well. One may contrast this with Meyer's experience when he went to Berlin as Professor of Celtic. As he wrote to Mrs J. R. Green, a principal supporter of the School of Irish Learning, lamenting the dearth of German students of Celtic: 'both Thurneysen and I have but one German among them, the rest are all English, Irish or American'.[37]

This marks the main difference between Celtic studies in the nineteenth century and what became of them in the twentieth. Increasingly the principal scholars in the field of early Irish have themselves usually been Irish, and it is even more true for Scottish Gaelic, Welsh and Breton that they are studied in their own countries. In Meyer's fine appeals to the Irish to set up the School of Irish Learning the appeal to nationalism is evident. The positive side of his appeal cannot be denied: it would indeed be strange if a people, such as the Irish, that now prided itself on a revival in its national life, nevertheless displayed no interest in early Irish language, literature and history. But there is, potentially, a negative side: if nationalism were to have a major place in scholarship, would the scholars of England, France, Italy and Germany continue to take an interest in Celtic? As we saw with Zeuss and Thurneysen, the reasons why they came to study Celtic had to do with the history, languages and literatures of Europe rather than merely their own countries. The argument is the same, only even stronger, if we take a smaller domain than Europe and consider only the British Isles. In these isles speakers of Celtic languages and of English have lived for a millennium and a half; and the conquests of Wales and Ireland by the English and the Union with Scotland have intertwined their histories yet more closely. That sometimes unhappy history has certainly not told us that life goes on better if one nation's scholars think the language and literature of another unworthy of serious attention. In the years before the First World War first-rate Celtic scholars held permanent appointments in Liverpool, Manchester, Oxford and Cambridge, though admittedly these posts were not generally in Celtic – it was normally a voluntary and unpaid extra labour added to such standard and prestigious subjects as Greek and German. Later, Liverpool and Manchester had posts usually held by Welsh scholars; yet students of Welsh were understandably attracted to the larger departments in Wales. Moreover, the study of Celtic was never likely to flourish in England if it were regarded merely as an outpost of Wales – or of Ireland or of Scotland. What was always exciting was the possibility of studying a range of languages and literatures that have co-existed with English. In the twenty-first century, so far as England is concerned, the study of ancient and medieval Celtic has retreated to the Golden Triangle, with the exception, that is, of London, where Whitley Stokes's library, given to University College, slept, when last observed, under lock and key. In England the political and intellectual climate was for a long time much less favourable to Irish studies than it was before the First World War, in particular after 1916 and even more so after the Treaty and the Civil War. Only in Cambridge has Celtic

Studies made any lasting advance beyond the level reached before 1914. The Department of Anglo-Saxon, Norse and Celtic, the brainchild of Hector Munro Chadwick, has been exemplary, but it has led where no one else has followed.

Notes

1 Vol. 1 was published in 1909; vol. 2 came out in two parts, 1911 and 1913 (Göttingen).

2 The period is covered, in greater detail than was possible here, by D. Ellis Evans, 'The Heroic Age of Celtic Philology', *Zeitschrift für celtische Philologie*, 54 (2004), pp. 1–30; for a general account from towards the end of the period, see V. Tourneur, *Esquisse d'une histoire des études celtiques* (Liège, 1905).

3 A. Morpurgo Davies, *History of Linguistics. IV: Nineteenth-Century Linguistics* (London, 1998), is an authoritative guide.

4 E. Lhuyd, *Archaeologia Britannica* (Oxford, 1707; reprinted Dublin, 1971).

5 A revised edition, edited by R. G. Latham, was published in 1857. The effect of Cowley's work is demonstrated by a review written by Jacob Grimm in *Göttingischen gelehrte Anzeigen*, 27 (1833), pp. 257–62, quoted in E. Poppe, 'Lag es in der Luft? – Johann Kaspar Zeuß und die Konstituierung der Keltologie', *Beiträge zur Geschichte der Sprachwissenschaft*, 2: 1 (1992), pp. 41–56, at 51.'.

6 For Schlegel's scepticism, see Poppe, 'Lag es in der Luft?'.

7 F. Bopp, 'Über die celtischen Sprachen vom Gesichtspunkte der vergleichenden Sprachforschung', *Abhandlungen der kgl. Akademie der Wissenschaften zu Berlin 1838* (Berlin, 1839), pp. 187–272; repr. in F. Bopp, *Kleine Schriften zur vergleichenden Sprachwissenschaft: Gesammelte Berliner Akademieabhandlungen, 1824–1854* (Leipzig, 1972), pp. 149–234 (this also gives the original pagination); also published separately as *Die Celtischen Sprachen in ihrem Verhältnisse zum Sanskrit, Zend, Griechischen, Lateinischen, Germanischen, Litthauischen und Slawischen* (Berlin, 1839). The change in Bopp's views is evident from comparison with his earlier work, 'Vergleichende Zergliederung des Sanskrits und der mit ihm verwandten Sprachen. Erste Abhandlung. Von den Wurzeln und Pronominen erster und zweiter Person', *Abhandlungen* (1824), p. 123 (*Kleine Schriften*, 7): 'Es liesse sich, ausser den oben erwähnten mit dem Sanskrit zu vergleichenden Sprachen, noch manche andere der gegenwärtigen Untersuchung anreihen, wenn es unsere Absicht wäre, all' diejenigen Sprachen zu umfassen, welche einzelne Spuren der Verwandtschaft mit dem Sanskrit an sich tragen. Es finden deren mehrere in der Celtischen Sprachfamilie, und das Finnische und die verwandten Mundarten, so wie das Ungarische und Albanische, bieten ebenfalls ... überraschende Aehnlichkeiten dar.'

8 Because of the importance of the numerals in early comparisons, it was especially convincing to be able to explain 'nasalization' of the initial sound of the following word by reference to the final nasal of such numerals as Latin *septem*: Bopp, *Kleine Schriften*, pp. 207–08 (23 of the separate edition).

9 A summary account of his life is H. Hablitzel, *Prof. Dr. Johann Kaspar Zeuss: Begründer der Keltologie und Historiker aus Vogtendorf/Oberfranken, 1806–1856* (Kronach, 1987). See also Bernhard Forssman, ed., *Erlanger Gedenkfeier für Johannes Kaspar Zeuss* (Erlangen, 1989).

10 P. Sims-Williams, 'Celtomania and Celtoscepticism', *Cambrian Medieval Celtic Studies*, 36 (Winter 1998), pp. 1–35.

11 Recent Celto-sceptics tend to underestimate the importance of language in culture: see the penetrating criticism by P. Sims-Williams, 'How are you finding it here?', *London Review of Books*, 28 October 1999: a review of S. James, *The Atlantic Celts: Ancient People or Modern Invention?* (London, 1999).

12 K. Marx, *Pre-Capitalist Economic Formations*, trans. J. Cohen, ed. E. J. Hobsbawm (London, 1964), p. 140.

13 Ibid., p. 88.

14 Aristotle, *Politics*, Bk. VII, 1327b18–37.

15 A good guide to Gaulish, the best attested of them, is P.-Y. Lambert, *La langue gauloise* (Paris, 1995).

16 C. W. Glück, *Die bei Caius Julius Caesar vorkommenden keltischen Namen* (Munich, 1857); cf. D. Ellis Evans, *Gaulish Personal Names: A Study of Some Continental Celtic Formations* (Oxford, 1967), pp. 2–3.

17 E. Poppe, 'John Davies and the Study of Grammar: *Antiquae Linguae Britannicae ... Rudimenta*', in C. Davies, ed., *Dr John Davies of Mallwyd: Welsh Renaissance Scholar* (Cardiff, 2004), pp. 121–45.

18 J. C. Zeuss, *Grammatica Celtica*, 2 vols. (Leipzig, 1853); a revised edition was brought out by H. Ebel in a single volume (Berlin, 1871).

19 The first two have been published in facsimile: *Epistolae Beati Pauli Glosatae Glosa Interlineali: Irisch-Lateinischer Codex der Würzburger Universitätsbibliothek*, ed. L. C. Stern (Halle, 1910); *The Commentary on the Psalms with Glosses in Old Irish preserved in the Ambrosian Library: Collotype Facsimile*, ed. R. I. Best (Dublin, 1936).

20 A facsimile is available: *Saint Dunstan's Classbook from Glastonbury*, ed. R. W. Hunt, Umbrae codicum occidentalium IV (Amsterdam, 1961).

21 E. F. Koerner, 'Holger Pedersen (1867–1953): A Sketch of his Life and Work', in his *Practicing Linguistic Historiography: Selected Essays* (Amsterdam/Philadelphia, 1989), pp. 417–33 (with a bibliography of Pedersen's main writings); H. Pedersen, *Scéalta Mháirtín Neile: Bailiúchán Scéalta ó Árainn*, ed. Ole Munch-Pedersen (Dublin, 1994). Munch-Pedersen's introduction, pp. xxi–xxx, gives a sketch of his academic career up to the publication of *Vergleichende Grammatik der keltischen Sprachen*.

22 *Original Letters and Papers of the Late Lord Strangford upon Philological and Kindred Subjects*, ed. Viscountess Strangford (London, 1878), p. 28. The interest of this passage is noted by D. Ó Cróinín, 'The Reception of Johann Kaspar Zeuss's *Grammatica Celtica* in Ireland and Britain, and on the Continent: Some New Evidence', in Michael Wollenschläger, Eckhard Kreßel, Johann Egger, eds, *Recht? Wirtschaft? Kultur. Herausforderungen an Staat und Gesellschaft im Zeitalter der Globalisierung. Festschrift für Hans Hablitzel zum 60. Geburtstag* (Berlin, 2005), pp. 83–93.

23 The obituary of Windisch by J. Vendryes, *Revue Celtique*, 37 (1917–19), pp. 420–25, takes full account of his Sanskrit as well as his Celtic work; similarly Vendryes's obituary of Zimmer, *Revue Celtique*, 31 (1910), pp. 410–12. As Vendryes noted of the latter, 'On pourrait dire de lui, en reprenant un mot de Heine, qu'il avait toujours en écrivant un œil fixé sur son papier et l'autre sur quelqu'un. Les attaques personnelles surgissent à chaque page de ses écrits.'

24 E. Windisch, *Irische Texte mit Wörterbuch* (Leipzig, 1880); volumes 2–4 in the series were edited by Windisch with Whitley Stokes (Leipzig, 1884–1909).

25 R. Thurneysen, 'Why do Germans study Celtic Philology?', *Studies: An Irish Quarterly Review*, 19 (March 1930), p. 30; the article is reprinted in his *Gesammelte Schriften*, ed. P. de Bernardo Stempel and R. Ködderitzch, 3 vols (Tübingen, 1991), II, pp. 272–84.

26 R. I. Best, 'Bibliography of the Publications of Whitley Stokes', *Zeitschrift für celtische Philologie*, 8 (1912), pp. 351–406, at 358, 360, 362.

27 I. Ll. Foster, 'Sir John Rhys', in D. Ellis Evans et al., eds, *Proceedings of the Seventh International Congress of Celtic Studies, Oxford, 1983* (Oxford, 1986), pp. 10–14. J. Morris-Jones, 'Sir John Rhys', *Proceedings of the British Academy*, 11 (1925), pp. 187–212, and also separately issued, provides a bibliography of his publications.

28 R. Cochrane and J. Rhys, 'Notes on the Newly-Discovered Ogam-Stones in County Meath', *Journal of the Royal Society of Antiquaries of Ireland*, 38 (1898), pp. 53–60.

29 R. Thurneysen, *Handbuch des Altirischen* (Heidelberg, 1909).

30 R. Thurneysen, *Zu irischen Handschriften und Literaturdenkmälern*, i = *Abhandlungen der Königlichen Gesellschaft der Wissenschaften zu Göttingen*, Phil.-hist. Klasse, N.F., 14, No. 2 (Berlin, 1912), and Zweite Serie, ibid., No. 3 (1913); *idem, Die irische Helden- und Königsage bis zum siebzehnten Jahrhundert* (Halle [Saale], 1921)

31 *Heldensage*, iii.

32 Professor of Greek at Owen's College, Manchester, 1885; from 1889 also Professor of Comparative Philology; from 1904 also Lecturer in Celtic (honorary).

33 L. Breatnach, 'An Mhéan-Ghaeilge', in K. McCone et al., eds, *Stair na Gaeilge* (Maynooth, 1994), pp. 221–333.

34 S. Ó Luing, *Kuno Meyer, 1858–1919: A Biography* (Dublin, 1991).

35 See J. Vendryes, *Revue Celtique*, 36 (1915–16), pp. 423–24: 'à la faveur de l'hospitalité anglaise, il préparait les voies aux hordes casquées qui devaient conquérir Liverpool et Londres, en passant par Dublin'. This was written while Vendryes was on active service; his obituary of Meyer, *Revue Celtique*, 37 (1917–19), pp. 425–28, is much more measured, beginning 'La mort éteint tous les ressentiments'.

36 See R. I. Best, 'Bibliography of the Publications of Kuno Meyer', *Zeitschrift für celtische Philologie*, 15 (1924), pp. 1–65.

37 Quoted by Ó Luing, *Kuno Meyer, 1858–1919*, p. 111.

The Use and Abuse of the Early Middle Ages, 1750–2000

IAN WOOD

Every country has used, and uses, the past for its own ends. Sometimes the use is conscious, sometimes it is unconscious. It can be official or unofficial, public or private, all at the same time.[1] Some periods of history come to have particular significance at certain moments.[2] The early middle ages as the period that saw the break-up of the Roman Empire can and has been presented as the moment in which the modern states of western Europe first took some shape – the idea is indeed explicitly central to Ferdinand Lot's three volumes on *les invasions germaniques* and *les invasions barbares*.[3] France has been seen as developing directly from the kingdom of the Franks, Spain from that of the Visigoths; the origins of England have been found in the settlements of Anglo-Saxons; rather different, but equally central to the debates about national development, is the role allocated to the Lombards.[4] Germany is different yet again, because the Germanic tribes of the early middle ages established no large state in what has come to be seen as their homeland. On the other hand, there has long been a debate as to whether those tribes were or were not the major catalysts of the changes that engulfed the Roman World in the fourth, fifth and sixth centuries.[5] In addition, for much of the eighteenth and nineteenth centuries, historians argued as to whether or not the origins of feudalism lay in the social institutions brought into the Roman world by the Germanic peoples. And in many parts of Europe for much of the early modern and modern periods feudalism was not just a concept used to categorize the past, it was an issue of contemporary politics.

The basic development of interpretations of the early middle ages, and the contexts in which those interpretations evolved, is relatively easily set out. Some parts of it are well known, other parts less so. What follows is an unbalanced account – unbalanced because I will do no more than touch on some of the big issues that are familiar, and need relatively little rehearsal, whereas I will pause at greater length on some lesser, but nevertheless important, aspects of the story that are not generally appreciated.[6] Indeed, I will spend longest on a small number of readings of the Frankish past which have been forgotten. As an early medievalist I am struck by some points that might appear to be of little interest to a specialist in the eighteenth and nineteenth centuries, but which, nevertheless, seem to me to deserve revisiting.

My coverage of the material, however, will also be unbalanced because I will leave on one side some very important regions of western Europe: I will say nothing of the Celtic lands, although they too have made much of the period from the fifth to the eighth centuries. I will also remain silent about Spain, which has long debated its Visigothic past, and the extent to which it survived the Muslim invasions, not least because those invasions and the subsequent ideology of *Reconquista* have spawned a debate which is unique to the Iberian peninsula.[7] Nor will I comment on Italy, although its historiography is intimately connected to that of France,[8] which will be the chief focus of my discussion. Coverage of England and Germany will be patchy in the extreme. But unless one is extremely selective it is impossible to provide a sense of even the broadest developments.

One could sensibly begin an analysis of interpretations of the early middle ages in the sixteenth century, or indeed earlier. The Gothic history of the the sixth-century writer Jordanes was consulted by the bishops present at the Council of Basel (1431–49) to determine whether the Spaniards or the Swedes should have pride of place.[9] A more sustained use of the early middle ages can be found in sixteenth-century England, where first the authors of the Anglican settlement, and then their opponents, looked to the history of the early Church and the mission of Augustine to defend or undermine the English Reformation.[10] Of more long-term significance was the use of the Anglo-Saxon past to determine the proper limits of royal authority which began in the seventeenth century.[11] Most of the great British constitutional thinkers of the eighteenth century had something to say about the Anglo-Saxons and their institutions, and when a professional class of historians emerged in the nineteenth century it largely followed their line of interpretation. I leave the seventeenth- and early eighteenth-century writers aside not because they lack interest, but because the techniques of historical scholarship were only in their infancy. Indeed it was such debates that led to the development of the study of Old English, and to the first publication of many of the sources for the period.[12] By the mid-eighteenth century, however, many of those techniques were in place, even if not to standards that we now regard as necessary.

The development of what we would nowadays call historical skills in the seventeenth and eighteenth centuries was especially apparent in France, where the Académie royale des inscriptions et belles lettres was founded in 1716. In 1738 Martin Bouquet was to publish the first volume of the still-valuable *Recueil des historiens des Gaules et de la France*, a series which was to continue until 1904. And these were only part of what was essentially a campaign 'to advance the historical and legal argument for strong royal authority'.[13] Politics thus lay at the foundation of modern historical scholarship. The resulting debates provide a convenient starting-point for the present survey.

Looking back on French historiography concerning the early middle ages from the vantage-point of the late nineteenth century, Numa Denis Fustel de Coulanges remarked that

> L'opinion qui place au début de notre histoire une grande invasion, et qui partage dès lors la population en deux races inégales, n'a commencé à poindre qu'au XVIe siècle et a surtout pris crédit au XVIIIe. Elle est née de l'antagonisme des classes, et elle a grandi avec cet antagonisme. Elle pèse encore sur notre société présente ...[14] [*The opinion which puts a major invasion at the start of our history, and which thereafter divides the population into two unequal races, only dawned in the sixteenth century, and only took root in the eighteenth. It was born of class antagonism, and grew with that antagonism. It still weighs on our society.*]

Among those who contributed to the debate, it is worth noting Henri comte de Boulainvilliers, whose works were only published after his death in 1722, having circulated privately during his lifetime. His contribution was important, not because it was especially scholarly, but because he set out his claims in the starkest possible manner. For him the Franks were a warrior nation who conquered and enslaved the peoples of Gaul. The descendents of these warriors constituted the French nobility, which could claim higher status and privilege than the rest of the population by right of conquest. Subsequently the monarchy ignored the claims of the hereditary nobility, and elevated members of the *Tiers État*. De Boulainvilliers wanted to see a reversal to a system in which the power of the nobility was reestablished. It goes without saying that he himself belonged to that hereditary nobility, which he thought of as hard done by.[15]

A reply was not long in coming. In 1732 abbé Jean-Baptiste Dubos published his *Histoire critique de l'établissement de la monarchie françoise dans les Gaules*, which has been described as his 'best-known work of historical propaganda'.[16] Dubos was very much an establishment figure. He was elected to the Académie française in 1720, and two years later he became *secrétaire perpetuel*.[17] Some have assumed that the government commissioned his *Histoire critique*, and it is commonly acknowledged that he was reasserting a governmental view of absolutist power against writers such as de Boulainvilliers.[18] No doubt this is true, but a recent study of Dubos' unfinished and unpublished *Traité sur la succession de la couronne* has noted that the logic of the argument ended up with something rather too radical for circulation.[19] In other words, his research did not always lead to a neatly packaged result. It is, therefore, not enough simply to see the *Histoire politique* as an absolutist treatise, though there are moments when it is exactly that. In fact it is a rather more surprising work. Even the famous refutation by Montesquieu, which takes up much of Books 30 and 31 of *L'Esprit des Loix*, gives no indication of its structure or argument. Indeed Montesquieu, while winning a few skirmishes against Dubos, totally failed to get to grips with the overall historical argument.

In the expanded three-volume (six-book) version of the *Histoire critique*, published in 1735, one briefly meets the Franks at the end of Book 1,[20] but they don't actually appear as a significant force until Book 3. Indeed the legendary Pharamond, who was regarded as a historical figure of some importance in the eighteenth century, is simply dismissed:

> De quelle Tribu étoit-il Roi? Je l'ignore. Ainsi je ne parlerai point davantage de ce Prince, dont je ne trouve rien dans les autres Ecrivains du cinquiéme et du sixiéme siecle. Il y a même des Critiques qui croyent que la Chronique de Prosper a été interpolée dans l'endroit où elle fait mention de Pharamond, et qu'on y a inseré le peu de mots qu'elle en dit.[21] [*Of which tribe was he king? I don't know. And so I will say nothing more of this prince, about whom I can find nothing in other fifth- and sixth-century writers. There are even some critics who think that the Chronicle of Prosper was interpolated at the point when Pharamond is mentioned, and that the few words about him are an insertion.*]

Dubos was actually refering to the Chronicle of 452, which parades under the name of Prosper, and discoveries since his day have proved his hunch

about interpolation. He is almost as dismissive of Chlodio, the first plausibly Merovingian leader for whom there is good, albeit slight, evidence:
'De quelle Tribu des Francs ce Prince étoit-il Roi? Parvint-il à la Couronne
par voye d'élection ou de succession?'[22] [*Of what Frankish tribe was this
prince king? Did he gain the crown by election or hereditary succession?*]
The issue of election or hereditary succession was, of course, of great
importance for anyone interested in the constitution, and was particularly
so in the context of the accession of Louis XV: it takes up a good deal of
space in other accounts of the early Franks (despite the near-complete
absence of relevant source material). Dubos rightly asserts that Frankish
kingship was hereditary and leaves it at that.[23]

Like Fustel de Coulanges a hundred and fifty years later, Dubos is
careful to establish his interpretation of late Roman Gaul in some detail
before considering the Frankish impact. His reading, however, is different
from that later offered by Fustel. His argument is summarized by his intellectual opponent, the abbé Bonnot de Mably, in a manner which slowly
degenerates into ironic savagery:

> L'abbé du Bos ne fait de Clovis qu'un officier de l'Empire, un maître
> de la milice, qui tenoit son pouvoir de Zénon et d'Anastase. Il imagine
> une république Armorique, des confédérations, des alliances, des
> traités; il se livre à des conjectures jamais analogues aux coutumes ni
> aux mœurs du temps dont il parle ... Il suppose que les Français, aussi
> patiens et aussi dociles que les soldats mercenaires, n'ont vaincu pour
> l'avantage de leur capitaine, et n'auront pas regardé leur conquête
> comme leur bien, et le droit d'y commander comme une partie de leur
> butin.[24] [*The abbé Dubos sees Clovis as nothing more than an officer
> of the Empire, a master of the soldiers, whose power came from Zeno
> and Anastasius. He imagines an Armorican republic, confederations,
> alliances, treaties. He offers conjectures which have no parallels in the
> customs or manners of the period he discusses ... He supposes that the
> Franks, as patient and docile as mercenaries, did not win for the sake
> of their captain, and did not regard their conquest as their possession
> or their rights to control the region as part of their booty.*]

Dubos sees the barbarian take-over of the western Empire almost entirely
in terms of treaties. This does admittedly lead to a remarkable, albeit brief,
comment on the legitimacy of the French monarchy, which is seen as
deriving its legitimacy from a grant by the emperor Justinian, who is
described as one of the successors of Tiberius, whose authority Christ had

recognized.[25] Such an assertion is genuinely breathtaking, but it should not be allowed to overshadow the extraordinary overall historical interpretation that Dubos offers, and which has, I think, never been adequately discussed: working largely from the Chronicles, notably those of Prosper of Aquitaine, Hydatius and 452, he sets out the notion that the end of the western Empire was really a long and extended sequence of treaties made by the emperors, culminating in the official cession of Gaul to the Franks by Justinian in return for help against the Ostrogoths.[26] This last concession was, admittedly, stressed by Fustel de Coulanges,[27] but it has been almost entirely forgotten in modern historiography.

In other words, whether or not the *Histoire critique* was an officially commissioned attack on the theories of limited monarchy implied by de Boulainvilliers and others, Dubos set about interpreting the evidence in a remarkably open-minded way. He was not always accurate, but then neither were his critics – and Voltaire, for one, thought he was more accurate than Montesquieu.[28] If one were going to provide a reason for his precise take on the end of the Roman Empire I would suggest that as important as his determination to reply to Boulainvilliers on behalf of the monarchy was his experience as a diplomat. He was intimately involved in the negotiations which concluded the War of Spanish Succession.[29] He was used to seeing the fate of nations decided by diplomacy. Of course, not all those involved in diplomacy interpreted history in the same way: Mably could boast a career in foreign affairs similar to that of Dubos,[30] but treaties do not impinge on his reading of the Frankish past. Whether or not Dubos was right, his take on the end of the West Roman Empire deserves more attention than it has received since the publication of Montesquieu's *L'Esprit des Loix*.[31]

Dubos' biographer and chief apologist, Alfred Lombard, writing in 1913, commented:

Pour le public entier, à l'exception des spécialistes de l'histoire, et pendant près d'un siècle, l'énorme travail de Du Bos a disparu dans quelques pages d'une critique spirituelle et sommaire. On ne se souvient guère du livre de Du Bos, et quand il arrive qu'on en parle, on l'abandonne aussitôt pour citer 'la brillante réfutation de Montesquieu'.[32] [*For the public, leaving aside specialists in history, and for almost a century, the huge work of Dubos has vanished into a few pages of spiritual and summary criticism. Dubos' book is rarely remembered, and when it is talked of, one immediately leaves it to cite 'the brilliant refutation by Montesquieu'.*]

The latter saw himself as taking a middle way between Dubos and de Boulainvilliers. He commented: 'M. le comte de Boulainvilliers et M. l'abbé Dubos ont fait chacun un système, dont l'un semble être une conjuration contre le tiers-état, et l'autre une conjuration contre la noblesse'.[33] [*The count of Boulainvilliers and abbé Dubos each created their own system: the former seems to be a conspiracy against the Third Estate, the latter against the nobility.*] In fact Montesquieu's whole approach is different from that of Dubos. Whereas for the latter the history of France emerges gradually from that of the Roman Empire, for Montesquieu the traditions of the Germanic tribes, as described by Caesar and Tacitus, are more important. He is concerned with the liberty of the assemblies of the forests of Germany rather than the laborious chronological history of fifth-century diplomacy. It is in the warrior relationships of the tribes that the origins of vassalage are to be found, and it is out of this that feudalism develops.

Montesquieu's approach, albeit not the detail of his argument, was taken up two decades later by Mably, whose *Observations sur l'histoire de France* was published in 1765. Like that of Montesquieu, his was a history of the Merovingians which began in the forests of Germany, and which was again concerned primarily with the origins of feudalism – an issue that has no place in Dubos' *Histoire critique*. Mably parted company with Montesquieu on a significant number of details, not least on the distinction between seigneuries, benefices and fiefs, which he carefully distinguished, whereas they are rather lumped together in *L'Esprit des Loix*.[34] It can scarcely be said, however, that his reading, any more than that of Montesquieu, stands up as anything likely to be accepted by modern historians. The problems of using Tacitus to interpret first- let alone fifth-century *Germania* have long since been recognized (if not always heeded). Fustel noted many of the difficulties in using Tacitus to elucidate *Germania* in the Age of Migration.[35] But even in Mably's own day Gibbon had little trouble in dismissing his arguments, though his critique had remarkably little impact.[36] Basically the line of interpretation which developed from de Boulainvilliers through Montesquieu to Mably triumphed in France. As Fustel de Coulanges remarked:

On se représente ordinairement, au début de l'histoire de la France, une immense irruption de Germains. On se figure la Gaule inondée, écrasée, asservie ... Il semble qu'il ait changé la face du pays et qu'il ait donné à ses destinées une direction qu'elles n'auraient pas eue sans lui. Il est pour beaucoup d'historiens, et pour la foule, la source d'où est venu tout l'ancien régime. Les seigneurs féodaux se sont vantés d'être les fils des conquérants; les bourgeois et les paysans ont cru que le servage de la glèbe leur avait été imposé par l'épée d'un vainqueur.[37] [*Usually a vast onslaught of Germans is placed at the start of French History. Gaul is seen as drowned, crushed, enslaved … It seems to have changed the face of the country and to have oriented its destinies in a direction that would otherwise not have been followed. For many historians, and for the man in the street, this is the source from which the Ancien Régime developed. Feudal lords presented themselves as the sons of conquerors: the bourgeoisie and the peasantry thought that they had been tied to the land by the sword of a conqueror.*]

It is difficult to see quite why this interpretation should have held sway with so much ease without invoking the French Revolution. What Montesquieu and Mably both conjured up was an image of liberty, exemplified by Tacitus' account of the Germanic assembly, with a further image of ensuing corruption and the formation of the feudal state. Both the utopian liberty of the distant past and its corruption into feudalism were important for the Revolutionaries. Fustel again: 'La féodalité a été présentée comme le règne des conquérants, l'affranchissement des communes comme le réveil des vaincus, et la Révolution de 1789 comme leur revanche'.[38] [*Feudalism has been presented as the rule of conquerors, the emancipation of the communes as the awakening of the defeated, and the Revolution of 1789 as their revenge.*]

To have spent so much time on the French eighteenth century may seem absurd, given the development of early medieval studies in France, Germany and England in the period from 1750 to 2000. One should, however, not see these debates as confined to a small number of *savants*. Most of the main works were published in a number of editions: some, moreover, were translated. Looking at the list of works on French medieval history, down to Augustin Thierry's *Récits des temps mérovingiens* of 1840, one may be struck by how many of them were translated into English and how quickly.[39] The cultivated Englishman of the eighteenth and nineteenth century was more likely to know his Merovingian history than is his modern counterpart. It is also remarkable how many of the issues that are still debating points today can be found expressed by Mably and Montesquieu. And it is equally remarkable that ideas as challenging as those of Dubos, whether right or wrong, have somehow got lost.

Of course there were major developments in the years that followed the Revolution and, equally important, the imperial rule of Napoleon, which like that of Louis XIV deliberately drew on images of the Merovingian past.[40] Many would argue that the most important was the foundation in 1819 of the *Gesellschaft für ältere deutsche Geschichtskunde*, which was to publish the *Monumenta Germaniae Historica*,[41] though one should beware of seeing 1819 as a radical new beginning. The *Gesellschaft* was not an official body, but rather a private association, which initially faced a good deal of difficulty in getting funding. Moreover, the notion of creating a national collection of sources was not new. We have already noted Bouquet's *Recueil des historiens*, and there was Muratori as well. Denmark had already established a series of *Scriptores rerum Danicarum medii aevi*, in 1772.[42] On the other hand, the ultimate success of the publications of the *Monumenta* was to prompt other countries to follow suit, and to lead to such collections as the *Rolls Series*. And by the end of the nineteenth century the *Monumenta* was raising the standard of textual editing to new heights.

All this was part of a wider development of scholarship. Although it mattered more for vernacular than for Latin texts, scientific philology developed rapidly in the early years of the nineteenth century: again Denmark was in the vanguard.[43] There was a strong streak of nationalism in this Danish scholarship: by emphasizing links with England, the Danes made their heritage look less German. Schleswig-Holstein was already a bone of contention: it would become more so, and in the late nineteenth and twentieth centuries would impinge in a very particular way on early medieval studies, because of the fate of the Nyddam ship, found in Denmark in 1863, but housed in Schleswig, which would eventually end up on the German side of the border.[44]

The English, not surprisingly, borrowed heavily from the Danes: Benjamin Thorpe translated Rasmus Rask's *Grammar of the Anglo-Saxon Tongue* in 1830, though he was careful to weaken the work's nationalism, first by leaving out the dedicatory epistle, and in the third edition of 1870 by omitting the introduction.[45] Meanwhile Thorpe's contemporary and friend John Mitchell Kemble was drawing increasingly on developments in German scholarship, notably the work of Jakob Grimm.[46] Technically Kemble's book *The Saxons in England*, published in 1849, is finer than anything previously written about the Anglo-Saxons, although his approach to their history (though not to *Beowulf*), and indeed the approach of those that came after, remained constitutional, in keeping with the tradition of Anglo-Saxon scholarship which had emerged in the seventeenth century.[47] The first major break would not come until 1907, with Hector Munro Chadwick's *The Origin of the English Nation*.

German scholarship was no less affected by the context in which it was produced than was that of France, Denmark or England. It is impossible to dissociate the work of Jakob Grimm or indeed the foundation of the *Monumenta* from the growing sense of German nationalism. The very idea of creating a scholarly body to publish works relevant to the history of *Germania* before Germany had been united is an indication of the ideological role that the *Monumenta* played in the nineteenth century. And while the Danes had taken as a motto for their collection of historical texts the phrase *Gloria et amor patriae*,[48] the Germans went one better claiming *Sanctus amor patriae dat animum*, even though their *patria* did not yet exist as a unified country.[49] In time the overtones of early German history would become a good deal more sinister, not least because of the influence of a French thinker, Joseph Arthur comte de Gobineau, whose *Essai sur l'inégalité des races humaines* (1853–55) first set out a theory of Nordic racial superiority – though one should note that claims that some barbarian groups could boast superiority of blood had been advanced since the seventeenth century, notably in England.[50]

It was physical rather than intellectual aggression, however, that prompted a reconsideration of the Frankish past in the later nineteenth century. Paris suffered greatly during the siege of 1871 – which for some called to mind a siege almost thirteen centuries earlier, when the city was defended against the Franks by Ste Geneviève – an event that would be recorded soon after in Puvis de Chavannes' decoration for the Panthéon. It is not surprising, therefore, that the Frankish conquest should be re-evaluated in the aftermath of the German invasion. The most challenging response came from Fustel de Coulanges. He had been professor in Strasbourg until just before the outbreak of the Franco-Prussian War, by which time he had moved to the Sorbonne. He had already established himself as the leading interpreter of the classical past. Now he planned a multi-volume *Histoire des institutions politiques de l'ancienne France*.[51] In the event six volumes appeared, heavily edited and expanded by his pupil Camille Jullian after Fustel's death in 1889.

Unlike Dubos, Fustel has never been forgotten, though few have read his *Histoire des institutions politiques*, or even know anything more than the broadest outline of his argument. Not surprisingly for a man whose first great work was on *La cité antique*, he made much of the survival of municipal institutions, which he saw as continuing under the early Franks, who he regarded as being few in number, a factor which helped explain continuity from the Roman past. Moreover, if they did have strong traditions of liberty – and Fustel doubted the value of the accounts of Caesar and Tacitus – these were relatively easily integrated into the Late Antique world, which itself was accustomed to the existence of assemblies. The Franks most certainly did not introduce feudalism. In certain respects Fustel's interpretation was an answer to French fear of the Germans. In the past the Germanic peoples had not been the great enemy of Rome, indeed they had been more occupied with war inside Germania: 'Ces violentes et aveugles haines qui remplissent aujourd'hui le cœur du Germain étaient inconnues à ces ancêtres. Pour les Germains d'alors, "l'ennemi héréditaire", c'est le Germain.'[52] [*These violent and blind hatreds that fill the heart of the German today, were unknown to his ancestors. For the Germans of those days, the hereditary enemy was the German.*] This scholarly assessment went hand in hand with Fustel's personal patriotism, which urged the celebration of the Gallo-Roman past: he even encouraged artists to depict 'la race gallo-romaine au travail, occupée à tisser, à bâtir les villes, à élever des temples, à étudier le droit, à mener de front les labeurs et les jouissances de la paix'. [*the Gallo-Roman race at work, busy weaving, building towns, erecting temples, studying law, experiencing at once the labours and pleasures of peace.*][53] Camille Jullian would make the stance even more explicit with his slogan 'Nos ancêtres, les Gaulois'.

Fustel's barbarians do not amount to a race or a nation. The Goths under Alaric were no more than an army.[54] Most German and English historians did not share the same point of view, though many would now subscribe to it.[55] For a growing number of late ninteenth-century scholars, however, the concept of the Teuton, which had been long been in existence, gained added gloss not just from Gobineau's racial theories, but also from the development of notions of biological difference as well as the idea of Aryan language, expounded by the German philologist working in Oxford, Max Müller: though it should be said that Müller retracted the notion of an Aryan race as early as 1888.[56] It was, however, another war, that of 1914–18, that undermined the concept of the Teutonic race, at least for many in England.[57] Thereafter, it was primarily in Germany that the Teutons had much currency.

The question of race and its implications for the late nineteenth- and twentieth-century understanding of the tribes of the migration period has naturally attracted a good deal of attention.[58] Theories of a Germanic *Volk* and archaeology of the 'early Germans' fed into the racial ideology and expansionist politics of the Third Reich, providing supposed justification for conquest and ethnic cleansing, notably in the Slav lands where the presence of 'Germanic' grave-goods were thought to show that the territory had once been German.[59] This contamination of scholarship with Nazi ideology not only rendered subsequently unusable much of the German historiography of the 1930s, but also meant that in the aftermath of the Second World War discussion of the barbarian peoples and their nature dried up almost completely. The subject was broached by Reinhard Wenskus in his *Stammesbildung und Verfassung* of 1961. It was a book that received relatively little attention immediately after its publication,[60] and was really first championed by Herwig Wolfram in Austria. Some recent discussion of the work of Wenskus, Wolfram and Walter Pohl has presented them all as continuing a tradition of earlier German scholarship.[61] Although Wenskus' work marks less of a break than was once thought – in particular, his ideas have much in common with a long tradition of Celtic philology[62] – there are distinctions between his work and that of earlier German scholars.[63] There is, therefore, much to be said for interpreting his work as looking to find a way to deal with the barbarian peoples which deliberately eschewed the dangerous area of biology, emphasizing instead the role of tradition in giving fluid population groups (often temporary) foci around which to define themselves.

Whereas the dominant issue in eighteenth- and early nineteenth-century discussions of the end of the Roman Empire and the early middle ages had largely been concerned with constitutional and institutional issues, increasingly, as the nineteenth century wore on, these were replaced with a concern about race – itself a developing concept throughout the period. After 1945, however, despite the impression given by recent arguments for and against Wenskus, other issues came to the fore. Some of them were not long-lasting. For instance, in France the Vichy government and the Resistance briefly became a model for reading the barbarian take-over of Gaul in the fifth century.[64] More complex was the impact of the Algerian crisis on the French understanding of late Roman and Vandal Africa.[65]

In so far as any dominant theme has replaced those of the constitution and race within the European imagination, it has been the more elusive issue of the significance of the early middle ages for the development of Europe. This has clearly been indebted to contemporary interest in the relationship between the regions of Europe and the Common Market, or more recently the European Union.[66] Moreover, this debate has been played out in a different forum than that of the academic paper and printed book. One of the notable developments of the late twentieth century has been the mounting of major exhibitions, open to the general public, and the simultaneous publication of large, scholarly catalogues, the prefaces of which, penned by heads of state or other leading political figures, brazenly reveal the political agendas behind the displays.

This particular phase in the modern use of the early middle ages is already apparent in the *Karl der Große* exhibition of 1965. Its official credentials are clear enough: it was the tenth exhibition held *unter den Auspizien des Europarates* (the Council of Europe) and was presented *unter der Schirmherrschaft* (patronage) *des Herrn Bundespräsident Dr. Heinrich Lübke*. Charlemagne was presented explicitly as the 'first *Kaiser* who wished to unite Europe'.[67] This vision of a united Europe was clearly the underlying rationale for the exhibition: there was scarcely a centenary to commemorate: 1200 years since Pippin III's first recorded visit to Aachen and 800 years since Frederick Barbarossa's canonization of Charlemagne seem contrived celebrations. Three years later would have marked the 1200th anniversary of Charles' accession.

Since the *Karl der Große* exhibition, the early middle ages have been used on a number of occasions to promote the image of a united Europe, or at least the new-found accord between France and Germany. Most obviously there is the exhibition entitled, in its German incarnation, *Die Franken: Wegbereiter Europas*: 'The Franks, trail-blazers of Europe'. It was shown initially in 1996 in Mannheim, before moving to Paris, where its title was *Les Francs – Pionniers de l'Europe*, and then back to Berlin in 1997. The description of the Franks as trail-blazers of Europe in an exhibition under the *Schirmherrschaft* of Jacques Chirac, the French president, and Helmut Kohl, his German counterpart, could hardly be more explicit. The academic justification of the title, however, took up a mere two pages of a catalogue of more than 1,000 pages.[68]

For the most part, the exhibition provided a remarkable illustration of the Merovingian kingdom and more generally of daily life therein.[69] Although the title of the exhibition suggested that it would be concerned with a people, it was instead concerned with a politico-geographical unit. The question of the settlement of the Franks within the Roman Empire and the establishment of the Merovingian kingdom was addressed in an opening section, but almost entirely from an archaeological point of view:[70] in so far as historical scholarship was brought to bear, it was largely German. There was no Fustel de Coulanges, no Camille Jullian, no Ferdinand Lot.[71] Curiously, despite the problematic development of the German interpretation of the *Völkerwanderungzeit*, Francophone scholarship was in the backseat.[72] The overall picture, however, was of Germanic peoples integrated into a sub-Roman world

Not that all Continental exhibitions devoted to the period have promoted the same line on the foundations of European unity. In 1997 and 1998, overlapping with *Die Franken*, there was an exhibition on their victims, *Die Alamannen*, which moved from Stuttgart to Zurich and back to Augsburg. While *Die Franken* was supported by Chirac and Kohl, the *Alemannen* catalogue is prefaced with words of greeting by the German *Bundespresident* Roman Herzog and the president of the Swiss confederation, Arnold Koller. The Migration Period could be presented with an eye to regional identity as well as supporting an image of a united Europe – and Germany could point to its links with a non-EU country, while claiming to be the homeland of the Frankish *Wegbereiter Europas*.

That exhibitions on the early middle ages really are intended to influence modern understanding of the world is nowhere more apparent than in that of 2003 which took as its point of departure the gift of the elephant Abul Abas to Charlemagne: *Ex Oriente, Geschichte und Gegenwart christlicher, jüdischer und islamischer Kultur*: 'From the East: History and the Present of Christian, Jewish and Islamic Culture'. It was mounted, like *Karl der Große*, in the Rathaus and cathedral of Aachen, and was funded by UNESCO and the Council of Europe. The title itself indicated the ecumenical aims of the organizers. The introductory address and essays make this more than apparent. The exhibition was intended to promote dialogue between the various religious groups: a dialogue made all the more important by the war in Iraq.[73] Remarkably, one of the organizers of the project records the opposition with which it was greeted.[74]

These and many other exhibitions all have motives which go beyond scholarship.[75] The need for backing to gain the necessary funding has made this almost inevitable. Relatively meaningless claims along the lines that the Franks and Charlemagne provide a model for a united Europe inevitably figure in the resulting publications. Nevertheless, such exhibitions have also been stimuli for a large amount of research: objects which are relatively inaccessible have been put on display, and they have been shown next to other material which sheds light on them and on the context of their production: the vast catalogues that accompany every major display contain some of the most valuable contributions to modern scholarship – particularly when it comes to the discussion of individual objects. Clearly one should not dismiss the resulting research because it has been commissioned or produced in the context of a drive towards European unification.

Scholarship can be produced for less than worthy motives, and it can be dishonestly exploited: the 1930s are a constant reminder. Yet even when written in response to patronage or commission, historical research can and does ignore or pass beyond what has been required. And it is not just in the late twentieth and twenty-first centuries that this has happened. The *Histoire critique* of Dubos would seem to me to be a case in point.

The writing of history is never going to be entirely separable from the circumstances of its production. The past will always be used and abused – we are no purer today than most of our forebears. It is, however, worth remembering that some circumstances, both private and public, have prompted individual scholars to look at their evidence from a particular and unexpected vantage-point. Sometimes the resulting observations are forgotten or ignored – as a result of political or social change. Sometimes the ideas that have been discarded deserve reconsideration, for a good idea is worth preserving regardless of the circumstances of its production.

Notes

1 This paper is essentially an interim statement on my current research: I have revised the lecture delivered at Liverpool in the light of work done subsequently at the British School at Rome.

2 For a recent overview of some of the main areas of debate (albeit inevitably more up-to-date in some areas than others), see S. Gasparri, 'L'Europa del Medioevo. Etnie e Nazione', in *Lo Spazio Letterario del Medioevo*, 2. *Il Medioevo Volgare*, ed. P. Boitani, M. Mancini and A. Varvaro, vol. 1, *La Produzione del Testo*, tomo 1 (Rome, 1999), pp. 17–56.

3 F. Lot, *Les invasions germaniques: La pénétration mutuelle du monde barbare et du monde romain* (Paris, 1935): idem, *Les invasions barbares et le peuplement de l'Europe. Introduction à l'intelligence des derniers traités de paix*: vol. 1, *Arabes et Maures – Scandinaves – Slavs du Sud et du Centre* (Paris, 1942): idem, *Les invasions barbares et le peuplement de l'Europe. Introduction à l'intelligence des derniers traités de paix*. Vol. 2, *Slaves de l'Est. – Finno-Ougriens. – Turcs et Mongols. – États issus de la décomposition des Empire du Centre et de l'Est* (Paris, 1937).

4 A clear introduction may be found in G. Falco, 'La questione longobarda e la moderna storiografia italiana', *Atti del primo congresso internazionale di studi Longobardi* (Spoleto, 1952), pp. 153–66, with the account by S. Gasparii, 'I Germani immaginari e la realtà del regno. Cinquant'anni di studi sui Longobardi', *Atti del 16o congresso internazionale di studi sull'alto medioevo* (Spoleto, 2003), vol. 1, pp. 3–28, for the subsequent fifty years.

5 A seminal text for the most recent stage of the debate is the first chapter of W. Goffart, *Barbarians and Romans, A.D. 418–584: the Techniques of Accommodation* (Princeton, NJ, 1980).

6 There is an excellent discussion of much of the French material in Claude Nicolet, *La fabrique d'une nation: La France entre Rome et les Germains* (Paris, 2003), though as a classicist by training and profession Nicolet emphasizes different aspects of the subject than might be stressed by an early medievalist.

7 For a discussion of one of the leading figures in the twentieth-century debates, see *Giornata Lincei per il centenario della nascita di Claudio Sánchez-Albornoz* (Rome, 1995).

8 To a remarkable extent Italian historiography of the nineteenth and early twentieth centuries is a replay of the debates begun by de Boulainvilliers and Dubos, but with Longobards substituted for Franks. The most important difference is that in France the debate essentially comes down to one about social structure and the rights of the monarchy, while in Italy it relates to the question of the role of outside powers within the Italian peninsula, which remained a significant issue down to the Risorgimento and beyond. For the context in which the French debate passed to Italy, see Cesare de Lollis,

Alessandro Manzoni e gli storici liberali francesi della restaurazione (Laterza: Bari, 1926).

9 A. S. Christensen, *Cassiodorus, Jordanes and the History of the Goths* (Copenhagen, 2002), pp. 7–8.

10 See M. Murphy, 'Antiquary to Academic: the progress of Anglo-Saxon scholarship', in C. T. Berkhout and M. McC. Gatch, eds, *Anglo-Saxon Scholarship: the first three centuries* (Boston, MA, 1982), pp. 1–17.

11 R. J. Smith, *The Gothic Bequest* (Cambridge, 1987).

12 Murphy, 'Antiquary to Academic'.

13 T. E. Kaiser, 'The abbé Dubos and the historical defence of the monarchy in early eighteenth-century France', *Studies on Voltaire and the Eighteenth Century*, 267, ed. H. T. Mason (Oxford, 1989), pp. 77–102, at p. 83.

14 Numa Denis Fustel de Coulanges, *Histoire des Institutions Politiques de l'Ancienne France*, vol. 2, *L'invasion franque et la fin de l'Empire*, ed. Camille Jullian (Paris, 1891), p. 533.

15 See, for instance, Henri comte de Boulainvilliers, *Essai sur la noblesse de France* (Rouen, 1732), which includes his 'Dissertation sur la noblesse de France' and his 'Dissertation abregée sur les premiers françois et sur leur origine'. The basic work on Boulainvilliers (the spelling of whose name unfortunately varies) is Renée Simon, *Un révolté du Grand Siècle: Henri de Boulainviller* (Lille, 1940), but there is a convenient summary of his life and works in J. Brethe de la Gressaye, ed., *Montesquieu, De l'Esprit des Loix*, vol. 4 (Paris, 1961), pp. 359–62.

16 Kaiser, 'The abbé Dubos and the historical defence of the monarchy', p. 92.

17 A. Lombard, *L'abbé Du Bos: un initiateur de la pensée moderne (1670–1742)* (Paris, 1913), pp. 158, 160.

18 Kaiser, 'The abbé Dubos and the historical defence of the monarchy', pp. 92–93.

19 Ibid., pp. 84–91.

20 J.-B. Dubos, *Histoire critique de l'établissement de la monarchie françoise dans les Gaules*, 3 vols (Amsterdam, 1735), I, pp. 207–44.

21 Ibid., I, pp. 360–61.

22 Ibid., I, p. 388.

23 Ibid., III, p. 279.

24 Abbé Bonnot de Mably, *Observations sur l'histoire de France*, in *Collection complete des Oeuvres de l'Abbé de Mably*, ed. l'abbé Brizzard (Paris, An III = 1794/5), p. 141.

25 Dubos, *Histoire critique*, III, p. 252.

26 Ibid., III, p. 220: the evidence comes from Procopius, *De Bello Gothico*, VII 33, 4:34, 37, ed. H. B. Dewing (Cambridge, MA, 1914–28).

27 Fustel de Coulanges, *Histoire des Institutions Politique de l'Ancienne France*, vol. 2, p. 509.

28 Voltaire, 'Questions sur l'Encyclopédie, s.v. Lois (Esprit des)', in idem, *Dictionnaire philosophique* (Paris, 1816), vol. 11, p. 57: citing Zosimus, *Historia Nova* VI, 5, in Dubos' defence.

29 Lombard, *L'abbé Du Bos*, pp. 118–41.

30 See Abbé Brizard, 'Éloge historique de l'abbé de Mably', in *Collection complete des Oeuvres de l'Abbé de Mably*, pp. 1–120.

31 For another enthusiastic assessment of Dubos see also Nicolet, *La fabrique d'une nation*, pp. 89–96.

32 Lombard, *L'abbé Du Bos*, p. 469.

33 Montesquieu, *L'Esprit des Loix*, Book 30, ch. 10, ed Brethe de la Gressaye, p. 163.

34 Mably, *Observations sur l'histoire de France*, p. 410.

35 Fustel de Coulanges, *Histoire des Institutions Politiques de l'Ancienne France*, vol. 2, pp. 236–39.

36 I. N. Wood, 'Gibbon and the Merovingians', in R. McKitterick and R. Quinault, eds,

Edward Gibbon and Empire (Cambridge, 1997), pp. 127–32.

37 Fustel de Coulanges, *Histoire des Institutions Politique de l'Ancienne France*, vol. 2, p. 531.

38 Ibid., p. 531.

39 The *Récits des temps mérovingiens* appeared as *Narratives of the Merovinian Era* in 1845.

40 For the use of the imagery of Childeric's grave-goods, see H. Neumeyer, 'Geschichte der archäologischen Erforschung der Franken in Frankreich', in *Die Franken – Wegbereiter Europas* (Mainz, 1996), pp. 35–42, at p. 35.

41 H. Bresslau, *Geschichte der Monumenta Germaniae Historica* (Hannover, 1921); H. Fuhrmann, *'Sind eben alles Menschen gewesen'. Gelehrtenleben im 19.und 20. Jahrhundert. Dargestellt am Beispiel der Monumenta Germaniae Historica und ihrer Mitarbeiter* (Munich, 1996); D. Knowles, *Great Historical Enterprises* (London, 1962), pp. 65–97. See also M. de Jong, 'Johann Friedrich Böhmer (1795–1863). Romanticus en rijkspatriot', in *Die Middeleeuwen in de negentiende eeuw* (Hilversum, 1996), pp. 63–72, for an important assessment of one of the leading figures in the initial years of the MGH.

42 R. E. Bjork, 'Nineteenth-century Scandinavia and the birth of Anglo-Saxon Studies', in A. J. Frantzen and J. D. Niles, eds., *Anglo-Saxonism and the Construction of Social Identity* (Gainesville, FL, 1997), pp. 111–32, at p. 117.

43 Bjork, 'Nineteenth-century Scandinavia and the birth of Anglo-Saxon Studies'.

44 See L. Jorgensen, B. Storgaard and L. Gebauer Thomsen, *The Spoils of Victory: the North in the Shadow of the Roman Empire* (Copenhagen, 2003).

45 Bjork, 'Nineteenth-century Scandinavia and the birth of Anglo-Saxon Studies', pp. 121–22.

46 G. P. Ackerman, 'J. M. Kemble and Sir Frederic Madden: "Conceit and too much Germanism?"', in Berkhout and McC. Gatch, eds, *Anglo-Saxon Scholarship: the first three centuries*, p. 169.

47 See the assessment in A. Dopsch, *The Economic and Social Foundations of European Civilization* (London, 1937), p. 13. For a more recent assessment see A. J. Frantzen, *Desire for Origins: New Language, Old English, and Teaching the Tradition* (New Brunswick, NJ, 1990), p. 35. Kemble does, however, give certain issues (notably the family) particular emphasis. One might note that his own marriage was breaking down at the time.

48 Bjork, 'Nineteenth-century Scandinavia and the birth of Anglo-Saxon Studies', p. 117.

49 P. J. Geary, *The Myth of Nations* (Princeton, NJ, 2002), p. 26.

50 H. A. MacDougall, *Racial Myth in English History: Trojans, Teutons and Anglo-Saxons* (Montreal, 1982). p. 272; see A. Brown Price, *Pierre Puvis de Chavannes, Catalogue, Van Gogh Museum, Amsterdam* (Zwolle, 1994), pp. 17, 26, n. 73.

51 See Nicolet, *La fabrique d'une nation*, p. 208.

52 Fustel de Coulanges, *Histoire des Institutions Politiques de l'Ancienne France*, vol. 2, p. 323.

53 Numa Denis Fustel de Coulanges, 'De la manière d'écrire l'histoire en France et en Allemagne', *Revue des Deux Mondes* (1 September 1872), trans. Price, *Pierre Puvis de Chavannes*, p. 26, n. 72.

54 Fustel de Coulanges, *Histoire des Institutions Politiques de l'Ancienne France*, vol. 2, p. 439: more generally see p. xi.

55 Much of the relevant bibliography is cited in M. Kulikowski, 'Nation versus army: a necessary contrast?', in A. Gillett, ed., *On Barbarian Identity: Critical Approaches to Ethnicity in the Early Middle Ages* (Turnhout, 2002), pp. 69–84.

56 MacDougall, *Racial Myth in English History: Trojans, Teutons and Anglo-Saxons*, p. 121.

57 Ibid., pp. 129–30. For the impact of the First World War on medieval scholarship in general, see C. Violante, *La fine della 'grande illusione': Uno storico europeo tra guerra e dopoguerra, Henri Pirenne (1914–1923): Per una rilettuta della "Histoire de l'Europe"* (Bologna, 1997).

58 For a point of departure, Geary, *The Myth of Nations*. Some of the most informative discussion is by archaeologists: see S. Jones, *The Archaeology of Ethnicity* (London, 1997) and the archaeological contributions of Sebastian Brather, Hubert Fehr and Florin Curta in Gillett, ed., *On Barbarian Identity*.

59 H. Härke, 'All Quiet on the Western Front? Paradigms, methods and approaches in West German archaeology', in I. Hodder, ed., *Archaeological Theory in Europe* (London, 1991), pp. 187–222: idem, '"The Hun is a methodical chap." Reflections on the German tradition of pre- and protohistory', in P. J. Ucko, ed., *Theory in Archaeology: a world perspective* (London, 1995), pp. 46–60.

60 One of the few scholars to note the importance of the work of Wenskus in the 1960s was John Michael Wallace-Hadrill: see his review in *English Historical Review*, 79 (1964), pp. 137–39.

61 See, for instance, A. Callander Murray, 'Reinhard Wenskus on "Ethnogenesis", Ethnicity and the Origin of the Franks', in Gillett, ed., *On Barbarian Identity*, pp. 39–68, with the reply by Walter Pohl, 'Ethnicity, Theory, and Tradition: a Response', in ibid., pp. 221–39. Criticisms of Wenskus, Wolfram and Pohl also tend, misleadingly, to present all three as having near-identical views.

62 See, for instance, the resumé of their ideas in Lot, *Les invasions germaniques*, p. 13.

63 Gasparri, 'L'Europa del Medioevo. Etnie e Nazioni', p. 37, rightly in my opinion, portrays the work of Wenskus and Wolfram as a reaction against earlier work.

64 A. Loyen, 'Resistants et collaborateurs en Gaule', *Bulletin de l'Association Guillaume Budé*, 23 (1963), pp. 437–50.

65 See, for example, G. Fourquin, 'Éloge funèbre de Christian Courtois', *Settimane di Studio del Centro Italiano di Studi sull'Alto Medioevo*, V, *Caratteri del saecolo VII in Occidente* (Spoleto, 1958), p. 68.

66 This is, of course, not the case with New World scholarship.

67 W. Braunfels, 'Vorwort', p. ix, *Karl Der Große: Werk und Wirkung* (Aachen, 1965).

68 F. Staab, 'Die Franken – Wegbereiter Europas', in *Die Franken – Wegbereiter Europas*, pp. 10–22, at pp. 21–22.

69 The exhibition was divided into two halves: 'Die Merowinger und ihr Reich' and 'Alltagskultur im Frankenreich', with an introductory section on 'Von der Vielfalt zur Einheit: Das Frankenreich ensteht'.

70 *Die Franken – Wegbereiter Europas*, pp. 55–170.

71 Jullian and Lot are cited elsewhere in the catalogue.

72 The tone is set by Staab, 'Die Franken – Wegbereiter Europas', pp. 10–12, which, despite citing non-German scholars, sees the development of a concept of the Franks ('der Wandel des Frankenbegriffs') almost entirely as an aspect of German intellectual history.

73 See the comments by Walter Schwimmer, General Secretary for the Council of Europe, and Wolfrang Thierse, Präsident des Deutschen Bundestages, in *Ex Oriente: Isaak und der Weisse Elefant: Bagdad-Jerusalem-Aachen: Eine Reise durch drei Kulturen um 800 bis heute* (Aachen, 2003), vol. 1, *Die Reise des Isaak*, pp. 10–11, 12.

74 W. Dressen, 'Aufklärung, Sichtbarkeit: ex Oriente Lux: ein Werkstattbericht', in *Ex Oriente*, vol 1, pp. 18–21, at p. 19.

75 Of particular interest and importance was the Copenhagen exhibition of the Danish bog-finds, 'The Spoils of Victory'. In order to secure the loan of the Nyddam ship from Schleswig, the Danes had to relinquish claims to ownership of the boat, and in so doing closed one part of the long-running saga of the Schleswig-Holstein question.

Whatever Happened to Your Heroes?
Guy and Bevis after the Middle Ages

David Matthews

In May 1767 the antiquarian Samuel Pegge read a paper to the Society of Antiquaries on the subject of the legendary English hero, Guy of Warwick. Less concerned with the Anglo-Norman and Middle English romances about Guy than the mentions of him by such historians as Leland, Camden, Heylyn and Dugdale, Pegge showed that almost nothing about the legend could be true.[1] One after another, events in Guy's story fall beneath Pegge's antiquarian sword. He demonstrated that the Anglo-Saxon setting was anachronistic and that the tale could only have been composed in the later middle ages. He argued that pilgrimage to the Holy Land, of the kind that Guy undertakes, was not a feature of English life before the Conquest (37). Though there might have been a Guy of Warwick, he could not have been earl of Warwick, and neither could he have fought a duel with Colbrond in order to save the throne of England from the Danes (29). In the reign of Athelstan the Danes did not besiege Winchester, and did not have 'it in their power to contest king Athelstan's title to the crown' (35–36). Pegge deduced that Guy must have been about 68 when he died, so at the time he was supposed to have fought with Colbrond he was 'rather too old to be engaged in such a perilous affair, and wherein so much was at stake, as the right to the crown of England' (35).

Plausibly concluding that the story of Guy of Warwick might have been a confection made by someone seeking to ingratiate himself with the real earls of Warwick of the later middle ages, Pegge takes apart the story's claims to factual status. At best, it is an example of invented tradition. Exit one legendary English hero.

It is impossible to judge, at this distance of time, what the mood might have been in the Society's Chancery Lane rooms after the paper was read. Perhaps there was sage nodding at a job well done. Perhaps congratulations, as the errors in Leland, Camden and other pre-Enlightenment historians were relentlessly chased down. What seems *un*likely to have happened is that anyone present thought there was any novelty in Pegge's conclusions. From a modern perspective, his performance looks a little like that of an academic at a film conference who demonstrates, by close reference to medieval chronicles, that the events in Mel Gibson's film *Braveheart* do not represent the historical actuality of the late years of Edward I's reign.

In 1767 the name of Guy of Warwick – along with that of Bevis of Hampton and to a large extent that of King Arthur himself – had been proverbial for its association with incredible fiction for more than a century and a half. At the time, the story of Guy of Warwick was readily available in any number of chapbooks, which placed an emphasis on the story's incredibilities as a major selling point. A short walk from the Society's rooms, for example, at the sign of the Looking Glass on London Bridge, *The Noble and Renowned History of Guy, Earl of Warwick: Containing A Full and True Account of his many Famous and Valiant Actions; Remarkable and Brave Exploits; and Noble and Renowned Victories*, originally produced by 'G.L.' in 1706, had appeared in its tenth edition by 1759. This duodecimo publication is the kind of cheap production, retold in modernized English prose and illustrated with woodcuts, that members of the Society of Antiquaries might have expected to see in the hands of the rustic poor, or perhaps their own servants.

It is true that there was a long tradition of acceptance of the story of the fight between Guy, earl of Warwick, and the Dane, Colbrond. William Dugdale, in his *Antiquities of Warwickshire* (1656), took it at face value, and in Pegge's own time, Thomas Percy mentioned the story in his *Reliques of Ancient English Poetry* (1765) without challenging it. It nevertheless seems unlikely that any of the gathered antiquaries had his eyes opened to the impossibility of Guy's story by Pegge's paper. His performance was either a spectacular example of preaching to the converted, or it was about something other than the need to straighten out the facts in the case of Guy of Warwick.

In the 1760s the understanding of late medieval literature and culture was on the verge of a great transformation. In expelling Guy of Warwick from history, Pegge's memoir represents part of an Enlightenment ordering of knowledge, in which one of the more persistent literary survivals of the middle ages was put in its place, its truth-claims rationally debunked, and the credulousness of pre-Enlightenment historians exposed. Pegge's memoir also represents a centralizing of knowledge. At the time, antiquarianism was taking an increasingly organized form.[2] The Society of Antiquaries itself was increasingly officialized; having been granted its Royal Charter in 1751, the body that had once met in taverns and coffee houses would move to Somerset House in 1780. In this period of antiquarianism, which has been called 'the great age of the county history', there was of course enormous interest in the provinces.[3] Pegge himself was a Derbyshire man who was very concerned with local antiquities. But in this instance, what is seen is a crushing centralization of truth-claims, with a provincial legend put firmly in its place by a scholar whose authority issues from an official, metropolitan body.

Today the English heroes Bevis of Hampton and Guy of Warwick are of very little interest to anyone beyond those scholars who specialize in the medieval romances about them. They have no place in modern popular culture and are not, like Beowulf, Robin Hood, Gawain, Arthur or Lancelot, the subject of cinema or novels. They belong with other near-forgotten provincial heroes, such as Horn, Havelok and Wade. Yet in the middle of the eighteenth century, all of these figures (except Beowulf) were bracketed together and thought of as the stuff of unbelievable fictions, most of which were reproduced in cheap books for sale to readers of non-'canonical, non-'polite' literature.

In the late eighteenth century, something happened which set Bevis and Guy on one trajectory, and Arthur and Robin Hood on altogether another. The last two were retrieved from life in the sub-literary chapbooks, and rapidly transformed into national figures in the nineteenth century. Bevis and Guy, on the other hand, became the preserve of scholars and were largely forgotten by everyone else. Pegge's memoir cannot of course be held responsible for this: in fact, it was not published until 1783 and does not seem to have had wide impact.[4] But Pegge's work represents a larger phenomenon, the late eighteenth-century reorganization of knowledge about the middle ages. In the context of that reorganization, this essay examines the post-medieval presentation of these English heroes up until the later eighteenth century, considering the implications of their disappearance.

I

The romances of Guy of Warwick and Bevis of Hampton are routinely linked because of their obvious similarities. Each is based on an Anglo-Norman original composed early in the thirteenth century; each was translated into Middle English around 1300; they are both purportedly set in the tenth century but in reality (as Pegge correctly said of *Guy*) their historical basis is negligible, and they more truly represent a kind of thirteenth- and fourteenth-century antiquarian interest in the Anglo-Saxon past. Both romances are long and involve the heroes in many adventurous twists and turns that take them to foreign lands. They both have pious endings. In neither case is there a single authoritative redaction of the romance; instead there are different adaptations made at different times.[5]

The reception histories of the romances of Bevis and Guy are also very similar. They were already the subject of satirical treatment as early as Chaucer's time. Chaucer was familiar with *Bevis* and *Guy*, both of which he mentions in his *Tale of Sir Thopas*, lampooning their subject matter and the tail-rhyme form in which they are partially composed. The strong implication is that metrical romances of this kind are quaintly old-fashioned in the context of Chaucer's emergent urban, professional and courtly audience. Around the same time, nevertheless, other medieval texts remain accepting of the metrical romance tradition. The *Laud Troy Book* (c. 1400) opens with an eclectic list of heroes which includes Bevis and Guy alongside Richard I, Gawain, Ywain, Tristram and Percival, Roland and Charlemagne, Cassivelaunus, and finally Horn, Havelok and Wade.[6] They are listed in order to set up a contrast – not necessarily an unfavourable one – with the heroes of the classical story of Troy.

Despite Chaucer's scorn, *Bevis* and *Guy* were among the small handful of Middle English writings that had some currency after the middle of the sixteenth century. The stories at least, if not the texts themselves, survived into the modern period in frequent reprintings. Although Caxton, so far as is known, did not print either romance, around 1500 both Richard Pynson and Wynkyn de Worde produced versions of *The History of Guy of Warwick* and *Sir Bevis of Hampton* (Pynson: STC 12540, 1988; de Worde: STC 12541, 1987). In the second half of the sixteenth century, although the interest in Middle English literature shown in the early Tudor period had begun to wane, and attacks on the immorality of romances increased, William Copland produced a version of *Guy of Warwick* around 1565 (STC 12542) and two impressions of *Bevis* c.1560–65 (STC 1988.8, 1989), while Thomas East produced another *Bevis* around 1585 (STC 1990). East's *Bevis* is in rhyming couplets which are printed on the page as long lines, a space-saving measure then copied by succeeding printers.[7]

In this period the tradition of Chaucer editing was tending increasingly towards what James Simpson has characterized as a model of recovery of the Chaucerian text by an editor whose methods look forward to philological recovery of medieval texts. Caxton aimed 'to reproduce the same text that Chaucer wrote, no more nor less...', an aim in which he was followed by the sixteenth-century editors.[8] Chaucer editions were folios, and by the end of the Tudor period these were lavish productions.

By contrast, the sixteenth-century prints of *Bevis* and *Guy* are quartos and, in the standard manner for such early volumes, give no sense of a coherent methodology or the drive to *recover* medieval writing. They simply present the texts without any learned discussion whatsoever. *Bevis* and *Guy* are also treated as resources to be mined and adapted at will rather than venerated and preserved. For example, the killing of the Dun Cow by Guy is a commonplace of the later Guy tradition. But it does not exist in the medieval romance; it is an early modern interpolation, deriving from a stall-ballad printed in 1592.[9]

In the minds of the booksellers and their clients there seems, then, to have been a clear distinction between this kind of medieval writing and that of Chaucer, Gower and Malory. The Bevis and Guy quartos, usually illustrated by woodcuts, are clearly appealing to a quite different readership from that which might have bought, for example, Thomas Speght's grand folio edition of Chaucer's complete works of 1602. Although it is difficult to specify the readership, it seems safe to say that the Bevis/Guy tradition was never invested with great cultural capital in the way that Speght's Chaucer was.

It is not surprising, then, that the Chaucerian verdict on Bevis and Guy in *Thopas* was endorsed in late Tudor and Jacobean courtly literary culture. A host of references makes it clear that courtly taste increasingly disdained (or affected to disdain) such texts as *Bevis* and *Guy*, which had evidently become proverbial for their incredibility. At the beginning of the Shakespeare and Fletcher collaboration, *Henry VIII* (1612–13), for example, the Duke of Norfolk describes the kings of France and England as vying with one another at the Field of the Cloth of Gold: 'they did perform / Beyond thought's compass – that former fabulous story / Being now seen possible enough, got credit / That Bevis was believed'.[10]

A self-consciously ordained split between courtly and popular culture had by then already been propounded in *The Arte of English Poesie* (1589) by George Puttenham. Discussing metre, Puttenham refers to popular tunes and poems. These are the work, he continues, of

> blind harpers or such like tauerne minstrels that giue a fit of mirth for a groat, & their matters being for the most part stories of old time, as

the tale of Sir *Topas*, the reportes of *Beuis* of *Southampton, Guy* of *Warwicke, Adam Bell,* and *Clymme* of the *Clough* & such other old Romances or historicall rimes, made purposely for recreation of the common people at Christmasse diners & brideales, and in tauernes & alehouses and such other places of base resort, also they be vsed in Carols and rounds and such light or lasciuious Poemes, which are commonly more commodiously vttered by these buffons or vices in playes then by any other person.

The chief characteristic of such verse is 'short distaunces and short measures', which might please the 'popular eare', Puttenham continues, but 'in our courtly maker we banish them vtterly'.[11] This 'utter banishment' is perhaps the rather exaggerated result of Puttenham's zeal to segregate popular and courtly literatures. But around the same time Thomas Nashe also derides the rhymes in *Bevis,* asking 'Who is it, that reading Beuis of Hampton, can forbeare laughing, if he marke what scambling shyft he makes to ende his verses a like'.[12] In 1622 Henry Peacham was slightly more tolerant when recommending various courtly literary works to his readers in *The Compleat Gentleman.* These consisted of such things as Sidney's *Arcadia* and Thomas More's *Richard III,* but Peacham added, 'Imagine not that hereby I would binde you from reading all other bookes, since there is no booke so bad, euen Sir *Beuis* himselfe, *Owleglasse,* or *Nashes* herring, but some commoditie may be gotten by it'.[13]

Peacham does not entirely write off the popular reading represented by *Bevis* and is perhaps more concerned to insult Thomas Nashe's 1599 work, *Lenten Stuffe ... With a new Play ... of the praise of the Red Herring.* But he does have a clear sense of a hierarchy in which *Bevis* occupies a low position. More specific information about readership from the same period is suggested by the satirist Henry Parrot's 1615 poem, 'Trahit sua quemque Voluptas'. Parrot imagines different kinds of readers looking at his own book at the stationer's stall. One after another they cavil and turn to other books. A 'Countrey-Farmer' is represented as saying, 'Shewe mee King *Arthur, Bevis,* or *Syr Guye*'. 'Those are the Bookes', Parrot comments, 'he onely loves to buye'.[14]

Parrot links Bevis and Guy with King Arthur; Puttenham put them in the same bracket with such outlaw tales as *Adam Bell, Clym of the Clough* and *William Cloudesley.* Later writers would just as readily link Bevis and Guy with Robin Hood. Much earlier, the *Laud Troy Book* also linked Bevis to Arthurian heroes, but the list there was generically consistent: its heroes were all the subject of romance. By the early seventeenth century, there is no generic consistency in the associations made between Bevis and Guy, and King Arthur, Robin Hood and even the English translation of the folk tale, *Till Eulenspiegel*. The common factors are that they are all unbelievable; they are all the objects of rustic approbation, all available in chapmen's bags: all things which disqualify them from polite canons of literature. In terms of their literary prestige, *Bevis* and *Guy* were on a downward trajectory, 'moving down-market', Tessa Watt suggests, 'as they were reprinted'.[15]

In the early fifteenth century, the *Laud Troy Book* counterposed Bevis and Guy to classical heroes without much disadvantage on the side of the native heroes. The same counterposition, however, was later used to create a distinct divide between native stories and the classics. It is routine in the seventeenth century. In an epigram to the Earl of Newcastle, Ben Jonson opens by praising the earl's horsemanship, comparing him to '*Perseus* upon *Pegasus*; / Or *Castor* mounted on his *Cyllarus*' before making a further comparison with 'our home-borne Legend.../ Of bold Sir *Bevis*, and his *Arundell*...'[16] Jonson's reference to 'home-borne Legend' seems quite neutral here, but more often the comparison between classical and native is made to burlesque effect. In Philip Massinger's play *The Picture* (1630), the hero Mathias goes into battle against the Turks. His deeds are related:

> bold *Mathias*
> Aduanc'd, and star'd like *Hercules* or *Golias*.
> A hundred thousand *Turkes*, it is no vaunt,
> Assail'd him, euery one a Termagaunt,
> But what did he then? with his keene edgde speare
> He cut, and carbonadode 'em, heere, and there,
> Lay leggs and armes, and as 'tis sayd truely
> Of *Beuis*, some he quarter'd all in three.[17]

Samuel Rowlands, in his *The Famous History of Guy Earle of Warwicke* (1609), writes a prefatory poem, 'To the Noble English Nation': '*Great* Hercules, *if he had breath'd on ground*, / When English Guy *of* Warwicke *liu'd renownd*, / There would have ben a combate t'wixt them two, / To try what stoute Alcides force could doe...'[18] Rowlands goes on to make further comparisons with Hector and Achilles, before pleading:

> Kinde English, yeald vnto your countriman,
> As gentle entertainement as you can:

Though he lye quiet, now transform'd in dust,
Sleeping in death, as other mortals must:
With your life-giuing breath, reuiue his fame,
That hath deseru'd an honourable name. (A3ᵛ)

In however apologetic a sense, Rowlands is at least making a plea here for the idea of Guy as a native-born hero who has fallen into dusty neglect in a way that has not occurred with the classical heroes. Rowlands' verse retelling of Guy was to become the standard version of the story for the seventeenth century, replacing the medieval original.

More often, this sense that Bevis and Guy (and King Arthur and others) deserve revival because they are *native* heroes is counterbalanced by a complete lack of faith that vernacular heroes can match those of classical legend. Again and again their names are invoked for the purposes of burlesque or bathos. Rowlands himself, in his poem 'A Drvnkards Duello', describes two drinking companions meeting in combat, the aggressor drunkenly proclaiming: 'I come like *Beuis* to the Bore, / Appear base coward...' He is further characterized as 'braue Sir *Lancelot* of the Lake' – before his adversary flattens him with one blow from a shovel.[19]

Despite a long tradition of scorn, it is clear that well into the seventeenth century both Bevis and Guy remained popular with booksellers, and the most likely reason for that is that they continued to sell well. Watt points out that such books as these were subject to an economy of scale which meant that they became more profitable the longer they remained in demand.[20] Among the larger expenses of such works were the illustrations. In the Bevis/Guy quartos, it is clear that the same blocks were used and re-used by different printers – perhaps acquisition of the blocks was enough in itself to persuade a printer to put out a new edition.

Notably, they retained this popularity while preserving something approximating the medieval romance versions of the tales. As late as 1639, *Sir Bevis of Hampton newly corrected*, printed by Richard Bishop, offered something in appearance very like a Middle English metrical romance in couplets (with each couplet written as a long line, following in the tradition of East). This was at a time when even Chaucer was in decline: in the same year, Francis Kynaston published part of a translation of Chaucer's *Troilus and Criseyde*, not into English but into Latin, which he regarded as the more durable language. There was a sense that Middle English had outlived any usefulness it had. In a prefatory poem to Kynaston's translation, the Oxford scholar Edward Foulis confidently predicted, 'the Translation will become / Th' Originall...'[21] Strangely, while interest in

Chaucer fell, the 'Originall' Middle English survived in *Bevis*. In however devalued a form, the metrical romances of Bevis and Guy were among the major representatives of medieval culture for the early seventeenth century.

The texts were not, however, exclusively the object of derogation. In the collaboratively written play *Sir John Oldcastle* (1600), whose authors included Anthony Munday and Michael Drayton, there is a scene in which the Bishop of Rochester has his summoner seek out Oldcastle's books, as part of his scheme to convict Oldcastle of heresy. The play goes to great lengths to make Oldcastle appear a favourable character – it is an implied riposte to Shakespeare's characterization of Oldcastle as Falstaff – while the Bishop is an obvious schemer. When the summoner appears with books the Bishop demands, 'What bring'st thou there? what? books of heresie?' The summoner responds, 'Yea my lord, heres not a latine book … / Heres the Bible, the testament, the Psalmes in meter, / The sickemans salue, the treasure of gladnesse…' The bishop commands them to be burnt, but Oldcastle's servant Harpoole intervenes: 'I haue there English bookes, my lord, that ile not part with for your Bishoppricke, Beuis of Hampton, Owleglasse, the Frier and the Boy, Ellen of Rumming, Robin hood, and other such godly stories which if ye burne, by this flesh ile make ye drink their ashes in S. Marget's Ale.'[22] At this point, the scene abruptly ends.

The audience knows that Harpoole's threat is not idle: in an earlier confrontation with the summoner, he forced the man to eat the warrant he had been trying to serve on Oldcastle. Centrally, this scene is concerned with the opposition between Latinity and the vernacular. At first it seems that the Bishop, representative of Latinity, will use Oldcastle's possession of vernacular books of religion to condemn him. Latinity is devious; either the summoner is lying for his master, or he is illiterate himself and is relying on the illiteracy of others so that his mis-identification of the books will not be discovered. They are certainly vernacular writings, but Harpoole shows that the books are simply innocent native writing. Native stories have a role to play here in turning the tables on the devious Church.

Bevis, *Guy* and *Elinor Rumming* are described as 'godly', which is perhaps more Harpoole's particular view rather than one likely to be shared by everyone in a seventeenth-century audience. But by this point in the play we have seen that Harpoole has an instinctive way with writing, spotting a false text and making the summoner eat his own words. Harpoole identifies a list of titles which might not receive favour from courtly culture, but which serve to identify an honest and uncomplicated Englishness counterposed to a courtly world of political scheming.

II

In the course of the seventeenth century, succeeding booksellers had no choice but to make Bevis and Guy less authentically medieval, at least in the linguistic sense, because their readership would not or could not go on reading medieval metrical romances. By the late seventeenth century, Guy and Bevis appeared principally in modernized form.

There is a host of printings of *Guy* and *Bevis* in the late seventeenth century, usually in the standard 24-page format of the three-sheet octavo, with woodcuts. These were such works as *The Gallant History of the Life and Death of that most Noble Knight, Sir Bevis of Southampton. Where is contained much Variety of Pleasant and Delightful Reading*, printed about 1690. Somewhat more generously, a black-letter prose chapbook printed in 1689 for William Thackeray and Jonah Deacon promised, in 78 pages, *The Famous and Renowned History of Sir Bevis of Southampton, giving an account of his birth, education, heroick exploits and enterprises, his fights with giants, monsters, wild-beasts and armies, his conquering kings and kingdoms, his love and marriage, fortunes and misfortunes, and many other famous and memorable things and actions, worthy of wonder; with the Adventures of other Knights, Kings and Princes, exceeding pleasant and delightful to Read.*

The verse versions earlier in the century had occupied volumes of 140–50 pages, which gave the equivalent of a romance of 4–5000 lines: comparable to the length of the Auchinleck *Bevis of Hampton*. Obviously, the chapbooks boiled the stories down. The Middle English romance of *Guy of Warwick* consists of up to 11,000 lines, but in such chapbooks as Charles Bates's printing of c. 1680, *The History of the Famous Exploits of Guy Earl of Warwick*, it is reduced to the standard 24 pages (on very cheap paper).[23] But even as this process of abridgement and apparent vulgarization occurs in the seventeenth century, there is a rising value placed on the vernacularity of the texts. The editions prepared by John Shurley, in contrast to earlier productions, tend to be prefaced with strident claims about the value of the material.

Shurley, a writer operating in the last two decades of the seventeenth century, produced versions of the stories of Amadis of Gaul and of Palmerin, the hero of a romance of Spanish origin. One of his earliest works was *The Renowned History, or the Life and Death of Guy Earl of Warwick* (1681). In an 'Epistle to the Reader', Shurley offered extravagant justifications for the printing and reading of *Guy of Warwick*, 'the far-famed and Most Renowned *English* Champion', supposedly basing his remarks on 'what can be Collected out of the best Historians, both Antient and Modern'. Shurley's is a prose retelling of the story in about 40 quarto pages, which he offers as a spur to martial conduct. Such stories, Shurley argues, fill men 'with a desire to imitate the same, and the very remembrance inspires them with courage…' This is particularly true 'in *English men*, who at this day are Famed for Courage and true Heroick Vallor through all the yet known World' (Epistle, n.p.).

The Guy story that then begins, however, has an unfamiliar look. Shurley first discusses the Roman invasion of Britain, concluding that the Romans never conquered Britain by the sword alone, but gave the Britons their own terms (A1^r). A brief account of the collapse of the empire and the invasion of Britain by the Saxons follows. For three hundred years the Saxons hold sway in Britain, in constant civil war, until the advent of 'Edgard the great King of the West-Saxons sirnamed Athelstone'. In his reign lived 'the very famous Champion Giraldus Cassibilanius, vulgarly called Guy of Warwick, who as credible historians do affirm, descended lineally from the British Royal blood, ever since Cassibilanius…' The British story is Shurley's addition; the story of Guy that follows is a standard version derived largely from Rowlands' verse retelling. It describes Guy's courtship of Felice, his travels in the Holy Land, his killing of the Dun Cow, his killing of a dragon in Northumberland and, finally, his return to England, the fight with Colbrond, and pious hermitage and death. Shurley's unusual prefaced material on Celtic Britain seems a gesture to a larger historical context, and hence to the imagined historicity of Guy. Notably, Guy is in this version not just a hero of the Saxon past, but a figure who effortlessly reconciles in himself the pre-Roman British heritage with the Anglo-Saxon English.

Shurley's version reappeared several times. At the same time, a tradition of very basic chapbook Guys continued, as in the 24-page prose version, *The History of the Famous Exploits of Guy Earl of Warwick*, printed for Sarah Bates around 1720, and the very similar chapbook, *The History of Guy, Earl of Warwick*, sold in Aldermary Church Yard, London, around 1750. These are highly condensed versions of the narrative, illustrated by woodcuts, in which the emphasis is on the ending of the Guy story, with its motifs of repentance and chaste life.[24] However, the more elaborate tradition represented by Shurley was continued in the version first printed by 'W.O.' for 'G.L.' in 1706, and reprinted at least ten times in the ensuing years. This was *The Noble and Renowned History of Guy, Earl of Warwick: Containing A Full and True Account of his many Famous and Valiant Actions, Remarkable and Brave Exploits, and*

Noble and Renowned Victories, which claimed to be based on 'Authentick Records'.

Like Shurley's, G.L.'s prefatory material emphasizes Guy as a national figure rather than as a pious exemplar, though there is no mention of him as descendant of a Celtic ruling family. The emphasis now is on Guy's final fight with Colbrond, 'Which he both undertook and perform'd, to the eternal Honour of the *English* nation' (A3ᵛ). The story is told in a prose version, in a generous 151 pages. Notably, it is presented in roman type, instead of the black letter which had been the norm up until the end of the seventeenth century. A prefatory poem offers an abstract of the story and suggests to readers: '*as thou read'st, be this remember'd too, / It was an English Man all this did do...*'

The printing tradition of *Bevis of Hampton* had taken a similar turn at the same time. *The Famous and Renowned History of Sir Bevis of Southampton*, printed for Thackeray and Deacon in 1689, features a prefatory epistle signed S.J. (conceivably John Shurley, who also used the initials J.S., in another guise). He suggests:

> Therefore for the honour of our Country, of which he [Bevis] has so well deserved, let his Memory live in the thoughts of every true English Man, and be to them a pattern of Heroick Virtue, that by imitating him, they may raise the very name of the British Empire, as formerly it was, to be the Terror of the World...[25]

It was these kinds of versions of the two legends that had been in existence for several decades when Samuel Pegge decided to take his stand against the historicity of Guy. What is interesting about the chapbooks' claims on historicity is not that they seem likely to have been taken very seriously by readers, but that they are clearly borrowing from antiquarian discourse. In a context in which serious investigation of medieval artefacts was just beginning (at the end of the seventeenth century),[26] the rewritings of Bevis and Guy are supplied with a veneer of historical-antiquarian knowledge. This would also explain the concern with the Roman-British past in the chapbooks, which was similarly an object of concern to antiquaries.[27] It was perhaps this pretension to antiquarian discourse that provoked Pegge more than anything else.

Like antiquarian discourse, which increasingly links itself to the honour of the nation in the period, by the early eighteenth century *Bevis* and *Guy* too were relocated within the terms of a nationalist discourse. As eighteenth-century national sentiment grew, particularly as the result of the effort, after the 1707 Act of Union, to forge Great Britain out of what was 'a less than united kingdom',[28] the booksellers and editors make more concerted attempts to link these medieval heroes to national concerns.

III

At the time that Samuel Pegge stood up to denounce the historicity of Guy of Warwick in 1767, he was well aware of the revival of interest in the middle ages that was going on around him. He participated in it himself, editing a medieval kitchen handbook, *The Forme of Cury*, in 1780, and presenting to the Society of Antiquaries a critique of Thomas Percy's theory of minstrelsy as propounded in the first edition of the *Reliques of Ancient English Poetry* (1765). In the 1770s Thomas Warton would publish his hugely influential *History of English Poetry*, the medievalist forgeries of Thomas Chatterton appeared, as did Thomas Tyrwhitt's new edition of the *Canterbury Tales*.

In the context of this general revival, two heroes from medieval literature, who had for two hundred years been confined to cheap chapbook productions, were now raised to high-cultural status. King Arthur, who with Bevis and Guy had been proverbial for outrageous fiction for so long, suddenly became respectable in the nineteenth century. The influence of the Arthurian cycle on Victorian Britain can hardly be exaggerated. At the same time Robin Hood emerged as a proper subject for antiquarians, particular in Joseph Ritson's two-volume anthology, *Robin Hood: A Collection of all the Ancient Poems, Songs, and Ballads, now Extant, Relative to that Celebrated English Outlaw* (1795). Within the overall rediscovery of medieval culture that began in the late eighteenth century, these figures became two of the most recognizable characters in all of medieval English culture – as the continuing appearance of films, television series, comics and books featuring Robin and Arthur suggests. But the reception of Arthur and Robin is not, of course, simply popular. By the late nineteenth century, the Arthurian cycle in particular was the object of serious scholarly editing and high-cultural refashioning.

Why then did two other English heroes, Bevis and Guy, so thoroughly fail to follow them in revival? Why, today, are the Holy Grail or Robin Hood's skill with a bow proverbial and instantly recognizable, while Bevis's fight with the boar, or Guy's saving of England by the defeat of Colbrond, are forgotten by everyone except a few scholars? As we have seen, in the course of the eighteenth century both were positioned in proto-

nationalist terms. Each had been regarded as completely unhistorical –
but so too were Robin Hood and Arthur, which had no detrimental effect
on their nineteenth-century reception. Even *Mandeville's Travels*, perhaps
regarded as the most mendacious of all medieval survivals, prospered
under the new conditions of interest.[29] But *Bevis of Hampton* and *Guy of
Warwick* were edited only once apiece in the nineteenth century, each time
by William Barclay David Donald Turnbull, in editions with tiny print
runs restricted to club memberships (Edinburgh: [Maitland Club], 1838;
Edinburgh: [Abbotsford Club], 1840).

I have already suggested that one of the things Pegge was enacting in
his talk on Guy of Warwick was a centralizing of antiquarian knowledge.
Antiquarianism was in many ways a heavily regional activity, because it
concerned ancient monuments and artefacts that were to be found in
provincial Britain, or in many cases texts that had a particular regional
focus. The importance of the county history has already been remarked
on. But at the same time antiquarianism was subject to more central,
metropolitan institutions, such as the London-based Society of Antiquaries, and the universities of Oxford and Cambridge. I would suggest
that in the late eighteenth century, the problem with Guy and Bevis was
not the affront to common sense posed by their manifest incredibilities,
as Pegge argued. Eighteenth- and nineteenth-century antiquaries and
literati dealt quite comfortably with such affronts: either by valuing, as
Thomas Warton did, incredible fiction for its own sake; or, as Robert
Southey did in his introduction to *The Byrth, Lyf, and Actes of Kyng
Arthur* (1817), by simply denying there was so much that was unrealistic:

> The authors of these books never supposed that they were outraging
> probability; none of the marvels which they feigned were regarded as
> impossible; they were all founded upon the received opinions of the
> age; the belief in magic, the science of gems, and the wonderful prop-
> erties of wells, fountains, and lakes, whose effects were described in
> books, the authenticity of which had never been questioned. Travellers
> and naturalists told of more monsters than the romance writers ever
> devised.[30]

Similarly, Southey continued, 'The prowess of the knights of Romance...
is not much exaggerated' (xxxi).

The problem was more that despite the efforts of the eighteenth-century
hack writers to put a patriotic and nationalist gloss on the efforts of Guy
and Bevis, they remained essentially provincial heroes – like Havelok and

Wade, and scarcely more popular than those figures. Arthur, as the product of French tellings of Celtic material about a Romano-Celtic figure, is the least likely national British figure. But as a leader and unifier of Britain, a national figure is what he became. Arthur could be regarded as having invented, in the Dark Ages, the entity that came into being with the Union of 1707. Robin Hood, not a king but still a leader, is also a unifying national figure, someone who effects a reconciliation between the conflicting identities of Saxon and Norman. It is perhaps this that John Shurley had in mind with his canny (if slightly bizarre) attempt at reinventing Guy as an amalgam of Roman, British and Saxon identities. Shurley might have seen that straightforward native appeal would not do in the case of these popular heroes; they needed to be positioned for national status. There is in fact nothing inherently stranger in his construction of Guy than there is in the various reinventions of Arthur as the Englishman he certainly was not.

* * *

When he was first delving into English romances in the early nineteenth century, Walter Scott read *Guy of Warwick* (probably in the Auchinleck manuscript, which he had in his possession for lengthy periods). He found it, as he confided to his friend George Ellis, very dull and almost as bad as *Bevis of Hampton*. 'I think nothing but national prejudice could have elevated it to the situation of eminence in which it is placed by Chaucer', he wrote to Ellis (not the first to miss altogether the fact that Chaucer's treatment of *Guy* and *Bevis* is ironic). '[I]t may serve however to show in what an ineffable degree our Ancestors possessd the virtue of patience or at least how heavy their time must have hung upon their hands.'[31]

In its early manifestation in the late eighteenth century, English medieval studies was an antiquarian/romantic enterprise. In the era of Warton, Hurd, Percy and Scott the possibility was first created of distinguishing medieval *studies* from medieval*ism*.[32] Scott's words underline the extent to which Guy and Bevis do not fit this paradigm. They are too provincially rustic and unable to shake off the stigma of the chapbook. Although they might appear ideally positioned for status as English heroes in an era of increasing national self-consciousness, in fact they are *too* English. They are not from the fringes, not Celtic, not bardic enough, for the era of romantic balladry. John Shurley saw the necessity for Guy to be converted into a British figure, but 'Guy of Warwick', by then, evidently had too much of the aura of good old English roast beef about him. The romances of Guy and Bevis were too individualistic – too much focused on the pious ending and the good deaths of their heroes, deaths that had appealed to seventeenth-century Protestantism, but that had nothing to say in the era of nationalism and nascent imperialism, in which such heroes as Arthur died in the cause of the nation. The near-disappearance of *Guy* and *Bevis* marks the centralizing of medieval literary tradition in an authorized form. This process both allowed the study of medieval literature to begin in an organized fashion, and at the same time removed some of its most popular texts from circulation.

Notes

1   S. Pegge, 'Memoir on the Story of Guy Earl of Warwick', *Bibliotheca Topographica Britannica*, vol. 4: *Antiquities in Bedfordshire, Berkshire, Derbyshire, Northamptonshire, Staffordshire, and Warwickshire* (London, 1790), Section VIII, pp. 29–39.

2   R. Sweet, *Antiquaries, The Discovery of the Past in Eighteenth-Century Britain* (London and New York, 2004), ch. 1.

3   Sweet, *Antiquaries*, p. xviii; on the county history see further pp. 37–42.

4   R. S. Crane, 'The Vogue of *Guy of Warwick* from the Close of the Middle Ages to the Romantic Revival', *PMLA*, 30 (1915), pp. 125–94, p. 191.

5   R. B. Herzman, G. Drake and E. Salisbury, eds, *Four Romances of England: King Horn, Havelok the Dane, Bevis of Hampton, Athelston* (Kalamazoo, 1999), pp. 187–99; J. Zupitza, *The Romance of Guy of Warwick*, Early English Text Society, es 42, 49, 59 (Oxford, 3 vols rpt. as 1, 1966).

6   J. E. Wülfing, *The Laud Troy Book: A Romance of about 1400 A.D*, Pt. 1, Early English Text Society 121 (Oxford, 1902), p. 2.

7   On the reception history of *Guy of Warwick*, see Crane, 'The Vogue of *Guy of Warwick*'. On early *Bevis* prints and sixteenth-century disapprobation of the tale, see J. Fellows, '*Bevis redivivus*: The Printed Editions of *Sir Bevis of Hampton*', in J. Fellows, R. Field, G. Rogers and J. Weiss, eds, *Romance Reading on the Book: Essays on Medieval Narrative presented to Maldwyn Mills* (Cardiff, 1996), pp. 251–68, esp. 252–54, 258.

8   J. Simpson, 'Chaucer's Presence and Absence, 1400–1550', in P. Boitani and J. Mann, eds, *The Cambridge Companion to Chaucer*, 2nd edn (Cambridge, 2003), p. 253.

9   J. Burke Severs, ed., *A Manual of the Writings in Middle English 1050–1500*, fascicule 1 (New Haven, CT, 1967), p. 30.

10 William Shakespeare and John Fletcher, *Henry VIII (All is True)*, ed. G. McMullan (London, 2000), I.i.35–38.

11 G. Puttenham, *The Arte of English Poesie* (London, 1589), p. 69.

12 T. Nashe, *The Anatomie of Absurditie* (London, 1589), Ci[r].

13 H. Peacham, *The Compleat Gentleman* (London, 1622), pp. 53–54.

14 H. Parrot, *The Mastive, or Young-Whelpe of the Olde-Dogge: Epigrams and Satyrs* (London, 1615), I1[r]. On the readership of early chapbooks, see further M. Spufford, *Small Books and Pleasant Histories: Popular Fiction and its Readership in Seventeenth-Century England* (London, 1981), ch. 45; T. Watt, *Cheap Print and Popular Piety 1550–1640* (Cambridge, 1991).

15 Watt, *Cheap Print*, p. 268.

16 'An Epigram. To, William, Earle of Newcastle', lines 7–8, 9–10, W. B. Hunter, ed., *The Complete Poetry of Ben Jonson* (New York, 1963), p. 210.

17 *The Picture* II.i.115–22; P. Edwards and C. Gibson, eds, *The Plays and Poems of Philip Massinger*, vol. 3 (Oxford, 1976), p. 219.

18 S. Rowlands, *The Famovs Historie, of Guy Earle of Warwicke* (London, 1607), A3ʳ.
19 S. Rowlands., 'A Drvnkards Duello' [*A Paire of Spy-Knaues*] (London, 1613?), B2ʳ.
20 Watt, *Cheap Print*, p. 262.
21 D. Brewer, *Chaucer: The Critical Heritage*, 2 vols (London, 1978), vol. 1:153; cf 1:211.
22 A. Munday et al., *The First Part of the True and Honorable Historie, of the Life of Sir Iohn Old-castle, the good Lord Cobham* (London, 1600), H2ʳ. 'Owleglasse' is an English translation of the folktale 'Till Eulenspiegel'; 'Ellen of Rumming' is presumably John Skelton's 'The Tunning of Elinor Rumming'; the popular poem 'The Friar and the Boy' was printed by Wynkyn de Worde c.1500.
23 Paper was a major expense: see Watt, *Cheap Print*, p. 262.
24 Such versions are condensed and cheap in appearance, but some of them are carefully compiled and 'identify and preserve a central core of experience in the romance...' See J. Simons, 'Romance in the Eighteenth-Century Chapbook', in J. Simons, ed., *From Medieval to Medievalism* (Basingstoke, 1992), pp. 122–43.
25 J. Shurley (?) 'SJ', prefatory epistle, *The Famous and Renowned History of Sir Bevis of Hampton* (London, 1689).
26 See Sweet, *Antiquaries*, ch. 7.
27 Sweet, *Antiquaries*, ch. 5.
28 L. Colley, *Britons: Forging the Nation 1707–1837* (New Haven, CT, and London, 1992).
29 See J. Waters Bennett, *The Rediscovery of Sir John Mandeville* (New York, repr. 1971).
30 R. Southey ed., *The Byrth, Lyf, and Actes of Kyng Arthur*, 2 vols (London, 1817), I, p. xxx.
31 Scott to [Ellis], 22 Oct 1801: H. J. C. Grierson ed., *The Letters of Sir Walter Scott*, 12 vols (London, 1932–37), XII, p. 201.
32 I have discussed this at greater length in my 'What was Medievalism?: Medieval Studies, Medievalism, and Cultural Studies', in R. Evans *et al.* eds., *Medieval Cultural Studies: Essays to Celebrate the Work of Stephen Knight* (Cardiff, 2006), pp. 9–22.

Nature, Masculinity, and Suffering Women
The Remaking of the *Flower and the Leaf* and Chaucer's *Legend of Good Women* in the Nineteenth Century

HELEN PHILLIPS

A Walter Crane wallpaper inspired by Chaucer's *Legend of Good Women* and the *Flower and the Leaf* won a Special Medal at the 1876 Philadelphia Centennial Exhibition.[1] Crane's three-section design, following a current fashion, makes possible an expressive interaction of symbols and themes: Nature, women, morality, love and domestic virtues, a list reflecting popular images of Chaucer during the previous sixty years. The dado, its lower section, depicts lilies and doves, symbolizing purity and faithful marriage. The middle section shows daisies and words from a song in the *Flower and the Leaf*: '*SI DOUCE EST LA MARGARETE*'. Another quotation joins this to the frieze: '*TO WHOM DO YE OWE YOUR SERVICE? & WHICH WILL YE HONOUR TELL ME I PRAY THIS YERE THE LEAF OR THE FLOWER?*'[2] In the frieze Alceste and Love hold hands, recalling Chaucer's *Legend of Good Women* (F 241–42), where they also command the poet to praise faithful women. Accompanying them are caryatid-like female figures representing Diligence, Hospitality, Order and Providence, virtues of the housewife symbolically holding up the roof. Yet domestic virtues figure nowhere in either medieval poem. They have emerged from half a century of remaking, together with many other elements that make up the complex figure of the nineteenth-century Chaucer.

This wallpaper illustrates what, to a modern eye, is the period's extraordinary admiration for the *Flower and the Leaf*, due only partly, I think, to belief that it was by Chaucer. The same admiration is found in Dryden's refashioning of it as a fiercely moral poem, and in the nineteenth-

71

century perception of it as the essence of Chaucer as a Nature-poet, an image derived from some genuine writings, especially Chaucer's dream poetry and the spring opening to the *Canterbury Tales*, plus apocryphal texts including the *Flower and the Leaf*, which appeared in editions of Chaucer from the sixteenth to the late nineteenth century, when scholarship proved the attributions false.

The imaginative power of the image cannot be overstated. Writer after writer hails Chaucer as a ruddy-cheeked, cheery lover of early morning walks and fresh air, a model for English masculinity. Fitzgerald, for example:

> How the fresh air of the Kent hills, over which he rode four hundred years ago, breathes in his verse still. They have a perfume like fine old hay [...] All his poetry bespeaks a man of sound mind and body...[3]

Landor:

> He slaps us on the shoulder, and makes us spring up while the dew is on the grass [...] We feel strong with the freshness around us.[4]

At the same time, Shakespeare was being memorialized more in Stratford than in London, becoming the Bard of Avon and of the Warwickshire birthplace, rather than of the complex commercial capital where he wrote his plays.[5] It is possible, as I have argued elsewhere, to see this Nature-loving Chaucer as a reaction to the trauma of the rapidly expanding, industrialized and polluted city between the 1820s and the 1880s.[6] English identity is another obvious contemporary presence. This article, however, will examine particularly links between Chaucer the Nature poet and gender issues. They are captured in the extrovert manly activeness of the quotations above and in Furnivall's description of Chaucer as 'The cheery dear old man, who so loved women and the "glad light green" of spring'.[7] Both the medieval poems celebrated women as well as springtime and represented in their own times innovative positions on gender issues – concerning 'good men' as well as 'good women'. Their nineteenth-century remakings, however, reflect major preoccupations of a later age.

The fifteenth-century *Flower and the Leaf* describes a young woman's vision of two retinues of the Flower and the Leaf, led by Flora and Diana and symbolized by plants and birds, including the daisy, medlar and goldfinch for the Flower and the laurel, oak and nightingale for the Leaf.

The Flower represents idleness, pleasure and beauty, the Leaf effort, self-control and chastity. Both companies contain knights and ladies. The Leaf knights compete in a tournament; knights and ladies dance and sing of love together. The Flower people are first burnt by the sun and then drenched by the rain, but succoured by the Leaf people, who lead them under their tree's shade, warm them up and feed them cooling leafy salads. They all ride home cheerfully together. The narrator is asked which side she chooses and she chooses the Leaf.

The poem reflects the fashion for chivalric orders, badges and liveries in French and English late-medieval courts, including courtly groups dedicated to the Flower and the Leaf. At Richard II's court, John of Gaunt's daughter Philippa led the English Flower faction: a connection suggesting the absence of any moral condemnation, at that period, of the Flower.

The *Legend of Good Women*, begun around 1386, and the *Flower and the Leaf* (both far more serious poems than their connections with such princely amusements indicate) exemplify, I would suggest, the development of a new kind of late-medieval feminism, whose defence of women against misogyny no longer relies solely on religious and moral arguments but uses glamorizing motifs from courtly literature and romance to create a model not only of female virtue but also male–female harmony and love. Earlier medieval writings on gender, whether pro- or anti-women, reflect clerical celibacy, its authors' usual background, and present the good woman, whether virgin, chaste wife or chaste widow, as the unsexual woman, and sexual morality as a matter of policing female behaviour.

The new feminism, from Chaucer's *Legend of Good Women* through Christine de Pizan's writings to the anonymous *Chevalier des Dames* and Martin Le Franc's *Champion des Dames* (c. 1440), opposes misogyny more from the perspective of the married laity and accepts sexual passion and marriage as potentially virtuous. This new feminism's defence of women often employs amorous and knightly adventures; looks favourably on virtuous male–female desire; and sometimes offers criticism of masculine behaviour and a distinctive ideal of the *good man* – a man of honour who is faithful, conscientious, combating misogyny and respectful to women – alongside its less monkish concept of the good woman. It is one of the early pointers forward towards the gradual romanticization and elevation of marriage, and the rejection of asceticism as the main arbiter of ethical issues in matters of gender. Chaucer's *Legend* also uses the issue of how literary tradition has forgotten or belied the truth about these heroines as an opportunity to explore questions about the poet's debt to literary tradition and nature and experience; some nineteenth-century poets would pick up themes from his poem in order, themselves, to consider the new poet's role in relation to past tradition.[8]

Chaucer's *Legend* reflects contemporary French and English poems where the daisy symbol is a compliment to ladies called Marguerite or Margaret. Chaucer's daisy, however, compliments Anne of Bohemia, who is also represented in Alceste, the perfect wife. The narrator abandons his books in spring to adore the daisy, and his dream follows on from this experience. The poem recounts stories of classical heroines who died because of love; they illustrate the 'oppressyoun' and 'tirannye' of bad men (Text F 1868, 1883).[9] Unlike earlier medieval catalogues of good women, Chaucer's heroines are neither ascetic saints, virgin martyrs nor warrior queens, but faithful and passionate lovers and wives: this is an endorsement of the values of secular women, women with sexual experience, not of the older criteria for good women, which privileged virginity or narrowly patriarchal conceptions of wifely duty. Chaucer is confronting existing criteria for good women as well as misogynist condemnations of women. His women are Cleopatra, Dido, Thisbe, Lucrece, Medea, Hypsipile, Ariadne, Philomela, Phyllis and Hypermnestra. Wherever the sources permit, Chaucer stresses their status as queens or royal heiresses and as wives, and presents several as powerful women of munificent generosity, sincerity and integrity. Most of his men are exploitative, unfaithful, lustful and ungrateful for everything women do for them, not true *gentil* men, though princes. He gives his women, albeit tragic, considerable emotional agency. These unconventional 'good women' led most twentieth-century critics to read the *Legend* cynically, as Chaucer's send-up of a defence of women.[10] The nineteenth century, like earlier centuries, read it with respect.

Remaking

The Flower and the Leaf does not demonize the Flower. Chaucer's *Legend* says he supports neither company above the other. The *Legend*, too, denies any contradiction between sexual desire and virtue (Text F 148–70). The villain in the *Flower and the Leaf* is that medieval usual suspect mutability, plus the Flower company's indolence and lack of foresight: Flower values may not last, but they are not evil. Later readings and remakings of the *Flower and the Leaf* see matters differently.

Remaking begins in 1700 with Dryden's *Fables*, which includes the *Flower and the Leaf* among adaptations from Ovid, Virgil and Chaucer.

Dryden's version would greatly affect nineteenth-century reception of the text and consequently of Chaucer. First, he adds a mystical dimension to its natural description. The attraction, even affinity, in this for readers in the Romantic age is obvious:

> The grove eccho'd and the Valleys rung;
> And I so ravish'd with her heav'nly Note
> I stood intranc'd, and had no room for Thought.
> But all o'er-pour'd with Ecstasy of Bliss,
> Was in a pleasing Dream of Paradice ...
>
> And what alone did all the rest surpass,
> The sweet possession of the Fairy Place;
> Single, and conscious to my Self alone,
> Of Pleasures to th'excluded World unknown,
> Pleasures which no where else, were to be found,
> And all *Elysium* in a spot of ground.   117–21, 140–45[11]

Did this inspire Wordsworth's 'spots of time'? Wordsworth, another translator of Chaucer, read Dryden's versions with attention.[12] Dryden also adds fairies and echoes of *A Midsummer's Night's Dream*. Reflecting his own conservative political attitudes and respect for his patron, the Duke of Ormonde, a Garter knight, he enhances the martial elements, and adds a general pattern of conflict which creates sharper moral opposition between Flower and Leaf. The Flower now becomes tainted with vice.

Dryden's *Fables* were widely read in the early nineteenth century. His contrast between the sinful Flower and virtuous Leaf, his sense of a sacred Nature, a heavenly moment of vision, and the proto-Wordsworthian presentation of the dreamer's vision in the grove as 'mystique truth, in Fables first conveyed' (601) were to feed (albeit somewhat distorted from what they had meant for Dryden) into shifts in the general perception of Chaucer that begin around 1810 or 1820. Thus the classicizing and pre-Romantic Dryden becomes a major catalyst in the development of Chaucer the Nature poet and moralist in the Romantic era.

In the early 1800s the eighteenth-century Chaucer still prevailed: a social Chaucer, the poet of people, urban life, satire and bawdiness, occasionally lapsing into crude language and metre – a primitive for some canons of taste (of course, primitiveness gained new significance in the Romantic period, and the nineteenth century made great advances in understanding Chaucer's metre and language). By about 1820 there is a swing of emphasis, from social poet to Nature poet, and from bawdy satirical poet to a champion of morality. Interestingly, in nineteenth-century France Chaucer remains the social observer of the *Canterbury Tales*. This seems not just a function of accessible translations: we find it in the most scholarly commentators (and the courtly poems were included in translations).[13] Nor does French medievalism draw with the fervour found in England on natural descriptions in the *Roman de la Rose* or its fourteenth-century successors, Chaucer's own sources for springtime descriptions.

Scott in this, as in so many things, is a meeting-point of Augustan and Romantic attitudes. His allusions to the *Knight's Tale* and the *Flower and the Leaf* in *Rokeby* (1813) and *Ivanhoe* (1819) centre, with clear influence from Dryden, on military, chivalric themes. Chapter ten of *The Antiquary* (1816) describes a tapestry and a dream depicting woodland scenes from the *Flower and the Leaf* and Chaucer's *Book of the Duchess*: these prefigure the future of the novel's hero, a soldier making his own way in the world through merit and effort (virtues of the Knights of the Leaf), and they also contribute to the novel's interfaces between the medieval Catholic past and a Protestant, modern world. Natural imagery is not an important inspiration Scott draws from medieval literature (was that because, being a lowland Scot, he had a different, national, resource to draw on for culturally significant landscape, and because the lure of the pre-industrial pastoral landscape exerted less pressure than on English writers?) These leafy visions connect with other tree symbolism in *The Antiquary* and reflect Scott's conservative political ideas, in which trees frequently symbolize ancient aristocratic securities, as much as Romantic delight in Nature.

The Poet's Morning Walk: *from Keats to Tennyson*

At the same time, Keats's sonnet on the *Flower and the Leaf* (1817) heralds a new Chaucer. It begins: 'This poem is like a little copse...' Written during a period of intense reading of Chaucer, the sonnet, with *Endymion* and *Sleep and Poetry* (all published in 1817), suggest Chaucerian inspiration in their model of the poet as a dreamer and symbolic wanderer through spring groves.[14] The sonnet echoes the language of the *Flower and the Leaf*; *Sleep and Poetry* begins with a quotation from it and talks of the poet's inspiration in a Drydenesque 'bowery nook' which is Elysium, a 'spot / Of awfuller shade or an enchanted grot', where a vision which is also 'an eternal book' will provide him with 'many a lovely saying / About the leaves and flowers' (64–66, 75–76). This inspiration in 'groves Elysian' reappears in *Endymion* (177), where art is also a 'bower' and 'sweet dreams' (4, 5), and Keats prays for 'ethereal dew' to fall on him so that he may 'in wayfaring / … stammer where old Chaucer used to sing' (131–34). Keats uses the medieval-Dryden motifs of the morning rambles, leafy bower and dream as Chaucer's genuine dream poems had done, both literally and to explore the situation of the poet, poised, as Keats felt himself to be, between the muses of nature and literary tradition (called 'preve' versus 'bokes' in the *Legend*, 1–39). Reynolds' perceptive sonnet in reply bade Keats continue in 'thine own green way', singing in Chaucer's 'key' in 'fields and olden wood' – old fields symbolize poetic tradition in the *Legend*, Text F 66–83.[15] Tennyson will develop this topos of the walk through (and for him also a flight over) landscape as the image of the poet, adding a sense of the morning woodland walk as a vista of past poetic tradition to which the young writer adds himself. Like Chaucer's *Legend*, Tennyson's walk will also introduce a series of unhappy women.

The nineteenth-century urge to search for indicators of individual personality in an author's writing means that many take Chaucer's first-person narrators simply and biographically: Leigh Hunt, who knew the material well – and had therefore read all the apocrypha's Maytimes – regularly talks of Chaucer's habit of morning walks.[16] Some portray Chaucer enjoying a rural retreat: Longfellow's charming poem 'Chaucer' has him hearing larks, linnets, a crowing cock and smelling 'odors of ploughed field or flowery mead', coming through his windows as he composes poetry.[17] While poets including Tennyson and Morris adapt the medieval springtime, with profound understanding into the original ideas and symbolism, to become a new, creative, image-resource for themselves, the popular groundswell of assumptions sees the Father of English Poetry as a hearty enthusiast for country walking, emanating morality and English manliness.

Keats's sonnet's first line, 'This poem is like a little copse', illustrates a particular claim made about Chaucer: that he creates a kind of writing where Nature itself is directly transferred onto the page. It is an enduring idea. Stopford A. Brooke writes in 1871 that Chaucer's delight in the daisy 'is more natural, less mixed up with reflection, more direct' than we find in Wordsworth or Burns.[18] Hazlitt's influential *Lectures on the English Poets* (1818) articulates this idea powerfully, and attempts to link it to processes in the poet-observer's mind. He says:

His words point as an index to the object, like an eye or the finger. There were none of the commonplaces of poetic diction in our author's time [a complete Romantic fantasy about Chaucer's rhetoric, of course], no reflected lights of fancy, no borrowed roseate tints; he was obliged to inspect things for himself, to look narrowly, and almost handle the object.[19]

Hazlitt and his contemporaries could not know that these natural descriptions often imitate earlier poets, but the notion in any case reflects a powerful ideology of their own period, not just ignorance. It also reveals a developmental conceptualization of the founder of English poetry as (in even Elizabeth Barrett Browning's estimation) childlike; and Chaucer, a poet at the beginning of aesthetic evolution, as it were, is seen epistemologically as resembling the first stages of perception, when the external world is grasped physically before it can enter the mind, here almost literally physically: 'eye', 'finger', 'inspect ... for himself', 'handle the object'.[20] Hazlitt goes on to say: '[Chaucer] exhibits [...] the naked object [...] He does not affect to show his power over the reader's mind, but the power which his subject has over his own.'

Chaucer's descriptions have 'a local truth and freshness, which gives the very feeling of the air, the coolness or moisture of the ground ... and render back the sentiment of the speaker's mind'. The *Flower and the Leaf* and its female dreamer's pleasure in the landscape, supremely exemplifies this:

the delight of that young beauty in the Flower and the Leaf, shrouded in her bower, and listening, in the morning of the year, to the singing of the nightingale, while her joy rises with the rising song, and gushes out afresh at every pause, and is borne along with the full tide of pleasure, and still increases and repeats and prolongs itself, and knows no ebb ...[21]

Hazlitt argues that Chaucer's direct apprehension of nature simultaneously engages human 'sentiment': this is his theory to account for the characteristics the century most prized, Chaucer's twin art of Nature and Human Nature (the latter to be found particularly in tragic women and an aesthetic evocation of pathos):

It was the same trust in nature that enabled Chaucer to describe the grief and patience of Griselda; the faith of Constance; and the heroic perseverance of that little child, who going to school through the streets of Jewry 'Oh *Alma Redemptoris Mater*, loudly sung' ... In depth of simple pathos, and intensity of conception, never swerving from his subject, I think no writer comes near him.[22]

Eagerness to credit that Chaucer wrote from raw experience received from Nature directly into his senses or sentiment represents a Romantic reaction against alleged Augustan artifice, allegory and unEnglishness. When late Victorian scholarship finally showed that many of the poems were not Chaucer's, and how indebted Chaucer's rural descriptions were to previous, particularly French writers, the *Flower and the Leaf* and the genuine *Legend* fell into critical and popular neglect. Simultaneously the *fin-de siècle* discovered renewed aesthetic respect for the eighteenth century and Regency, a rejection of realist style, a perception of beauty in the modern city, and resistance to the cultural hegemony of the image of the bluff, manly, uncomplicated and heterosexual Englishman. In the twentieth century a new ironic Chaucer was born. His career allegedly emerged from youthful callow dependence on French conventions to full, 'virile' Englishness (Kittredge's word in 1916) with the *Canterbury Tales* – another reason for despising the early dream poems, the Victorians' favourites, with their Maytimes and courtly love.[23]

The Chaucer of early morning walks attracts recurrent epithets: manly, hale, healthy, rural, fresh, tender and, of course, English. George Meredith, one among so many, encapsulates this:

> Fresh-featured and ruddy
> As dawn when the drowsy farm-yard has thrice heard Chauntecleer.
> Tender to tearfulness—childlike and manly, and motherly;
> Here beats true English blood, blood richest, joyance on sweet
> English ground.[24]

Ford Maddox Brown's famous 1851 picture, though showing Chaucer reading aloud to the court (a tragic passage about Constance and her baby son), and based on a medieval illustration of the same scene, contrives – awkwardly – an outdoors setting. The court is represented as a family group, equally mixed in gender, including fresh-faced young girls and children, and with domestic relationships and familial dramas uppermost: Alice Ferrers beside Edward III; the ailing Black Prince, the dying heir, leaning against the sheltering arms of his wife, with their son, the future boy-king Richard, at their feet; John of Gaunt, in full armour, brooding protectively apparently over his nation and his kindred's potentially dysfunctional future, and so on.[25]

Foucault famously argued that, rather than simple repression, the nineteenth century gave greater visibility and articulation to sexuality by talking about it, giving it terminology and categories – especially in terms of medical diagnoses, definitions, and the demarcation of norms and perversities. He sees a cluster of dynamics here, which includes measures for public health and hygiene in cities, the general idealization of a model where men work outside the home and women are imprisoned in the domestic, private, sphere, and the 'hysterization' of women: their characterization as neurotic and vulnerable, identifiable wholly in their biological functions as wives, objects of male desire, and mothers. Women become 'saturated with sexuality'.[26] From its capacity to merge the public and private spheres, Foucault sees this cluster of ideas as a new kind of power ('bio-power').

Foucault's analysis of history depends to a fault on generalization from French institutions and French social history, but this cluster of ideas has clear parallels with the images of Chaucer that so repeatedly caught popular imagination in nineteenth-century England. The rural, 'healthy' and 'hale' Chaucer, walking amid flowers, clean air and water, proclaims, as I have already suggested, repulsion from the polluted contemporary city; the Chaucer who is so insistently called 'manly', and free of French artifice and vice, and yet at the same time preoccupied with vulnerable, emotionally agonized women, and (equally insistent word) 'tender' towards them – this paradoxical figure, with such sharply differentiated 'masculine' and 'feminine' elements yoked together in its makeup speaks of heterosexual norms and of the hysterization of women. This founding father of the nation's poetry, of its literary mirror of itself, establishes, at the birth of that national self-image, values which, in Foucauldian terms, valorize certain typically nineteenth-century operations of power, even though the Chaucer of the age is treated by the Victorians as a man detached from the political forces and causes of his own, fourteenth-century, time. Cheery old apolitical Dan Chaucer, walking through the daisies and dreaming of sorrowful women, is a Foucauldian figure.

The power of such hidden clusters of ideals, driving values in a particular society, can explain why the Victorian Chaucer, even in the same comments from a single author, may yoke together disparate ideals: a master of poetry, yet childlike; manly, yet preoccupied tenderly with pathos and vulnerable women; admitted to be obscene, yet judged to be fresh and healthy. The popular image of Chaucer is perhaps all the more powerful because it holds together otherwise irreconcilable tendencies.

Chaucer as quintessential Englishman could be harnessed to contemporary political and factional causes. An 1849 reviewer finds in him 'that same joyous and exuberant reality, that hatred of "humbug" which distinguishes us now'; in Chaucer we meet 'that same spirit which now sneers in Punch and wrestles in the Times'. The same paragraph (in a political moment, 1849, of European nationalist revolutions) enlists this commonsensical, yet Protestant and outspoken, Chaucer–John Bull to the topical cause of combating radicalism and revolution. Chaucer's opposition to Popish superstition is (somehow) at one with a true Englishman's natural reluctance to – we are warned – jeopardize present gains for the false promises of revolution! Chaucer's attitude, 'though it was revolutionary in appearance ... was conservative at heart'.[27] Doubtless because this article's occasion is the 1845 edition of Chaucer's collected works, it acknowledges, more strongly than much Victorian comment, the social content of his writing, at least the anticlerical satires. It also acknowledges there are 'passages in old Dan Chaucer unsuited for the eyes and ears of juvenile gentlewomen', but criticizes Charles Cowden Clarke's 1835 selections from Chaucer (dedicated to 'the ingenuous, intelligent, well-informed and artless young women of England') for drawing attention to these, even while omitting them.[28] Contemporary admiration for the *Flower and the Leaf* and other springtime descriptions, and their regular appearance in anthologies, is, of course, partly due to such perils lurking for ladies in the wider oeuvre.

Chaucer, then, was a poet of human nature, but not the satirical, masculine, urban human nature that pleased the eighteenth century. This Chaucer (now the *ur*-novelist, a Victorian writer, excelling in character and feelings) is located especially in suffering female nature and motherhood: Griselda, Constance, the *Prioress's Tale*, as well as the tragic heroines of the *Legend of Good Women*. Meredith, in his lines above, tries to reconcile this topic of female pain, and masculine appreciation of it, with the bluff manly Chaucer: he is 'tender to tearfulness' – the phrase's syntactic uncertainties betray underlying tensions. The taste for pathos, if seen thus as quasi-parental protectiveness in Chaucer towards woman, together with delivery of a moral message, can be integrated with those ideals of wholesomeness and uncomplicated vigour that Meredith and many other commentators associate with their active, country-loving Chaucer, a poet who worked so immediately – indeed, so unreflectingly – from Nature. When we recall how much Chaucer, within the conventions of his period, actually uses his themes of 'pité' and women's adversities to present forms of female strength and questions about aristocratic 'gentillesse', the complex but very different Victorian handling of this material reveals some illuminating and disturbing links and contradictions.

Leigh Hunt's serio-comic 1837 *Blue-Stocking Revels* contains, like Chaucer's *Legend*, celebratory catalogues of women: ancient heroines and contemporary female writers. But, within an ambiguously feminist and humorous piece of uncertain tone, it describes Chaucer thus:

> Great Chaucer. As humbly as a maiden went he.
> Young queens held their diadems of him in fee;
> Young mothers and young beauties, clear angels of earth;
> I know not which grac'd them most, sorrow or mirth.[29]

The radical Hunt here perceives that Chaucer's innovative concept of 'good women', his young queens of the *Legend*, creates 'angels' of this world, not the next; and he also detects as feminine the passive persona in Chaucer's poetry – two elements generally unnoticed by the tide of nineteenth-century opinion. But Hunt is at one with his century in frank relish for the suffering Chaucerian heroine: sorrow graces her. Elsewhere, in his own pastiche of Chaucer, 'The Tapiser's Tale', he manages to juxtapose in short compass a saintly maiden burnt at the stake ('Oh puré blood, swiche feendlich thirst to slake! / Alas for the soft flesche and gentil herte! ... To put a poore young creature to the fire!') with a prelude describing a field with roses, just as English Maytime 'feeldés ben daysies and cuppés alle!'[30] Enjoying daisies and contemplating the tormenting of women seem to inhabit the same aesthetic sphere worryingly often in the nineteenth-century appreciation of Chaucer.

Chaucer's unhappy women, however, also inspired several of the greatest Victorian writers; Karen Hodder, for example, has examined how Elizabeth Barratt Browning, who translated *Anelida*, reworked it.[31] Tennyson creatively reworks the *Legend*'s associated themes of feminism and wider social evils. He also sees Chaucer's concern with the poet's role, questions Chaucer had first broached in the *House of Fame*. Begun in 1831–32, Tennyson's *Dream of Fair Women*, elaborating the image Keats and Reynolds used, makes that morning walk the literary tradition into which the young poet inserts himself, with the Father of English Poetry as the first singer in the dawn chorus of English literature. Tennyson begins with Chaucer's own device of the poet moving from reading an existing book to a dream bringing new creativity:

I read, before my eyelids drop't their shade,
    '*The Legend of Good Women*', long ago
Sung by the morning star of song, who made
    His music heard below;

Dan Chaucer, the first warbler ...

At last methought that I had wandered far
    In an old wood: fresh-washed in coolest dew ...
                The Dream of Fair Women, 1–5, 53–2[32]

Tennyson's earliest, 1832, version starts by merging Chaucer's eagle-flight from the *House of Fame* with the contemporary thrill of a balloon flight: the young poet, uplifted, thinks of his own fame and the great past poets.[33] In his pre-dream sequence of literary inspirations, Tennyson gathers echoes of Dante's pre-vision 'selva oscura', and the 'dewy drops' and 'ethereal dew' which Keats used for Chaucerian inspiration in his 'Flower and the Leaf' sonnet. The picture of the poet walking in an English dawn, hearing birdsong, turns into complex symbols of tradition and the individual talent. Tennyson's 1832 prelude, like Chaucer's in the *Legend*, links sexual oppression to a wider oppressive tendency: of the strong and 'selfish' always to overbear the 'gentler mind' – which ideally might one day rule.[34]

Tennyson's heroines are a puzzling assembly: adulteresses (Helen, Cleopatra, Rosamund) and innocent maiden victims (Iphigenia, Jephtha's daughter). Perhaps, united as Fair Women, their attractiveness to men unites them: men's responses create their fates and tragedies (men's 'wolfish eyes', predatory towards women). All have a severely restricted sphere of action, imprisoned in their sex, whether they glory in men's reactions (Cleopatra), bitterly regret the consequences (Iphigenia), or transcend them (Jephtha's daughter). Clashing word-choices point up the sexual exploitation beneath macho erotic glamour: a 'cavalier', snatching a female victim of war onto his horse; conquering 'heroes tall' bursting through 'shrine doors' with 'heated blasts'; and 'seraglios' which are 'vaults with iron grates' – deathlike and prison-like for women (29, 35–36).

Adultery and physical sex become moral issues in Tennyson's remaking, as they were not for Chaucer. But, in his own way and period, he joins with Chaucer in exploring the role of the male poet towards female subjects. His language is sexual, and Tennyson's passage through the 'rank dark wood-walks' (75), which seem in this poem not just Nature, or the past, or poetic tradition, but also a quasi-sexual penetration, brings him to Helen of Troy, and prompts thoughts of lost innocence (77–80). Though direct Chaucerian inspiration is rare amid Tennyson's oeuvre, arguably when he does evoke Chaucer it is for a capacity for ambiguous, dialogical perception of gender and social conflict, and not just to quarry the medieval poet for charming tropes, archaic language or costume drama. Robert Pattison discerns in *St. Simon Stylites* a figure analogous to Chaucer's Pardoner in its deception, its identity corroded by duplicity, and troubled outsidership; Eagleton describes the *The Princess* and *In Memoriam* as embodying disquiet about political and gender aspects of patriarchy.[35] Did young Tennyson as early as 1832 glean from Chaucer's *Legend* the same complexities and anxieties?

Tennyson's *Dream* towards its close swerves back from the air of relatively open speculation with which it treats the first six heroines, problematizing the relationship of female attractiveness to male cruelty and the male author's relationship to his 'fair women', finally to pay homage, when he comes to his last three heroines, to patriarchal obligations. Tennyson's last three women each represent duty to patriarchy in close association with death: duty to father and religion (Margaret Roper, recovering her father's head), to monarch and nation (Joan of Arc facing burning), and to husband and monarch (Queen Eleanor, risking poison). Tennyson's writing seems here to manifest a nervous over-emphasis on their patriarchal devotion, yet also a recurrence of grim and deathly terms, analogous to his earlier iron grates around seraglios. Jephtha's daughter, for example, says goodbye to natural 'bliss' and the chance of marriage, to serve 'my God, my land, my father' (209, 210) – in death. We return therefore to the puzzle over the criteria for inclusion. The contrast between adultery and chastity noted earlier seems to be subsumed in an even more problematic pattern: there is an unquestioned association, in all the 'fair women', between 'fairness' and suffering. While the suffering is caused by male actions, whether warfare or individual violence against women, the only virtue or strength with which these women can redeem the pessimistic dynamic of their situations is, itself, an abject bending under patriarchal domination.

After a text whose strength nevertheless seems today to lie in its moments of openness to uncertainty and exploration in matters of gender, Tennyson's coda returns from these patriarchal rigidities to his own version of Chaucer's theme, in the *Legend*, of the poet's role, seeming to admit inadequacy in grasping his feminine subject-matter. The earlier voice of experimental and exploratory thinking returns. Chaucer's description of writing as 'remembraunce' that preserves the truth of the past (the true virtues of women of the past) in the *Legend* (26) engenders an extraordinary passage where Tennyson describes failing to recall his dream of women with exactitude (273–80); then the poem ends with a social concern voiced at the start, the pain and oppression of the real world: no art can capture the 'bitter of the sweet' (288), and, as art fails, the heart fails to care strongly enough. Here the aesthetic 'grace' received in contemplating suffering women, acknowledged above by Hunt, is momentarily reversed into the real-life 'bitter' of social oppression, a truth about oppression that art betrays while representing it. While the under-lying misogyny that Chaucer attacks is the stereotypical accusation of female infidelity, the evil that Tennyson seems aware of as the background to his subject-matter of suffering women is male oppression.

Morris and the Pre-Raphaelites

Morris's *Earthly Paradise* also shows how, amid popular reception of Chaucer as a reassuringly manly (yet childlike) and moral nature lover, original poetry could still be inspired by the difficult and probing ideas in the *Legend*. Morris produces the most sparkling of all Victorian evoca-tions of Chaucer as the poet of an England before the polluted modern city, yet that very evocation embraces the world of urban work and commerce, from which most Victorian celebrations of Chaucer's Nature are in retreat, though they were a central element in Londoner Chaucer's own work:

> Forget six counties overhung with smoke,
> Forget the snorting steam and piston stroke,
> Forget the spreading of the hideous town;
> Think rather of a packhorse on the down,
> And dream of London, small and white and clean,
> And clear Thames bordered by its gardens green ...

> While nigh the thronged wharf Geoffrey Chaucer's pen
> Moves over bills of lading ...[36]

The poem's opening, 'Of Heaven or Hell I have no power to sing', recalls the *Legend*'s own first lines, about the unknowability of heaven and hell. The final 'Go Little Book' *envoi* prays modestly that his 'friend', Chaucer, who understands the 'joy and woe' of love, may not 'scorn thee [his poem], and thereof thou die': Morris feels Chaucer to be a fellow-sympathizer towards men who suffer in love ('he and his shall know whereof we cry') and also as someone beloved from whom scorn would be a death-bringing rejection.[37] This is a story collection with the *Legend*, not the *Canterbury Tales*, as inspiration for its tales of lovers, including Alceste in its June section. The often melancholy bemusement it conveys about the pain and rejections accompanying love may have other sources, including Morris's own life, but Chaucer's betrayed lovers clearly contributed. Morris's 'May' section reworks the *Legend* dream of the God of Love and, like Chaucer's dreamer, Morris's dreamer finds the God is alienated from him, but for a more personal failing than writing misogynist poetry: Love passes him by, he finds Love has gone and, in the dawning, 'shuddered at the sight of Eld and Death'. The impulses to self-doubt, and a questioning about attempting solutions to human wrongs and complexities, also echo Chaucer ('Dreamer of dreams, born out of my due time, / Why should I strive to set the crooked straight?', the socialist's question despairingly recalling *Truth*, 8).[38] Reviewers, as Florence Boos shows,[39] expected something prettier and lusher, and either pretended they had found it or complained at the sense of conflicted emotions and despair.

Morris's complex, tragic approach to love was pilloried for lacking manliness. One reviewer even contrasted it with the robust Chaucer of popular Victorian myth: the trouble with Morris's poem was that 'the strange disease of modern thought' had infected it and, instead of Chaucer's and Homer's 'manly cheerfulness and manly decisive tone', we find 'the morbid melancholy sentiment, the fluctuating chaos of ideas that belongs to the modern sceptic'.[40] Ironically, it can be argued that it is Morris who, unlike many other writers, values Chaucer as a fellow-male, and less for his male gaze at vulnerable women than as a sympathetic presence, a friend from the past, with whom to work through questions about work and relationships, and a writer blessedly free from the limiting masculinity of a 'manly decisive tone'.

Morris's medievalism includes the vision of reinvigorated, unalienated Labour, and unlike others who dwelt on the image of Chaucer in his cleaner England, idling in a country dawn, Morris identifies above with the poet who is, like himself, a busy man working amidst urban production and business. The ideal is linked to the Pre-Raphaelites' use of medieval motifs, many from the *Legend* and the *Flower and the Leaf*, in the visual arts and design, together with the revival of both men's and women's handwork, and the revolution of the domestic sphere by crafts-manship and art. This included raising the artistic status of women's traditional crafts of embroidery and weaving. William and Jane Morris, for instance, both worked on the design and execution of tapestries for the Red House depicting classical and medieval heroines. An analogous attitude, linking Chaucer and the ideal household, appears in Hannah Lawrance's history of English queens, published just after Victoria's accession, where (possibly with an eye to the young Victoria's court) she depicts Chaucer as composing his poetry under the benign influence of two gracious queens with virtuous courts: Philippa of Hainault and Anne of Bohemia.[41]

Chaucer's daisy had multiple meanings, including the poet's muse, and this becomes a popular theme both for nineteenth-century writers and artists. The so-called G version of the *Legend*'s prologue was unknown until Skeat's edition of 1889. The F text familiar to earlier decades, with its curious erotic-mystic presentation of the daisy, particularly stresses this motif of the daisy as Chaucer's muse. A sixteenth-century portrait of Chaucer shows him with a daisy, and Burne-Jones designed several pictures of Chaucer dreaming his poetry among daisies and poppies. One of Wordsworth's 'daisy' sonnets calls the flower 'the poet's darling'.[42]

Pre-Raphaelite designs based on the *Legend* must be the best-known aspects of its nineteenth-century reception. They have often overlapping histories: Burne-Jones cumulatively produced cartoons and finished versions, for a variety of places and patrons. The Peterhouse, Cambridge, combination room's windows (1869) depict the good women in pairs, plus Alceste with the God of Love, together with roundel windows of poets from Homer on. Despite the all-male academic community, the feminine subjects perhaps fit the specifically domestic and social nature of a common room, as well as the aesthetic opportunity offered by a linked sequence of bay-window panes. The static display of the figures of women famous for love dramas itself represents the urge to conceive the female as biologically impelled towards the fragile and neurotic.[43]

Birket Foster commissioned a similar set of stained-glass windows for his house, and Ruskin commissioned embroidered panels. Some of both of these programmes, and the cartoons, survive in Birmingham City Art Gallery and elsewhere.[44] The *Legend* and the *Flower and the Leaf* provide designers, practically, with opportunities to combine female figures and plants, and with themes from classical and English national cultural traditions that make them suitable for both the homes of connoisseurs and national buildings. Other women, from Chaucer, hagiography and the classics, were freely added to designs inspired by this concept. Such designs, because of the history of the poems' reception, could be suitable for august and moral messages in public buildings. The goddesses of the *Flower and the Leaf*, chosen above all Chaucer's works except the *General Prologue* and *Truth*, for the 1869 Chaucer window in Westminster Abbey, provided not only one half of the dual Chaucer of the age (poet of Nature, while the *General Prologue* exemplified the poet of Human Nature), but also a message of sexual and social probity (while *Truth* conveyed an unworldly invitation, appropriate for the sacred surroundings, to 'flee from the press').

Coleridge delighted in Chaucer's 'chearfulness, a manly hilarity' in the 1817 *Biographia Literaria*, repeating the praise in *Table Talk*, 1834, with the additional observation, 'how exquisitely tender he is, yet how perfectly free from the least touch of sickly melancholy or morbid drooping'; it is possible to see the hardening cultural taste, during the seventeen years between the comments, for both Chaucerian pathos and Chaucerian masculinity. Recurrent praise of Chaucer's manly health comes to connote wholesome outdoor exercise, together with morality, heterosexuality and the essence of Englishness. The 1849 reviewer already cited declared:

> no writer was ever more healthy than Chaucer; and we dwell on this characteristic with the greater pleasure that it seems proof of the thoroughly good constitution with which our English life began. Even when he comes in contact with grossness and immorality, they never seem to taint him ... there is no morbid gloating over impurity, or lingering around vice. There is nothing French in him ... His poems seem everywhere strewn with flowers, and wherever we go we encounter the breezes of spring.[45]

Hazlitt's lectures had contrasted Chaucer, 'stern and masculine', with 'effeminate Spenser'. An 1866 essay declares: 'He has been called a Wycliffite. He is not that. He is simply an Englishman. He hates friars, because they are not English and not manly.'[46]

No radical then, but a bluff xenophobe and homophobe. There may be a recall of the apocryphal story that Chaucer beat up a friar while a student. G. H. Kingsley comments with evident approval that it is easy to sympathize with a Chaucer ('hale Dan Chaucer') who felt the urge to lash out at the 'feminine powers of invective' typical of such men.[47] The defensive heterosexualism that clings at times round Chaucer's popular image in the mid-nineteenth century, in his approved roles as a country-lover and as a protective sentimentalist towards female vulnerability, can be interestingly related to the decline in those images of Chaucer after the *fin-de-siècle*, which displaces heterosexual Englishness from the forefront of literary commentators' models of the history of poetry. Matt Cook has examined the conflicting homosexual attitudes towards urban and pastoral cultural values in the *fin-de-siècle*.[48]

While it is risky to take different writers' comments at different points in the century together, there seems an interest in asserting that Chaucer is not effeminate, while foregrounding the pathetic and 'tender' impulses in his writing (always focusing on his tragic women, with curiously little interest in, for example, Troilus, the Man in Black, or Palamon and Arcite, his prostrated, swooning and often suicidal male heroes of tales of tragic passion).

And the conviction of his morality seems, as the century advances, to lessen public advertence to the bawdiness in his comedy, which had either delighted pre-Victorian culture or occasioned apologetic acknowledgement (as Coleridge does in an 1818 lecture, presenting it as a lamentable, but lesser, shadow of that found in the Italians Boccaccio and Ariosto).[49] Whereas William and Dorothy Wordsworth enjoyed the *Miller's Tale*, the mid-nineteenth century often managed to ignore the existence of the fabliaux: the popularity of anthologies and selections of his writings meant many readers never needed to encounter them. Wordsworth deplored the omission of bawdy lines from the modernized version of Chaucer's *Reeve's Tale*.[50] Ruskin, however, shunned the *Canterbury Tales*, rating the courtly and dream poems highest. He prized the *Flower and the Leaf* for expressing what he believed to be the middle ages' dislike of sensuality, and excluded the *Tales* from a proposed edition of Chaucer.[51] Burne-Jones omitted the fabliaux, despite Morris's protests, from the Kelmscott illustrations (c.1893).[52] His woodcut pages concentrate on scenes of love, desire and tragedy. With their flat perspective, askance gazes and still, androgynous women, framed by wide flower-design borders, these panels transmute both Chaucer the Nature Poet and Chaucer the poet of Human Nature and passion, into design. Yet, working within his own penchant for further, internal, architectural framings around the protagonists, he also achieves an at times subtly powerful expression of lack of freedom, agony and lone despair (well illustrated in his 'Lucrece' for the *Legend*).[53]

It is easy for a later age to see the century's biases and distortions, amid the highs and lows of nineteenth-century responses to Chaucer. What comes across most strongly, however, is readers' and artists' unceasing enthusiasm, and that is most articulately expressed by one, among so many, who was outstanding in using the Chaucerian inspirations in both visual and poetic art: William Morris. His work has left its own major impact on the way modern imagination still conceives Chaucer's nature and Chaucer's women. As he begins to write the last book of *The Life and Death of Jason*, of the betrayal of love between Jason and Medea (a subject Chaucer treated in the *Legend*), it is Chaucer he feels close to. He writes, with a characteristic mixture of modesty towards himself and zest for what he loves:

> Would that I
> Had but some portion of that mastery
> That from the rose-hung lanes of woody Kent
> Through these five hundred years such songs have sent
> To us, who, meshed within this smoky net
> Of unrejoicing labour, love them yet.
> And though, O Master! – Yea, my master still,
> Whatever feet have scaled Parnassus hill
> Since, like thy measures, clear, and sweet, and strong,
> Thames stream scarce fettered drave the dace along
> Unto the bastioned bridge, his only chain.
>
> *The Life and Death of Jason*, Book 17, 5–15[54]

Morris's last three lines reminds us that, though Chaucer's 'songs' may recall the bucolic lanes of Kent, he was by birth and for much of his working life a Londoner, born in Thames Street, and working at Westminster and on the Customhouse wharf.

Notes

1 See C. Smith, 'A Marriage of Convenience: Walter Crane and the Wallpaper Industry', in G. Smith and S. Hyde, eds, *Walter Crane: Artist, Designer, Socialist,* Catalogue, Whitworth Art Gallery (London, 1989), pp. 59–67; illustration p. 131.

2 See D. Pearsall, ed., *The Floure and the Lefe and the Assembly of Ladies*, TEAMS Middle English Texts (Kalamazoo, 1990), pp. 1–28.

3 E. Fitzgerald, *Euphranor, A Dialogue of Youth*, in G. Bentham ed., *Poetical and Prose Writings*, 7 vols (New York, 1967), I, p. 210. Generally on the reception of Chaucer see S. Ellis, *Chaucer at Large: The Poet in the Modern World* (Minneapolis, 2000); W. Finlay and J. Rosenblum, eds, *Chaucer Illustrated: Five Hundred Years of the Canterbury Tales in Pictures* (New Castle, Delaware and London, 2003).

4 Walter Savage Landor, *Blackwood's Magazine* 1842, quoted in C. F. E. Spurgeon, *Five Hundred Years of Chaucer Criticism and Allusion, 1357–1900*, 3 vols (Cambridge, 1925), II, p. 244.

5 S. During, *Foucault and Literature: Towards a Genealogy of Writing* (London and

New York, 1992), pp. 218–20.

6 H. Phillips., 'Chaucer and the Nineteenth-Century City', in A. Butterfield, ed., *Chaucer and the City* (Cambridge, 2006), pp. 193–210.

7 F. J. Furnivall, ed., *Robert Mannyng: Handlynge Synne*, Roxburghe Club 61 (London, 1862), p. iv.

8 See Delany's discussion of issues of poetic choice, testing the praxis of aesthetic theory, and the literary representation of women, in 'Women, Nature, and Language', in Delaney, *Medieval Literary Politics: Shapes of Ideology* (Manchester, 1990), pp. 151–77, at 151.

9 Line references are to L. D. Benson, ed., *The Riverside Chaucer*, 3rd edn (New York and Oxford, 1987). All Chaucer references are from this edition.

10 Certain (arguable) misreadings contributed to the cynical view: see H. Phillips and N. Havely, eds, *Chaucer's Dream Poetry* (Harlow, 1996), pp. 290, 292, 323 note.

11 John Dryden, *Poems 1697–1700,* vol. 7 of V. A. Dearing, ed., *The Works of John Dryden,* 7 vols (Berkeley, 2000).

12 R. H. Horne, ed., *The Poems of Geoffrey Chaucer Modernized* (London, 1941); B. E. Graver, ed., *William Wordsworth, Translations of Chaucer and Virgil* (Ithaca, NY, and London, 1998).

13 The important publication, containing summaries and extracts, is H. Gomont, trans., *Geoffrey Chaucer: Poète anglais du XIVe siècle. Analyses et fragments* (Paris, 1847).

14 M. Allott, ed., *Keats, The Complete Poems* (London and New York, 1970).

15 J. H. Reynolds, *Poetry and Prose* (London, 1928), p. 174.

16 E.g. J. Strachan, ed., *Leigh Hunt, Selected Writings,* 6 vols (London, 2003), II, p. 258, V, p. 776.

17 H. W. Longfellow, *The Poetical Works of Longfellow* (London, 1904), p. 711.

18 Quoted in D. Brewer, *Chaucer: The Critical Heritage,* 2 vols (London, 1978), II, p. 166.

19 W. Hazlitt, *Lectures on the English Poets, The Spirit of the Age* (1818; London, 1910), p. 22.

20 Elizabeth Barratt Browning, quoted in Spurgeon, *Chaucer Criticism and Allusion*, II, p. 243.

21 Hazlitt, *Lectures*, pp. 26–27.

22 Ibid., pp. 28–29.

23 G. Kittredge, *Chaucer and his Poetry* [1916] (Cambridge, MA, 1970), pp. 26–27, 72–73.

24 G. M. Trevelyan, ed., 'The Poetry of Chaucer', *Poetical Works* (London, 1919), p. 14. On the manly image see S. Ellis, *Chaucer at Large: The Poet in the Modern World* (Minneapolis, 2000), pp. 20–23.

25 Fisher and Allen discuss the picture in 'Victorian Illustrations to Chaucer's *Canterbury Tales*', in Finlay and Rosenblum, *Chaucer Illustrated*, pp. 258–62.

26 M. Foucault (trans. R. Hurley), *The History of Sexuality, Volume One: An Introduction* (London, 1981), pp. 104, 154.

27 [Anon.], 'Chaucer', *North British Review* 20 (1849), pp. 293–328, at 295–96.

28 Ibid., p. 297, commenting on Clarke's *Riches of Chaucer*.

29 H. S. Milford, ed., *Poetical Works of Leigh Hunt* (London, 1923), pp. 176–92, at 189.

30 Ibid. pp. 128–29.

31 K. Hodder, 'Elizabeth Barratt and the Middle Ages' Woeful Queens', in L. J. Workman and K. Verduin, eds, *Medievalism in England* II, *Studies in Medievalism* 7 (1995), pp. 105–30.

32 C. Ricks, ed., *Poems of Tennyson,* 3 vols (Harlow, 1987), I, pp. 479–92.

33 Ibid., notes, pp. 479–81.

34 Ibid., note, p. 481.

35 R. Pattison, *Tennyson and Tradition* (Cambridge, MA, 1979), pp. 79–80; T. Eagleton, 'Tennyson: Poetry and Sexuality in *The Princess* and *In Memoriam*', repr. in R. Stott, ed., *Tennyson* (Harlow, 1996), pp. 76–86.

36 M. Morris, ed., *William Morris, Collected Works*, 24 vols (London, 1910), III, p. 3, IV, p. 1.

37 Ibid., IV, p. 441.

38 Ibid., III, p. 1.

39 Florence Boos, 'Victorian Response to *Earthly Paradise Tales*', *The Journal of the William Morris Society*, 5/4 (1983–84), pp. 16–29.

40 Henry Howlett, *Contemporary Review*, 1868, pp. 631–33, quoted in O. Maurer, Jr, 'William Morris and the Poetry of Escape', in H. Davis, W. C. Devane and R. C. Bald, eds, *Nineteenth-Century Studies* (Ithaca, NY, 1940), pp. 246–76, p. 263.

41 H. Lawrance, *Historical Memoirs of the Queens of England*, 2 vols (London, 1838), II, p. 133.

42 E. de Selincourt, ed., *William Wordsworth, Poetical Works* (Oxford, 1944), vol. 2, p. 135.

43 Foucault, *History of Sexuality*, p. 104.

44 C. A. Sewter, *The Stained Glass of William Morris and his Circle* (New Haven, 1974), pp. 44–45; J. Banham and J. Harris, *William Morris and the Middle Ages*, Catalogue, Whitworth Art Gallery (Manchester, 1984), pp. 40–41, 200–07.

45 Anon, 'Chaucer', *North British Review*, pp. 325, 327.

46 F. D Maurice, *Chapters from English History on the Representation and Education of the People* (London, 1866), p. 58.

47 Quoted in Spurgeon, *Chaucer Criticism and Allusion*, II, p. 77.

48 M. Cook, *London and the Culture of Homosexuality, 1885–1914* (Cambridge, 2003), pp. 122–42.

49 *Lectures 1808–1819 On Literature*, in R. A. Foakes et al., eds, *Coleridge, Collected Works* (Princeton, NJ, 1971–2001), vol 5, p. 95; *Biographia Literaria*, in *Collected Works*, vol. 7, p. 76.

50 Quoted in Spurgeon, *Chaucer Criticism and Allusion*, II, p. 242.

51 E. T. Cook and A. Wedderburn, eds, *The Works of John Ruskin*, 39 vols (London, 1903–1912), vol. 7, p. 474; letter, vol. 27, p. 631; vol. 28, pp. 500–01.

52 D. Robinson, 'The Kelmscott Chaucer', in Finlay and Rosenblum, *Chaucer Illustrated*, pp. 282–83.

53 See Robinson's discussion, ibid., pp. 297–303.

54 Morris, *William Morris, Collected Works*, I, pp. 259–60.

Riding with Robin Hood
English Pageantry and the Making of a Legend

John Marshall

The medieval proverb, 'many men speak of Robin Hood that never bent his bow', has had limited effect in discouraging uninformed opinion.[1] Nor, if it was the intention, has it curbed the enthusiasm to speak of Robin Hood since the late fourteenth century when the priest Sloth confessed, in *Piers Plowman*, that:

> I kan noght parfitly my *Paternoster* as the preest it syngeth,
> But I kan rymes of Robyn Hood and Randolf Erl of Chestre.[2]

Resisting all constraints, Robin Hood has remained firmly in the popular imagination and on the lips of successive generations for eight centuries, an achievement that earned him the only properly fictional character entry in the first edition of the *Oxford Dictionary of National Biography*. Although the outlaw myth acts, centrally, as a reference point for contesting the concepts of freedom and justice, it fluctuates in emphasis according to the tastes and anxieties of each age. In addition to transformations fashioned by audience sensibilities and social and political conditions, the myth is moulded by the practical demands of the different media through which it is transmitted. This has seen Robin shift in shape over the years from the sometimes violent, anti-authoritarian yeoman of the late medieval ballads and games through the genteel, dispossessed nobleman of Renaissance plays and Victorian novels to the Green Lord of the Wildwood, the incarnation of spring, of new age literature. He is, undeniably, one of the best-known and most enduring secular figures in the western world.

But Robin has another string to his bow. Since the early nineteenth century he and his adventures have epitomized the middle ages. For film and television generations in particular, the visualizations of character, costume and scenery have created an image and evocation of the period uninhibited by historical correctness. This cinematic medievalism is the culmination of years of conflating fact and fiction in an attempt to make the Robin Hood myth seem 'real'. Many narrative developments and historical details now so familiar would have been unrecognizable to the ballad and game audiences of the fifteenth century. The setting in the reign of Richard I, the noble status of the dispossessed outlaw (Earl of Huntingdon or Loxley), the principle of robbing the rich to give to the poor and the love of Maid Marian are all late sixteenth-century elaborations of the myth.[3] They become, though, consistent and memorable features of Robin Hood tales in the nineteenth and twentieth centuries as, after *Ivanhoe* in 1820, does the emphasis on Robin's Saxon heritage. From that moment, Robin becomes the patriotic figure and emblem of English identity that audiences take for granted today.

This creeping process of historical definition encouraged the belief, without much evidence, that Robin Hood actually existed. Growing interest in the indigenous literature of the past led the radical literary scholar Joseph Ritson to publish in 1795, for the first time, a two-volume edition of nearly all the extant Robin Hood ballads.[4] Ultimately as influential as his gathering of texts was the 'Life of Robin Hood' that began the first volume. Based on a variety of manuscript and published sources it sought, with an impressive academic apparatus, to provide the nearest thing Robin had ever received to a biography. Some of the references are more convincing than others. Least believable of all now is Ritson's uncritical adoption of William Stukeley's pedigree of Robin Hood that ennobled the outlaw and traced his descent from the non-existent earl of Fitzooth and lord of Kyme. The genealogy may have lacked authority, but the gist of authentic nobility it generated survives.[5]

A distinct advantage of noble origin, even though it robs us of the common man and contradicts the content of the ballads, is that it adds context to the outlaw narrative. The early ballads and May game plays are essentially brief, episodic depictions of frequently violent action. In them – and, presumably, to early audiences – it was not so important who Robin was, other than a yeoman, or where he came from, but what he did to whom and why. In these early treatments of the myth where, with the rare exception of a rather perfunctory death scene, the story never ends, biography and history are unnecessary constraints. In the extended forms of full-length plays, popular novels and films, on the other hand, where stories begin and end, and characters are subject to the processes of change, the ups, downs and restoration of noble birthright within a defined historical period are essential devices.

Romanticism, antiquarian interest, the fashion for biography and developments in the novel produced, by the early nineteenth century, the Robin Hood that flourishes today. He became, for the first time, in Thomas Love Peacock's novel *Maid Marian*, a fusion of features that had previously been kept separate; a noble and patriotic outlaw with an inheritance, who also possessed the physical skill and courage of the English yeoman.[6] Other aspects of his 'life' were consolidated to give some biographical consistency. He no longer lived, as in the *Geste of Robyn Hode*, in the nebulous reign of an unnumbered Edward, but securely in the time of Richard I. His devotion to Mary was transferred to Marian. He became a freedom fighter with a nationalist cause rather than an opportunist bandit. He embodied the qualities of Englishness and typified chivalry, fellowship and loyalty that made him an ideal role model for adolescent boys and classic material for the soon-to-emerge cinema.

For all the undoubted impact on the Robin Hood myth in the nineteenth century of ballad anthologies, historical biographies and novels, they were literary in form and, for the most part, solitary in audience experience. The communal aspect of live exchange fundamental to the sharing of tales told through ballad and game endured, somewhat diluted, in the guise of comic operettas and plays with incidental music. Popular as many of these anodyne entertainments were, the myth of Robin Hood reached a significantly larger and more engaged audience through another performance medium. English pageantry has a long and illustrious, if rather neglected, history in which Robin plays his part. One of the attractions of its revival in the nineteenth century was that it resonated with the image and spirit of the 'medieval'.

What actually furnished that resonance was not always strictly medieval. Rather it was an idealized form of antique presentation, owing more to the seventeenth century than to the fifteenth, inhabited by figures from a romanticized past. Historically, English pageantry is an elusive combination of spectacle and speech in which metaphor, allegory, symbolism, mythology and history combine to commemorate and honour a person or an event. For the most part, early civic pageants were vehicles for propaganda that demonstrated allegiance to the crown and staged relations of power within the city. In later years they would celebrate local and national identity by depicting momentous occasions and honouring public worthies. The elite auspices of the early pageants made them an uneasy medium in which to raise a potentially subversive hero like Robin Hood. But this is precisely what was done for the 1615 Lord Mayor's Show in London. The reputation of this pageant, in which Robin Hood appears as a historical figure, rests mainly with the author and devisor. Better known for his contribution, with Shakespeare and others, to the play of *Sir Thomas More*, Anthony Munday wrote two plays, acted by the Admiral's Men at the Rose Playhouse in the late 1590s, on the downfall and death of Robert, earl of Huntington. An anti-Catholic government spy, Munday later became a prolific devisor/author/producer of Lord Mayor's Shows.[7] In one capacity or another he was involved in fifteen of them between 1602 and 1623. In 1615, for the second year running, Munday was asked by the Drapers' Guild, of which he was a member, to devise an entertainment to celebrate the election to mayor of Sir John Jolles. He called this pageant *Metropolis Coronata; the Triumph of Ancient Drapery* and, as before, relied on a mixture of history, mythology and moral allegory to convey his heady mixture of flattery and instruction.[8]

The devices on the River Thames were occupied by Jason, Medea, representations of Neptune and Thamesis, Fame and Time as well as the figure of Henry fitz Ailwin, a draper and the first lord mayor of London. On land the new mayor encountered the Monument of London inhabited by the city herself and her Twelve Daughters representing the twelve companies. They were attended by the 'foure especiall qualities' necessary for civic happiness; Learned Religion, Military Discipline, Navigation and Homebred Husbandry.

Somewhat incongruously, these 'shewes' acclaiming drapery, the golden fleece and London were followed by a 'device of Huntsmen, all clad in greene, with their Bowes, Arrowes and Bugles, and a new slaine Deere carried among them' (ll. 200–01). Munday explains Robin Hood's presence through genealogy; Henry fitz Ailwin is Robin's father-in-law. This is a subtle but expedient change in name from the Robert Fitzwater who occupied the role in his play, *The Downfall of Robert Earl of Huntington*. In order not to upset the protocol of the occasion this is no rough-handed Robin Hood disposed to theft. He is the gentrified, 'Earle Robert de la Hude, sometime the noble Earle of Huntington' (ll. 202–03). Even his outlawry lacks a criminal basis, being blamed instead on 'the cruell oppression of a most unnaturall covetous Brother ... Gilbert de la hude, Lord Abbot of Christall Abbey, who had all, or most of his Lands in morgage' (ll. 207–09). For the purposes of eulogizing guild culture, Munday emphasizes the gallantry of Robin's company of men and praises them for honouring him as their 'Lord and Master' (l. 211).

In the evening conclusion to the show, the brave huntsmen present themselves before the mayor to whom Robin speaks directly:

Since Graves may not their Dead containe,
Nor in their peacefull sleepes remaine,
But Triumphes and great Showes must use them,
And we unable to refuse them;
It joyes me that Earle Robert Hood,
Fetcht from the Forrest of merrie Shirwood,
With these my Yeomen tight and tall,
Brave Huntsmen and good Archers all:
Must in this Joviall day partake,
Prepared for your Honours sake. (ll. 310–19)

For Munday, 'Triumphes' and 'Showes' are not only enough to wake the dead but let the sponsor influence the choice of an outlaw's in-laws. Munday's reason for deviating from the biography he had created for Robin in his plays may have been because fitz Ailwin's inaugural mayoralty, allegedly, coincided with the reigns of Richard I and John. Never one to be over-bothered by historical accuracy, it does not seem to have concerned Munday that fitz Ailwin had no daughters. He was, though, predeceased by his eldest son, Peter, who left two girls. The eldest of these became Henry's heir. Robert Fitzwater may have had the better claim, if only mythically, to father-in-law of Robin, but in 1615 he lacked the essential virtues of being a draper and the first lord mayor of London.

This was not the first instance of Robin Hood being used to display prowess by association. Henry VIII, with twelve noblemen, entered the queen's chamber on the morning of 18 January 1510 dressed as 'Robyn Hodes men'. Abashment on the ladies' part was eased with some dancing before 'thei departed'.[9]

Henry VIII's encounter with Robin Hood and his men on Shooters' Hill in 1515 is usually categorized as an elaborate aristocratic version of a May game, but it owes as much, if not more, to the aesthetic and form of the 'royal entry'. It was highly organized, if not choreographed, and involved Robin with 200 archers, made up of the king's guard, speaking directly to and in honour of the king and queen. Returning from the Greenwood, the king and queen meet Lady May and Dame Flora, richly apparelled in a chariot drawn by five horses. On each horse sat a lady representing in turn 'humidite', 'vert', 'vegetave', 'pleasaunce' and 'swete odour'. The king was saluted with 'diverse goodly songes' and the whole occasion brought 'great solace and confort' to the large number of people, estimated at 25,000, who witnessed the event. It may have been May that was being celebrated, and the Robin Hood game acknowledged as a popular means of observance, but the artistic devices employed were those of pageantry.[10] It has echoes of what may be the earliest ceremonial royal involvement with Robin Hood. In late May 1357, Edward the Black Prince and the captive King John of France were ambushed, on their way from Winchester to London, by 500 men in a forest. The men dressed in green were, the prince explained, foresters behaving like robbers as was their custom. By the time the king reached Cheapside and the magnificent display mounted by the London Goldsmiths he must have realized that he had been exposed to a performance of pageantry rather than a threat to his life. The time of year, the costume and the nature of the encounter suggest, in spite of the early date, that Robin Hood or some other outlaw tradition was being invoked.[11]

This crossover between customary game and pageantry may also explain Queen Elizabeth's interest in the London Midsummer Day May game of 1559. The event comprised a giant, drums and guns, the nine worthies with speeches, a 'goodly' pageant with a queen and divers others with speeches, St George and the dragon, and a morris dance followed by Robin Hood, Little John, Maid Marian and Friar Tuck who all had speeches around London.[12] This does not sound much like the contemporary May games of the Thames and Severn Valleys over which Robin presided and it probably would not have been the sort of thing to set before the queen at Greenwich the following day if it was. The reference, which uses both generic terms 'May game' and 'pageant', is a useful reminder that there probably never was an archetype of the Robin Hood game and that differences in local circumstances and audience constituency inevitably conditioned custom and practice. It is possible that the arrangement of diverse scenes in procession of the May game lent itself to the formality of pageantry whereas the games of village parishes were less structured and emblematic in their performance and less ceremonious in their relationship with the audience.

Although pageantry as a form of presentation clearly had an influence on the making and diffusion of the Robin Hood myth before the Commonwealth, the number of instances where Robin actually appears seems fairly limited. This is perhaps because early pageantry tends to concentrate on personifications rather than persons, unless they are royalty. Robin Hood fits uneasily in an art form that is populated by embodiments of cities, countries, continents, rivers, mountains, time, seasons and the months – although he is often associated with May – as well as figures from classical mythology. Moreover, what he represents socially, even when gentrified, is too specific in a world of servitude and injustice to appear in the glorification of authority. This changed in the last quarter of the nineteenth century.

Robin reappeared as a star of pageantry when pageantry remodelled its ideological purpose. From the late eighteenth century to the middle of the nineteenth century the art of pageantry, particularly the Lord Mayor's Show, was in serious decline, becoming little more than a shabby military parade. For whatever reason, not least to do with confidence in international expansion and a growing sense of national identity, the Lord Mayor's Show of 1884 discarded the symbolism and pseudo-history of an individual company and celebrated instead the history of the City of London and Britain's Imperial greatness. Perhaps more importantly, the show that year stressed, for the first time, the educational value of the past it was celebrating. Its purpose was to present before the public 'some of the glorious traditions of our ancient city – to show how, from time almost immemorial, the Corporation has been both loyal to the Crown and true to the people'.[13] Unsurprisingly, the show began with Dick Whittington who was followed by William the Conqueror, Richard Coeur de Lion, Richard II and Queen Elizabeth, and a tableau of Lord Mayor Walworth standing over the slain Wat Tyler. The procession continued with the City's first charter, a Nile boat, a herd of camels and elephants ridden by representatives of Rajahs with a group 'symbolical of India'. Although Robin does not feature in this show, it is possible to see how this forerunner of the Victorian educational pageant, with its emphasis on chronology rather than moral allegory, might accommodate him. Chronology as a means of establishing an evolutionary national history that erased contradictions, smoothed differences and celebrated continuity became the dominant organizing principle of late nineteenth- and early twentieth-century English pageantry.

Robin had previously made an appearance in a pageant that was part military, part history and part allegory. On 23 June 1862 the Coventry pageant, which celebrated Lady Godiva, was revived after an interval of eleven years. The procession was fronted by two heralds and a detachment of the First Life Guards. They were followed by the band of the menagerie, consisting of twelve men with tureens and porringers, and St George with a Templar attendant. After them came members of the city guilds and a fire engine. Next processed the Ancient Order of Foresters with, indicating perhaps the thinking behind the inclusion, Robin Hood and Maid Marian accompanied by Will Scarlet, Friar Tuck and other Merry Men. After the Black Prince in armour, more bands and guilds preceded the long-awaited Lady Godiva on a white horse. Bringing up the rear was a tableau containing handsome Florizell and pretty Perdita dressed as shepherd and shepherdess, seated in a bower with sheepdog and lamb at their feet.[14]

Around the same time, Knutsford participated in the vogue for a 'Merrie England' experience by reviving, or rather reinventing, the May Day celebration. What this involved in the early years from 1864 is unclear but in 1913, and possibly earlier, Robin, Marion and Will Scarlet took their place in the procession that escorted the May Queen and her attendants. Their presence had some seasonal purpose to it, as did the involvement of Jack-in-the-Green and the morris dancers, but it is more difficult to account for the inclusion of King Cnut, Scottish highlanders, Night, Spanish and Swiss girls, John Bull and Britannia, a special Canadian tableau complete with Miss Canada and a trooper on a pony, Japanese girls, a Turk, Grace Darling and her father, some cricketers and Alice in Wonderland.[15]

Robin, though, was getting used to keeping odd company. In 1893 he appeared in the Lichfield 'Greenhill Bower'. This Whitsuntide procession of uncertain origin began at the Guildhall and made its way to the 'Bower House'. Robin, Friar Tuck and Little John processed behind Wombwell and Bailey's 'World Renowned Menagerie', with their brass band, in the company of Shylock, Portia, Buffalo Bill, Mexican Joe, a Toreador, a Chinaman, John Bull, a Yellow Dwarf and Mephistopheles. They were followed by tableaux that juxtaposed fairy tales with royal and political figures. Succeeding them, in keeping with the fashion of the time, was the 'Grand Mediaeval Display of Ye Olde Court of Arraye, consisting of Knights and Men at Arms'.[16]

The events at Coventry, Knutsford and Lichfield seem more like fancy-dress celebrations of past glories and present fascinations than a history lesson. Even so, the bias of the Lord Mayor's Show of 1884 concurred with the educational tenor of the times and was cultivated by Louis N. Parker, the man usually credited with the invention and founding of modern pageantry. A schoolmaster at Sherborne School, he planned, throughout his time there at the close of the nineteenth century, to put on a musical 'folk-play'. It was not, though, until he had left the school that an opportunity arose. He deliberately used the term 'folk-play' to distance himself from earlier forms of pageantry but it was considered misleading and dropped. Parker was aware that the earlier techniques of allegory and symbolism presented visually in procession were unsuitable for learning history. Instead he chose to present his pageants at static open-air sites and emphasized their educational and dramatic potential. Historical accuracy was a guiding principle. He insisted upon archive research to find precise words for speeches and songs as well as evidence for reconstructing costumes and props. It was also important to him that the dramatic episodes presented should relate specifically to the history of the place. The Sherborne Pageant of 1905 was the culmination of Parker's thinking. There were eleven episodes in all, written and performed by amateurs. It began with 'The Coming of Ealdhelm' in 705, encompassed the defeat of the Danes and the introduction of the Benedictine Rule to Sherborne in 998, and concluded with 'Sir Walter Raleigh comes to Sherborne' in 1593.[17]

Somewhat strangely for a man committed to authenticity and evidence, he interpolated between episodes seven and eight 'a Morris Dance, in which Robin Hood, Maid Marion, and their band take part'.[18] As both episodes represent events occurring in 1437 it is possible that Parker was thinking of Robin Hood games rather than a historical figure. No evidence for such games exists in the local parish records, although from their beginning in around 1505 to the Reformation there are receipts from the King game or revel and, in the earliest account, for a 'Morys daunce'.[19] The list of Sherborne episodes further indicates that Robin and his band 'play a small part in the action of the seventh'.[20] It does not say what this 'small part' was, although it is easy enough to guess from the title: 'The Quarrel between the Town and the Monastery'. During the fifteenth century there was fierce animosity between the parishioners and the monks of Sherborne, caused, not least, by the dispute over a new baptismal font for the parish church which the monks opposed. The quarrel intensified and in 1436 townsmen reputedly set fire to the roof of the abbey church with a flaming arrow.[21] From such flights of fancy legends grow.

Parker's primary aim was the education of a community in its own past. He saw this as a protest against modernity: 'this modernising spirit, which destroys all loveliness and has no loveliness of its own to put in its place, is the negation of poetry, the negation of romance … This is just precisely the kind of spirit which a properly organised and properly conducted pageant is designed to kill.'[22] Although Parker deserves the credit for transforming English pageantry and finding yet another campaign for Robin Hood to fight, he was not alone and not the first. There was another exponent of the pageant who believed in the redemptive power of the past, the character-building quality of the sports and pastimes of old England, the obligation to research, the significance of place and the need for Robin Hood. He was D'Arcy Ferris.

The Ripon Millenary Festival of 1886 established D'Arcy Ferris as the nation's leading Master of Revels and Pageant Master of the nineteenth

Fig. 1 D'Arcy Ferris in costume as Master of the Revels/Lord of Misrule (reproduced by kind permission of the De Ferrars family)

century. The initial idea for a celebration to mark the 1000th anniversary of Ripon came in the form of an innocent rhetorical question from the vicar of Trinity Church. He wondered out loud before his congregation what the citizens of Ripon had to look forward to in 1886.[23] Plenty it seemed. It was fifty years since the recreation of the bishopric of Ripon and, according to the Corporation Calendar, 1000 years since King Alfred had given the city its foundation charter.[24] The vicar thought a 'splendid service in the Cathedral' was a worthy commemoration. He could not have known then how his simple idea would generate gargantuan ambitions and become the focus for political jealousies and religious dissent. It started the way of all millennial celebrations; was 1886 the right date? Was the calendar entry genuine? Then the dean of Ripon, agreeing to the service in the Cathedral, mused on the possibility of a festival for the Corporation. The mayor concurred and stated at a public meeting that the subject had been before the council who referred it to the finance committee who, in turn, thought it should be discussed further by an appointed sub-committee who should give consideration to the content and proper title of the event. The composition of the sub-committee caused ructions in the council chamber. Ancient prerogatives had not been fully recognized. All members of the Corporation should be on the committee claimed those who were excluded. Even the proposed title of the event, 'The Festival of the Existence of a Thousand Years of the See and the City of Ripon' was attacked. It wasn't accurate; the see had not existed uninterruptedly for 1000 years. It was sectarian and divisive in that it described a united civic and ecclesiastical celebration that excluded Nonconformists.[25]

When the programme of events drawn up by the sub-committee was put before the city council the majority of members treated the matter with 'unbecoming levity'. They mocked and ridiculed the committee's choice of activities and bayed at them, 'who is going to pay?' Eventually the proposal to hold the festival was accepted, but only on the casting vote of the mayor. The festival was to be over three days at the end of August. On the Wednesday there would be a procession through the city to a service in the Cathedral followed by a subscription luncheon. In the afternoon a public meeting would be held in the market place where addresses appropriate to the occasion would be given. A torchlight procession in the evening would bring the first day to a close. On the Friday and Saturday – Thursday was market day – old English sports and pastimes would be performed at Fountains Abbey. The whole event would come to be known by its finally agreed short title, 'The Ripon Millenary Festival'.

For the purposes of the history of pageantry and Robin Hood, the most significant meeting was that of the Millenary Sports Committee held on Saturday 24 April. It was there that the programme for the Friday and Saturday was agreed prior to its presentation before Lord Ripon, as owner of Fountains, for his approval. It read:

> Play of Robin Hood, with choruses, on the traditional spot near the Abbey where the famous encounter took place with the Curtal Friar, Old English Revels, to include Morris Dancers, May Pole, &c., at the west end of the Abbey, Procession of the Ancient Guilds of Ripon.[26]

At a meeting of the Millenary Festival Committee on 1 May it was decided to offer a prize of £10 10s for the best open-air play written on the legendary encounter. Competitors were to pay special attention to dramatic effect and provide suitable solos, duets and choruses, 'as the play will be set to music, and should occupy about one hour'.[27] Advertisements placed in national papers and literary journals set the first day of June as the deadline for receipt of entries.

Although D'Arcy Ferris was not formally engaged by the Festival Committee as Master of the Revels until 19 May 1886, it is highly probable that the play was his idea. He was in contact with the Ripon town clerk earlier in the year before the first public meeting in February called by the mayor to discuss the possibility of a festival. A letter from Ferris survives in the festival archive in which he explains to the town clerk that he did not reply sooner as he was away from home. He goes on to say that he has already been in correspondence with the editor of the *Ripon Chronicle*, from whom he may have heard about the festival, to make suggestions for the event. He promises to set a programme before the committee after consulting the Bodleian, Guildhall and British Museum libraries, anticipating Parker's methods by almost twenty years. He attaches great importance to the 'fete', as he calls it, 'as being a revival of ancient civic pageants'. If entrusted with a function in it he promises a worthy presentation that is 'at once of antiquarian as well as spectacular interest'. He concludes in a way that suggests he had previously discussed the possibility of including a play with the town clerk:

> ... within 2 or 3 days I will submit a programme. In the meantime Birch's 'Merry Men of Sherwood Forest' might be selected & choruses practised by a choir of about 50 voices or more who would form the chorus of Foresters & forest maidens in a play of Robin Hood in which

Fig. 2 The River Skell and Fountains Abbey where, according to tradition,
Robin Hood met and fought with the curtal friar

the well known incident of his fight with the friar of Fountains might be introduced. Should you have no one to write the play (which will be necessary in order to be suitable for open air performance) perhaps Oscar Wilde – who is really a clever poet – might do so, or I could undertake it. I will write to Mr Wilde in any case.[28]

Wilde's response is unfortunately not known. Ferris's ambitions for the play may now seem unrealistic, but it is worth remembering that at this time Wilde was not a household name. He had published *Poems* to mixed critical reviews in 1881 and had only a single play performed in New York in 1883; *Vera: or The Nihilists* was not a success, instant or otherwise, running for just a week. It is a rather immature and laboured melodrama about Russian revolutionaries that debates the difference between terrorism and idealism and ends in a parody of *Romeo and Juliet*. It is a poor predictor of the talent to emerge and unlikely to have been seen by Ferris. It is possible, though, that it was Wilde's youthful enthusiasm for liberty, expressed in the early poems as well as *Vera*, which made Ferris think he would be attracted to the subject of Robin Hood. Equally disappointing as Wilde's lost reply is the fading from performance history of

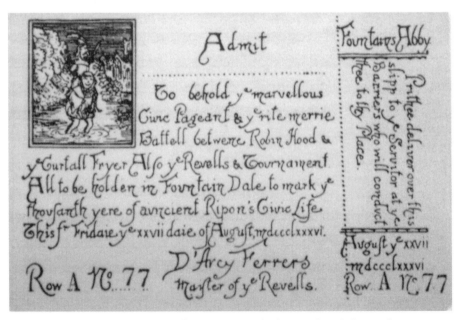

Fig. 3 Ticket to the Ripon Millenary Festival, designed and drawn by D'Arcy Ferris (W. Harrison, *Ripon Millenary*, Ripon, 1892)

D'Arcy Ferris. There is not space here to give him the biography he deserves; a few cuttings will have to do.[29] His business card described him as 'Tenor of the Royal Albert Hall and Professor of the West London Conservatoire of Music and Dramatic School, Conductor of various choral societies'. Although music was his profession – member of the chorus in the original production of *HMS Pinafore*, conductor of the premiere of Holst's operetta *Lansdown Castle*, musical arranger and choir master for Lady Archibald Campbell's open-air production of *As You Like It* at Coombe House, Kingston-upon-Thames (coincidentally reviewed by Oscar Wilde in the *Dramatic Review*, 6 June 1885) – he had many other interests. He was, almost single-handedly, responsible for the revival of the 'Ancient English Morris Dance'.[30] His interest in the morris and pageantry sprang from the same source. He was passionate about improving the social condition of the people and believed that revival of the old (medieval) English sports and pastimes would encourage a 'spontaneous attempt among the masses … to amuse themselves … lightening the life of the poor by innocent pastimes … with the additional hope that by breaking down class prejudice, we may, as a nation, live more happily together'.[31] This romantic notion of the redeeming potential of recreation inevitably brought Robin Hood into Ferris's crusade. Ferris described him as 'the representative of Democratic Freedom in his day' and 'of never-ending interest to "Merrie England" and her bards'.[32] At the same time as his morris dance revivals he was devising a series of pageants. Robin made an appearance in at least three of them: 'The Festival of ye Summer Queen' at Lockinge House for Lord and Lady Wantage, 'Ye Progress of ye Harvest Quene' for the Lord Lieutenant of Yorkshire at Grimston, and in the 'Red, White and Blue Bazaar' May revels at Islington.[33] The first two involved Robin as a character in a play, possibly written by Ferris, although the programme wryly credits 'Mayde Playne', and the third in procession with Little John, Friar Tuck and Maid Marian as Queen of the May. Such were his credentials and renown – he went on to take responsibility as Pageant Master for the highly successful Liverpool Pageant of 1907 – that when Ripon planned their millenary festival they were unlikely to look further than D'Arcy Ferris for their Master of the Revels. They offered him a fee of 30 guineas and 10 per cent of the profits.[34]

One of his first tasks was to judge the short list of plays that had been submitted after the committee had ascertained that he had not entered himself. Opportunistically, and in the absence of an entry from Oscar Wilde, he had, but it was three days late and disqualified.

It may have been a disappointment to the Festival Committee that only seventeen scripts were received, although more than this number requested details of the project. Potential authors may have been put off by the four-week deadline or the subject matter. As one contributor put it, 'the subject of the ballad, and the ballad itself, are utterly devoid of dramatic interest'; consequently he 'looked in another story'.[35] Unsuccessful entries were returned with a single exception. Mr Sayle of Dresden was late in seeing the advertisement for the 'Prize Play' competition and sent in a 'sample' of an unexceptional dramatic treatment of the ballad, with Martin Parker, the seventeenth-century professional ballad writer, as the poet prologue.[36] More colourful is Sayle's accompanying letter setting out his plan of action for the play, particularly when he reaches the point where the friar's bandogs enter to attack Robin and his men. As he says,

> Now comes the *crux*. Can you or can you not get 50 dogs to be so trained several days before so as to be let loose at a certain time and rush on to the stage? It is my belief that you can by this expediency, viz. that they shall be fed only once a day *and fed on the spot of the play*. Being kennelled up mean and then let loose they would run every day to the spot to be fed; and they would do so on the day of the play. But if this is asking too much we can vary the play.[37]

The winning entry, recommended by Ferris, came from Augustin Dawtrey of Nottingham who used as his motto, to preserve anonymity during the selection process, 'Son of York', where he returned to live just before the festival.[38]

While D'Arcy Ferris was preparing, as Master of the Revels, to direct the play he was also devising the historical pageant that would precede it. As planned, the pageant cars and participants assembled at Studley Hall and processed through the estate grounds to Fountains Abbey. It was, by all accounts, an impressive spectacle. Ferris's pageant philosophy is described in his own words:

> The procession was designed to be historical and emblematical, with a few of the masquerading elements inseparable from mediaeval pageantry. Appropriate subjects for representation was my first aim, historical accuracy the second, and beauty and artistic arrangement the last.[39]

As he had promised, he researched his subject in the major academic libraries of England to ensure visual accuracy, especially in costume, wher-

Fig. 4 C. H. Knowles as Robin Hood by John Jellicoe (W. Harrison, *Ripon Millenary*, Ripon, 1892)

ever possible. The historical portion of the pageant began with the 'Druidical Period', progressed through the Roman, Danish and Saxon eras, included Robin Hood and concluded with Charles I, 'nothing specially noteworthy in the history of Ripon being suitable for presentation in the subsequent periods'.[40] It is almost as if anything after the Restoration and the golden age of English pageantry is not a proper subject for 'historical and emblematical' treatment, or, perhaps, is too closely associated with the 'modernising spirit that destroyed all loveliness' that so offended Louis Parker. The rest of the pageant comprised the classical groups as an emblem of Ripon triumphant, with the Genius of the City played by the mayoress. It was in this section that Ferris's confidence in his organizational and artistic skills was tested to the point of irritation. When suitable children could not be found for one of the cars, causing his 'logical allegory' to be upset by 'illogical re-arrangements', he remarked, 'Alas! On what delicate ground do we walk when novices attempt to tread the domain of metaphor!'[41]

The rear of the procession was brought up by the civic authorities preceded, in Ferris fashion, by Maypole dancers and the specially invited Kirkby Malzeard Sword Dancers, emphasizing the spirit of the middle ages.

It is evident that for Ferris and the Millenary Festival Committee, if not for all the citizens of Ripon, Robin Hood and his men took their rightful place in the historical part of the pageant. The group was made up of the actor/singers who would perform the play at the 'traditional spot', wearing costumes of sober character and hue so that they would be 'a relief from the gorgeous colouring of the majority'.[42] The phrase, 'traditional spot', seems to have acquired the potency of a magical mantra. It is repeated over and over again in the festival publicity and minutes and was quoted by nearly all the newspaper reviews. It is as though the tangible evidence of place was sufficient proof of Robin's existence and that the re-enactment of his encounter with the friar would render the past ritualistically present. It is also indicative of Ferris's scholarly desire for accuracy.

The 'traditional spot' is situated on the bank of the River Skell just to the east of the remains of the abbey kitchen, chapel and garderobes. For all its public avowal, it is not certain how this came to be the 'traditional spot'. The two versions of the ballad, *Robin Hood and the Curtal Friar*, surviving from the seventeenth century do not even name the River Skell, never mind the spot. In fact, all extant copies of the 'B' broadside and garland version have Robin only going as far as Fountains Dale, rather than the abbey, to meet with the friar.[43] The tradition may have a pictorial origin. When illustrators depicted the scene for broadside or garland publication they are likely to have included the abbey in the composition. This not only adds visual interest; it determines the location. The perspective of foreground river and background abbey spontaneously produces the 'traditional spot'. As though to reinforce the location, Robin Hood's Well was built, probably in the eighteenth century, into the wooded bank on the south side of the Skell adjacent to the 'spot'.

The text of Dawtrey's play pays homage to location from the start.[44] It begins, 'Scene: The Traditional Spot, near Fountains Abbey'. The performance began with an 'Invisible Chorus' made up of local men and boys, 39 in all but representing 50, as Foresters. Concealed behind the abbey, their voices filled the empty space, allowing the 'spot' itself to take centre stage before the entrance of human actors. But, it seems, nature can always be improved upon. As the official review of the play put it:

> Care had been taken to restore to the scene of the combat some of its pristine appearance, by the collection of brushwood, heather, and logs of wood; the stage had been 'dressed' like a piece of forest land, by the insertion of trees where none before existed.[45]

This sits somewhat uneasily with the reasons D'Arcy Ferris gave, at a public lecture in Ripon Town Hall, for preferring open-air plays. He told his audience that they

> differ most from the ordinary stage, in that they present living pictures of nature in contrast to the artificiality of stage scenery. In place of the counterfeit we have the real, instead of art we have nature, real flowers grow, and birds in the real boughs overhead offer their gratuitous services. Real perspective of distance too, in which perhaps the tuneful lay of foresters grows faint, till nothing but the gentle rustling of the trees, or the bleating of a far-off flock is heard.[46]

As the audience gazed upon the 'spot' restored, the Invisible Chorus established the historical credentials of the encounter:

> In Fountain's dale, long years ago,
> Before the Abbey's overthrow,
> Met Friar and Robin – foe to foe,
> Long years ago, long years ago.

And as though conscious of performance as an act of resuscitation, the Chorus incants the heroes' return:

> To try a bout *again* they come,
> *Again* the verdant dale they roam;
> From cloisters and from forest home.
> *Again* they come, *again* they come. (my italics)

Having linked the past with present and place, the 'tuneful lay of foresters grows faint' and is shattered by three blasts on horns heralding the entrance of Robin Hood on horseback followed by Little John, Will Scarlet and the 50 Merry Men on foot. The entrance was made to a rousing excerpt from the cantata *Robin Hood* by Liverpool-born composer John Liptrot Hatton.

The powerful presentation of Robin is maintained as he sings his first solo on horseback. It establishes him as the model of alternative but just authority. He compares his kingdom and courtiers favourably with any in existence and sets out his characterizing philosophy of wealth redistribution. His laws are 'simple and few'; to take from the lord and the bishop and give not to the poor – this is the fiftieth year of Victoria's reign after all – but to the 'halt and the lame', the weak and the old; in other words to the deserving poor whose poverty is faultless and visible. In the second verse of his solo, Robin extols the virtues of his pastoral idyll and, like Duke Senior in the opening of Act II of *As You Like It*, despises the pomp of the court. This is a noble Robin Hood who barely mentions his outlaw status.

It is not just in sentiment that Dawtrey's text borrows from Shakespeare's Robin Hood play. As *Robin Hood and Ye Curtall Fryer* draws to a close, Will Scarlett is borne on the shoulders of two foresters and a slain deer is carried on a pole by two others as the Merry Men sing 'What shall he have who killed the deer' from Act IV sc. ii. As soon as they finish, Robin calls for 'Rob the Songster', played by D'Arcy Ferris, to sing a lay. He responds with 'Under the greenwood tree' from Act II sc. v. Slightly less obvious, but undoubtedly still a literary debt, is the similarity between the punning banter exchanged between Robin and the Friar and that between Orlando and Oliver in the opening scene of *As You Like It*. In addition, Robin's observation that 'The fat capon that lines thy paunch' will disturb the Friar's digestion rather than his meditation looks to be lifted from Jaques' description of the justice, 'In fair round belly, with good capon lin'd' (Act II sc. vii).

Fig. 5 'A Group of Ye Foresters': the cast of Robin Hood & ye Curtall Fryer
(W. Harrison, *Ripon Millenary*, Ripon, 1892)

Although Dawtrey's play relied for its plot, action and some dialogue upon the ballad of *Robin Hood and the Curtall Fryer* published by Ritson, it is clear that its dramatic sensibilities were Victorian Shakespeare (at one point hideous witches enter and bid Robin 'beware') rather than late medieval May game. Dawtrey, and Ferris, seem to have been unaware of Copland's sixteenth-century printing of a May game play of the same episode, or, if they were, chose not to use it. The Shakespearean influence is unlikely to have been Dawtrey's alone; he was paid a further £1 six weeks before the festival to revise his play.[47] D'Arcy Ferris may have instigated the changes. He had been involved in the prestigious open-air production of *As You Like It* at Coombe House the year before.

The ballad may have provided the plot, *As You Like It* the spirit, Victorian England the sentiment, but it was to pageantry that Ferris turned for the aesthetic. In his lecture he stated that he favoured pageant and movement over lengthy dialogue and went on to observe;

The tableaux formed by groups of actors during the play are striking pictures which will remain in the memory. These should be as natural and unstagy as possible, in fact, the more you can dispense with stage traditions, and the nearer you approach real life, the more truthful will be the presentation.

Testimony and photographs of the production seem to verify Ferris's beliefs: an actual, *the* actual, river was used for the dunking, arrows were fired and deflected by the Friar's buckler, a real deer was brought on stage, 50 dogs fought with Robin and his men. Well, not quite. Twenty boys dressed up as dogs scuffled with the foresters. This may have stretched a desire for naturalism to the limit; 'reverse-of-realistic' the *Dramatic Review* of 4 September 1886 memorably called it. Nevertheless, the text wastes no time in making the dogs' presence thematic as well as dramatic. To the Victorian home-spun philosophy that permeates the play, the loyalty of dogs is added to the virtues of nature, obedience, temperance and mirth. Before the dogs enter the fray the Friar sings;

The friend of man, a faithful friend
When others turn aside,
A service his which hath no end
Whatever luck betide.
A guardian he o'er childhood's feet,
A gentle guard and kind;
A comrade in the city street,
And eyes unto the blind.

The play, the revels and the procession were an enormous success and repeated, under Ferris's direction, ten and twenty years later. The festival made a profit of £178 5s 7d divided between Jepson's Hospital for orphans and the Ripon Dispensary. The local, national and international press lavished praise upon the event, with one extreme exception. The journalist sent to cover the occasion for the *Yorkshireman* tellingly head-lined his report, published on 4 September 1886, 'High Jinks at Ripon'. He was not easily impressed and things started badly: 'from the moment you set foot in Ripon you were expected to delude yourself into the belief that you had suddenly dropped back into the Middle Ages'. Neither did he find the speeches at the Market Cross to his liking. According to him they became 'so solemn and lugubrious that people who had come for the week began to wonder when was the next train home, while others, who were forced to stay, wished they might die before the next millenary'. Nor was food a way to his heart. He noted that anyone sceptical of the antiq-

uity of Ripon would have had their doubts removed by the cold fowl
served at the luncheon which must have been hatched for the occasion a
thousand years ago. He was, though, brief but generous in his appreciation of the pageant. His mood did not last and he either filed the most
honest review of the play or saw a different performance from the others,
possibly that on the Saturday when admission was less than half that of
Friday to accommodate the poorer citizens of Ripon. It is worth quoting
in its entirety:

> The play of *Robin Hood and ye Curtall Fryer* was somewhat disap-
> pointing, the book being poor and the delivery somewhat halting and
> disconnected. There were many funny incidents. The crowd, of course,
> got into the background and spoiled the set; and the Master of the
> Revels hastily donning the gown of the Town Clerk of Ripon, had to
> come on and expostulate. When he had done with the crowd Mr Ferris
> had to settle with one of the wild men of the pageant, who, in order
> the better to sustain his character of primaeval man, mounted a pictur-
> esque bit of ruin belonging to the set and tried to pose. He was,
> however, 'posed' off and the play then proceeded. It had not gone far,
> however, before the wild man again asserted himself, and this time
> neither threats nor entreaties could drive him from his lofty perch. The
> Friar, who appeared in the parti-coloured trunk hose of the Jester, occa-
> sionally forgot his role, and returned to the business of fooling which
> had occupied him in the procession from Studley to Fountains; Robin
> Hood lost his wig in the affray; the music went hideously wrong all
> through the play; the bugle was sounded when Robin did not blow,
> and Robin blew in vain for the music that did not come; the foresters
> came bouncing in to the arena before the bugle called them, and the
> spectators had to wait an unconscionable period for the appearance of
> the monks. But somehow the business got through, and of course
> brought down the 'house'. Then there was a rush for refreshments
> which were not to be obtained.

Whatever histrionics may have resulted from what sounds like last-
night euphoria, not to say frenzy, or over-confidence brimming from a
successful first night, it would be wrong to detract from the contribution
D'Arcy Ferris made to the revival of interest in medieval popular culture.
He and the justifiable faith put in him by the Ripon Millenary Committee
contributed to the creation, with Augustin Dawtrey and others, of a
Victorian Robin Hood, masculine, fair and philanthropic, a lord of the

greenwood that was both heritage and refuge. He did so by placing Robin in a 'spot' of history that was material in place and medieval in imagination. Ferris may not have been a professional academic, although his business card titled him 'professor', but he subscribed to the practices of scholarship in pursuit of research-based productions. Although less permanent in memory and lasting in legacy than the ballad collectors Ritson, Gutch and Child, he, like them, promoted the study as well as the continued enjoyment of Robin Hood. Ferris deserves his self-appellation 'apostle of pageantry' and to be better known as one who legitimately 'bent his bow'.

Notes

1 References to the early use of this proverb can be found in R. B. Dobson and J. Taylor, *Rymes of Robyn Hood: an Introduction to the English Outlaw* (Stroud, rev. edn, 1997), pp. 289–90.

2 William Langland, *The Vision of Piers Plowman: A Critical Edition of the B-Text Based on Trinity College Cambridge MS B.15.17*, ed. A. V. C. Schmidt (London, 2nd edn, 1995), p. 82, Passus V ll. 395–96.

3 For the evolution of the myth see Stephen Knight, *Robin Hood: A Mythic Biography* (Ithaca, NY, and London:, 2003).

4 *Robin Hood: A Collection of all the Ancient Poems, Songs and Ballads Now Extant Relative to the Celebrated English Outlaw (To Which Are Prefixed Historical Anecdotes of His Life)*, ed. Joseph Ritson, 2 vols (London, 1795).

5 William Stukeley, *Palaeographia Britannica: or discourses on antiquities in Britain No. 1–3* (London, 1743–52), 2, p. 115.

6 Thomas Love Peacock, *Maid Marian* (London: Hookham, 1822). I am grateful to Stephen Knight for this observation.

7 For a recent assessment of Munday see Tracey Hill, *Anthony Munday and Civic Culture: Theatre, History and Power in Early Modern London 1580–1633* (Manchester, 2004). For criticism of his Lord Mayor's Shows see David M. Bergeron, *English Civic Pageantry 1558–1642* (London, 1971).

8 Anthony Munday, *Mertropolis Coronata, The Triumph of Ancient Drapery* (London, 1615). For a modern edition see *Pageants and Entertainments of Anthony Munday: A Critical Edition*, ed. David M. Bergeron (New York, 1985), pp. 85–99. Quotations in the text are from this edition.

9 Janette Dillon, *Performance and Spectacle in Hall's Chronicle* (London, 2002), p. 31.

10 Ibid., pp. 56–57.

11 *The Anonimalle Chronicle 1333 to 1381*, ed. V. H. Galbraith (Manchester, 1927), pp. 40–41. Anne Lancashire, *London Civic Theatre: City Drama and Pageantry from Roman Times to 1558* (Cambridge, 2002), pp. 44–45.

12 *The Diary of Henry Machyn*, ed. John Gough Nichols, Camden Society OS 42 (1848), p. 201.

13 Robert Withington, *English Pageantry: An Historical Outline*, 2 vols (Cambridge, 1918, repr. New York, 1963), II, pp. 122–23.

14 Ibid., II, p. 170.

15 Ibid., II, pp. 153–54.

16 Ibid., II, pp. 148–51.

17 Ibid., II, pp. 194–233.

18 Ibid., II, p. 210.

19 *Dorset/Cornwall*, ed. Rosalind Conklin Hays, C. E. McGee, Sally L. Joyce and Evelyn S. Newlyn, Records of Early English Drama (Toronto, 1999), p. 250.
20 Withington, *English Pageantry*, II, p. 210.
21 Joseph Fowler, *Medieval Sherborne* (Dorchester, 1951), pp. 264–66.
22 Withington, *English Pageantry*, II, p. 195.
23 *Ripon Millenary: A Record of the Festival. Also A History of the City arranged under its Wakemen and Mayors from the year 1400*, ed. W. Harrison (Ripon, 1892), p. 205.
24 Ibid., p. 205.
25 The minutes of the committees of the Ripon Millenary Festival and other archive materials are kept by the North Yorkshire County Record Office DC/.RIC VII 2/37/1-36. The planning, presentation and reception of the festival are reviewed in Harrison, *Ripon Millenary*.
26 NYCRO DC/RIC VII 2/37/1, p. 25.
27 NYCRO DC/RIC VII 2/37/1, pp. 26–27.
28 NYCRO DC/RIC VII 2/37/2, no. 1.
29 There is a brief entry for him under the later spelling of his name, de Ferrars, by Roy Judge in the *Oxford Dictionary of National Biography: From the Earliest Time to the Year 2000*, ed. H. C. G. Matthew and Brian Harrison (Oxford, 2004).
30 Roy Judge, 'D'Arcy Ferris and the Bidford Morris', *Folk Music Journal*, 4:5 (1984), pp. 443–80.
31 Ibid., p. 444.
32 D'Arcy Ferris, 'A Review of ye Pageant', in Harrison, ed., *Ripon Millenary*, p. 160.
33 *Faringdon Advertiser*, 29 August 1885 (Lockinge House), *York Herald*, 2 September 1885 (Grimston), *Morning Post*, 10 May 1886 (Islington) and the Ferris Collection in the Vaughan Williams Memorial Library of the English Folk Dance and Song Society.
34 NYCRO DC/RIC VII 2/37/1, p. 31.
35 NYCRO DC/RIC VII 2/37/2, no. 149.
36 NYCRO DC/RIC VII 2/37/9.
37 NYCRO DC/RIC VII 2/37/10.
38 Little is known about Augustin Dawtrey. His name does not appear in the census for 1881 or 1891 although a number of Dawtreys record their birthplace as Yorkshire in the 1861 census. He gives his address, when sending in his play, as 75 Woodborough Road, Nottingham. He may have been a lodger at this address located in the Robin Hood Municipal Ward as White's directory for 1885–86 lists the occupant as Henry Lowry, boot and shoemaker. It is possible that Augustin Dawtrey was a pseudonym. The local Catholic church, also in Woodborough Road, was dedicated, in 1876, to St Augustine, Apostle of England. Under the name Dawtrey he was the author of a serial, 'The Family Skeleton', that appeared in the *Notts Figaro* during 1885. I am grateful to Christina Raven Conn, the Team Librarian of the Local Studies Library, Nottingham for her help with this information.
39 D'Arcy Ferris, 'Review', p. 151
40 Ibid., pp. 157–58.
41 Ibid., p. 158.
42 Ibid., p. 155.
43 *The English and Scottish Popular Ballads*, ed. Francis James Child, 5 vols (Boston, 1882–98), III, pp. 120–27.
44 The text is printed in Harrison, *Ripon Millenary*, pp. 105–24.
45 Ibid., p. 26.
46 The lecture was given on 29 June 1886 and extensively reported in the *Ripon Gazette and Times*, 1 July 1886.
47 The sum also covered writing music for the play and words for the festival march composed by Ferris: NYCRO DC/RIC VII 2/37/1, p. 45.

The Antiquarians and the Critics
The Chester Plays and the Criticism
of Early English Drama

David Mills

In 1955 Hardin Craig affirmed confidently that 'the Chester Cycle, almost certainly the oldest Corpus Christi play in England, and certainly, as preserved, the one that retains most perfectly the original form and spirit of the Corpus Christi play, somehow escaped the excessive and unregulated changes undergone by other cycles in pursuit of fifteenth-century modernization'.[1] Craig was repeating a critical belief about Chester's civic play-cycle that had been propagated for over three centuries. This paper examines the origins of that belief, the evidence for its truth, and the ways in which it informed, and was informed by, the early scholarly attitudes towards medieval drama and its audience. In conclusion, it briefly describes some of the changes in our approach to and understanding of early English drama in general and Chester's plays in particular during the last forty years

The Tudor Image of the Plays

The earliest published critical assessment of Chester's mystery cycle was written in the later sixteenth century. It appears in the Post-Reformation Banns, the verse announcement describing the plays, which was proclaimed in the city on St George's Day in a performance-year by a herald, accompanied by representatives of the participating trade and manufacturing companies in play-costume.[2] That such an announcement was necessary indicates that the plays were not by that date performed regularly. Chester had had a play on Corpus Christi day by 1422, which some time before 1521 had been replaced by a play at Whitsun. Probably by 1531–32 it was being performed in three parts over three days. Since 1498–99 the town had also developed a carnivalesque show at Midsummer, and thereafter each year the mayor could choose whether to stage the plays or to put on the Midsummer Show. In the times of religious controversy under the Tudors the show was the safer option.

The Post-Reformation Banns have a defensive tone which predicates objections to the plays. The civic play-cycles were regarded by many as relics of the unreformed Church, particularly in view of their frequent association with the Feast of Corpus Christi which honoured the miracle of Transubstantiation. So these Banns defend the plays not as devotional or proselytising but as an established tradition reaching back to the city's medieval past: '... in this cittie dyvars yeares the have bine set out' (28).[3] As such, they bear the hallmarks of that past age, its tastes and its abilities; they have become, as it were, 'heritage'. The Banns set up an opposition between the popular, low culture of the past and the more discriminating theatrical 'high culture' of the present.

> By craftesmen and meane men these pageauntes are playde,
> And to commons and contry men accustomablye before,
> If better men and finer heades now come, what canne be sayde?
> But of common and contrye players take yow the storye.
>
> (203–06)

The plays write their audience. The social standing of the players – tradesmen and members of the lower social orders – accords with the low expectations of the onlookers – common people and mere country bumpkins. The Banns recognize that 'we do things differently now':

> ... not possible it is those matters to be contryved
> in such sorte and cuninge and by suche players of price
> as at this daye good players and fine wittes coulde devise.
> For then shoulde all these persones that as godes doe playe
> in clowdes come downe with voyce, and not be seene.
>
> (193–97)

In defending the presentation of God in human form on stage, the Banns suggest a knowledge of the devices of the professional indoor theatre, though we have no documentary evidence until the 1580s of visits by professional players to the town.[4] The Banns champion the cause of the unskilled amateur against the paid actor:

And if anye disdayne, then open is the doore
that lett hime in to heare. Packe awaye at his pleasure!
Oure playinge is not to gett fame or treasure.

(207–09)

Since the plays were performed on movable stages or carriages in the
street, the reference is humorous, but implicitly contrasts the open-air
performance with indoor professional players who act for favour or
reward from a nobleman.

The audience is therefore asked to make an imaginative leap, from 'the
tyme wherein we presentlye staye' (38) to 'the tyme of ignorance whearein
we doe straye' (39). While originally offering medieval Cestrians access
for the first time to the biblical narrative in their native tongue, the plays
presented only a simplified account of the basic material:

and every playe of the matter gave but a taste,
leaveinge for better learned the cercumstance to accomplishe.

(15–16)

And, with the audience in mind, the author is

interminglinge therewithe onely to make sporte
some thinges not warranted by anye wrytte
which glad the hartes – he woulde men to take hit.

(11–13)

While this defends non-biblical material in the plays. it also suggests a
tension between the biblical and the entertaining in the cycle, implying
that, unlike a medieval audience which required its religion admixed with
fun, the Tudor audience will find that mixture unacceptable.

Although the Banns admit that the text has been somewhat revised,
they defend unauthorized material as fidelity to a prior authorial text, in
phrases such as 'your author his author hath' (68), 'the author tellethe his
author' (95). They therefore claim a conservative revision which still
preserves an older underlying text. The traces of this text are said to be
evidenced within the language of the plays:

Condemne not oure matter where groosse wordes you heare
which importe at this daye smale sence or understandinge …
At this tyme those speches caried good lykinge.

thoe if at this tyme you take them spoken at that tyme –
as well matter as words – then all is well fyne.

(49–50, 53–55)

The language is not merely obsolete, imparting 'smale sence or under-standinge', it also includes 'groosse' words, acceptable to the original crude audience ('caried good lykinge'), for which the Tudor audience should make allowance. The language offers its own proof of the antiquity and crude taste which the Banns affirm.

These Banns therefore present an image not merely of the plays but of the medieval context in which they emerged and to which they responded. It is a condescending view of the plays as a primitive form of drama, pioneering in its evangelizing mixture of Bible and entertainment, unsophisticated in its staging and performance, but worth preserving as an achievement of the city's past. And it projects an equally condescending image of the medieval Cestrian, whose tastes the plays reflect. Such a defence takes no regard of the plays as major civic events, vast in scale and costly to stage, constantly under revision. But this self-constructed 'otherness' anticipates and reinforces later trends in academic criticism.

The Critics' View of the Plays

Thomas Warton's *History of English Poetry*, the first volume of which appeared in 1774, provides a convenient starting-point for modern critical approaches to the early drama. His *History* was the first chronological account of English poetry. As Clarissa Rinaker observes:

> Although Warton properly excluded dramatic poetry from his design, he was unable to resist the temptation to discuss its origin and early development, and his two long digressions constitute the first valuable study of that subject and complete his interpretation of medieval life. On the basis of his reading of French memoirs on the subject, and his first hand acquaintance with the 'originals' in books and manuscripts not easily found nor often examined, he discussed the religious, secular and scholastic beginnings of the drama in a way that was not only valuable for its originality at the time it appeared, but authoritative as late as the second quarter of the next century when Collier quoted it as the most valuable source of information on the subject.[5]

Warton's account links the plays and their audience in a mutually confirmatory picture of primitive art and taste: '[The medieval audience and playwrights] had no just idea of decorum, consequently but little sense of the ridiculous.' In support of this claim, he cites an example from Chester. Evidently led by Eve's words,

Naked wee bine bothe forthy,
and of our shappe ashamed

(Play 2, 267–68)[6]

he concludes:

> In a play of *the Old and New Testaments*, Adam and Eve are both exhibited on the stage naked, and conversing about their nakedness; this very pertinently introduces the next scene, in which they have coverings of fig-leaves. This extraordinary spectacle was beheld by a numerous assembly of both sexes with great composure: they had the authority of scripture for such a representation, and they gave matters just as they found them in the third chapter of Genesis.[7]

Since women's roles were played by men, Warton's imagined audience would have gained a very novel notion of Man's first disobedience! Warton sees a solidarity between this simple, pious and unrestrained presentation of the Fall in Chester and the attitude of his 'Medieval Man' in his or her primitive innocence and faith.

Warton's condescending views gained additional currency and authority in the following century from the authoritative Shakespearean biographer and editor Edmond Malone in his *Historical Account of the English Stage*, which was reissued in an enlarged version in the posthumous edition of *The Plays and Poems of William Shakespeare* prepared by James Boswell.[8] Since Malone held that modern drama began with Shakespeare, he contemptuously dismisses all that had gone before: 'The drama before the time of Shakespeare was so little cultivated or ill understood, that to many it may appear unnecessary to carry our theatrical researches higher than that period' (III, p. 5). In particular: 'The Miracle Plays or Mysteries were totally destitute of invention or plan; they tamely represented stories, according to the letter of the Scripture, or the respective legend' (III, p. 27).

Nevertheless, Malone acknowledged a social and civilizing benefit from the performances for a primitive and violent medieval populace:

'Rude and even ridiculous as they were, they softened the manners of the people, by diverting the publick attention to spectacles in which the mind was concerned, and by creating a regard for other arts than those of military strength and savage valour' (III, pp. 22–23). Although I doubt whether Malone ever examined a mystery-play text, for him and for later critics these plays were 'pre-Shakespearean', a cultural benchmark for later progress.

J. H. Markland, in 1818 the first to edit any of Chester's plays, also attributes civilizing value to the cycles, but he acknowledges, despite their obvious deficiencies, their potentially educative function for an audience ignorant of the scriptures:

> It has often been urged, that Mysteries and Moralities taught little except licentiousness and impiety. The coarse language, the irreverent use of sacred names, and the familiar exhibition of the most awful events, must now be acknowledged extremely offensive; but we must be cautious not to judge the simplicity of those times by the sensitive delicacy of our own. They at least conveyed *some* scriptural knowledge, and diverted the mind from an exclusive devotion to war and warlike sports.[9]

Markland may well have been influenced directly by the Post-Reformation Banns, which he prints in his edition. He shares their condescending retrospective view of past taste, their demand to consider the context for which they were written, and their emphasis on bringing scripture to the ignorant citizens.

Thomas Wright's introduction to his two-volume edition of *The Chester Plays*, published in 1843 and 1847, offers members of the Shakespeare Society a detailed justification for reading mysteries and miracle plays such as Chester's. He proposes three reasons: 'as illustrating the history of the stage in its infancy', emphasizing therefore the evolutionary view of drama; 'as pictures of the manners and condition of our forefathers', as a socio-historical document, reflecting the audience; and 'as indicating the quantity and the peculiar character of the religious knowledge inculcated into the populace in Catholic times', a strongly positioned statement of religious attitude (p. v). Like previous critics he finds no inherent literary or dramatic value in the text itself.

Thus a consensus emerged that medieval drama represented a low, popular genre which nevertheless was the forerunner of Tudor high dramatic culture. This view underpins A. W. Ward's acclaimed *History of English Dramatic Literature* of 1875. His account of the 'origins' of English drama, which incorporates the mystery plays, precedes a chapter significantly entitled 'The Beginnings of the English *Regular* Drama' [my italics]. For this Professor of History and English Literature, the development of drama was inseparable from a nationhood that was fully formed only under Elizabeth: 'Renascence and Reformation and the political changes which ensued upon them contributed to prepare and fertilise the soil into which was to descend the seed of genius, the gift of Heaven [William Shakespeare]' (p. xxxii).

Finally, Sir E. K. Chambers, whose two-volume *Medieval Stage* of 1903 provided for over half a century the definitive account of the development of English drama, restates the undiscriminating and unsophisticated response of a medieval audience to plays:

> Literary critics have laid stress upon the emergence of the rude humour of the folk, with its love of farce and realism, in somewhat quaint juxtaposition to the general subject-matter of the plays. I can only add here that the instinct which made the miracle plays a joy to the mediaeval burgher is the same instinct which the more primitive peasant satisfied in a score of modes of rudimentary folk-drama.[10]

The self-confirming assumption of early primitive form and early primitive expectation thus guides the later criticism of the medieval theatre. As the archetypical primitive mystery play, so affirmed by the Tudor authors of its Banns, Chester came to occupy a significant role in the subsequent histories of English drama.

The Author

The Banns' account of the origins of Chester's cycle complements their characterization of the plays. Its importance is indicated by placing the story of its origins at the beginning of the Banns, the first words the citizens would hear:

> … sometymes there was mayor of this cittie
> Sir John Arnewaye, knighte, whoe moste worthelye
> contented himselfe to sett out in playe
> the devise of one Rondall, moncke of Chester Abbaye.

(4–7)

The Banns explain that 'Rondall' risked his life by setting out the stories from the Bible in English at a time when 'these storyes of the testamente … in a common Englishe tonge never reade nor harde' (21–22). Ranulf Higden was the author of the *Polychronicon*, the best-known monastic universal history. He entered St Werburgh's Abbey in Chester in 1299 and died in 1364. Sir John Arneway was for long held to be first mayor of Chester, in consecutive mayoralties; but in 1594 the mayoral list was corrected, and Arneway was shown to have been mayor successively from 1268 to 1276. The two men's historical dates do not coincide but Arneway's fictive mayoralties allow an overlap at c.1327–28. Tudor annalists therefore ascribed the start of the play productions to that year, which would make Chester's the earliest English play-cycle by half a century. The phrase 'the author tellethe his author' in the Banns seems therefore to mean that a reviser faithfully recalls his source-copy, by implication Higden's original device.

Politically, the Banns reconstruct the plays as a proto-Protestant initiative to bring the Bible to the people in their own language, and in so doing present Higden, their alleged deviser, as a monk in rebellion against his Church. The plays become a joint venture by the monk and the mayor. But the Banns are also responding to an alternative thesis of origin, also published orally. A proclamation 'newly made by William Newhall, in his first year as clerk to the Pentice, 1531–2' ascribes a double benefit to the plays:

> not only for the Augmentacion and incres **of the holy and catholick** faith of **our** sauyour Jhesu Crist and to exort the myndes of the common people **to good deuotion and holsome** doctryne therof but also for the commenwelth and prosperitie of this Citie.[11]

This advantage to both Church and town focuses upon two men: Mayor Arneway who 'devised' the plays 'to the honor of God'; and 'one sir Henry Francis' who 'devised and made' the plays. Moreover, Francis

> gate of Clement then beyng **bushope of rome a 1000** daiez of par**don** and of the Busshop of Chester at that tyme beyng xlti daiez of pardon **graunted from** thensforth **to** every person resortyng in pecible manner with gode devocion to here and se the **sayd playes** frome tyme to tyme asoft as they shalbe plaied within this Citie.

The name Henry Francis appears on three lists of monks at St Werburgh's Abbey of 1377, 1379 and 1382. Again, the dates do not coincide with those of Arneway. It is not clear which Pope Clement is intended, though Pope Clement 5 (1305–14) instituted the Feast of Corpus Christi, with which the plays were formerly associated. Newhall's Proclamation, which was probably read immediately before the performance began, appeals for peaceful assembly and threatens offenders with the anathema of the Church and the justice of the realm, broadening the reference from the local monastery and town to the national government and the international Church.

After Elizabeth's accession, a number of 'puritan' clerics in Chester, led by the returned Genevan exile Christopher Goodman, rector of Aldford, opposed plans to perform the plays in the 1570s. Writing to the earl of Huntingdon, President of the Council of the North, on 10 May 1572, Goodman referred to the traditions of origin:

> Where-as certain plays were devised by a monk about 200 years past in the depth of ignorance, & by the Pope then authorized to be set forth, & by that authority placed in the city of Chester to the intent to retain that place in assured ignorance & superstition according to the Popish policy. against which plays all preachers & godly men since the time of the blessed light of the gospell have inveyed & im-pugned as well in Sermons as otherwise when occasion hath served...[12]

Presumably intending Francis's authorship, Goodman argues that the plays are rooted in the unreformed Church and that their production 'giveth great comfort to the rebellious papist, & some greater occasions of assembling & conference than their intentions well considered is at this present meet to be admitted'. It is probable that the Post-Reformation Banns sought to counter this claim by substituting a different, Protestant-focused, narrative of origin while continuing the claims of promoting true faith.

Tudor antiquarians perpetuated this later narrative of origin. Robert Rogers, archdeacon of Chester, who was hostile to the plays, nevertheless left, at his death in 1595, lengthy notes about their origin, production and content on which his son David based his account in his 1609 history of Chester, under the chapter-heading of 'the lawdable exersises yearelye vsed within the Cittie of Chester'.[13] We owe our five extant manuscripts of Chester's cycle to antiquarians of impeccable Protestant allegiance who, between 1591 and 1607, copied a now-lost master text.

These conflicting and internally contradictory accounts were investigated by F. M. Salter in 1955 and require no discussion here.[14] Both traditions reinforce Chester's claims to be, at heart, a fourteenth-century play cycle. But while the Proclamation envisages a political alliance of Church and city for mutual benefit, the Banns suggest a proto-Protestant revolutionary enterprise, and also a 'deviser/director' relationship of Higden and Arneway.

The civic cycles were constantly modified to allow for changes in the organization and resources of companies, the demands of the city-organizers, changing politico-religious demands, and just possibly a concern for dramatic effectiveness. York's official text, BL MS Add. 35290, the only extant civic register of a play-cycle, was, according to its editors, 'compiled in the late 1460s or 1470s almost certainly from the craft copies of the individual pageants, and presumably by order of the Mayor and Council'.[15] It seems that until that time the companies had been largely responsible for their own play-scripts. Chester seems to have held a master text which could serve as a mechanism of control. The first reference to the plays, in 1422 when they were held on Corpus Christi, is to a dispute among companies about respective responsibilities; the mayor refers them firmly to their responsibilities as set down 'secundum Originale', in accordance with the Original or, as it is later termed, the Reginall.[16]

Goodman, writing to the archbishop of York in 1572, confirms that Chester's text has been modified over the years though not by anyone properly authorized, but he also says that the performance had not always followed the text:

> albeit divers have gone about the correction of the same at sundry times & mended divers things, yet hath it not been done by such as are by authority allowed, nor the same their corrections viewed & approved according to order, nor yet so played for the most part as they have been corrected.[17]

A new 'Reginall' was probably reconstituted from company copies after the 1567 production, since in 1568 the mayor sought the whereabouts of the Original from a Randle Trevor who swore on the gospel that, though he had had the book, he had returned it.[18]

A contemporary attempt to resolve the contradictions between the Higden and Francis traditions was made in 1628 by the Chester antiquarian Randle Holme in a note to the 1607 manuscript of the cycle. Holme argues that Francis gained pardon for the plays, but they were 'made' by Higden 'who was thrise at Rome before he could obtaine leaue of the Pope to haue them in the English tongue'. Warton elaborated this claim, which accommodates to the thesis of dramatic evolution from earlier liturgical and religious plays in Latin:

> If it be true, that these mysteries were composed in the year 1328, and there was so much difficulty in obtaining the pope's permission that they might be presented in English, a presumptive proof arises, that all our Mysteries before that period were in Latin. These plays will therefore have the merit of being the first English interludes.[19]

Malone reaffirms, with due acknowledgement, Warton's view that Chester's plays were written by Higden in 1328, and that pope and bishop gave remissions from periods in purgatory for their orderly audiences.

Later critics were less convinced by the authorship traditions. Liverpool-born William Roscoe, writing in 1795, was an early sceptic, but based his scepticism upon the confidence that Italy must have had the earliest vernacular plays in Europe: '[I do not] conceive it possible to adduce a dramatic composition in the English language, that can indisputably be placed before the year 1500, previous to which time they were common in Italy'. Conversely, Chester-born J. H. Markland in 1818 proposed 'that the Chester Mysteries are even of an earlier date than the year 1328', attributing them to an Arneway mayoralty of 1269.[20] Wright dismissed the authorship-claims as 'too improbable to deserve our serious consideration' (I, p. xvii) and was followed by Ward in 1875 (I, p. 45) and by ten Brink in 1893, who regarded the Higden ascription as 'not sufficiently proved and... not free from self-contradictions'.[21] But the claim did not go away. Chambers appeared to endorse Higden's authorship: 'Up to a certain point these fragments of tradition are consistent and, a priori, not improbable. About 1328 is just the sort of date to which one would look for the formation of a craft-cycle' (II, p. 352).

Despite his characteristic qualifications, Chambers *wants* to believe the tradition. Without quite saying so, he implies that he accepts Randle Holme's division, that Higden made the plays and Francis obtained the pardon. On the Arneway dates he unconvincingly argues that the antiquarians confused Arneway with another mayor, Richard Erneis or Harneis, who held successive mayoralties in 1327–28 and 1328–29. And Chambers, again hedging bets, follows his predecessors in seeing Higden's pioneering role as that of translator:

> The Chester tradition represents Higden's work as an affair rather of translation than of anything else. It is not quite clear whether translation

from Latin or from the Norman French is intended. In any case it is probable that the earlier English playwrights made use of French models.[22]

Such was the force of Chambers' persuasively argued thesis that even F. M. Salter, who had definitively exposed the authorship-myth in 1955, was reluctant to dispel the Chester tradition entirely. Why, he asks, did Newhall choose an otherwise obscure monk called Henry Francis as author of the plays, unless it was true? He concludes: 'It would be a shame to take away from Chester that pride of priority in which she has gloried for four centuries. Let us date her plays 1375'[23] – a piece of sentimentality that some have read as a statement of fact.

The French Connection

The French connection, to which Chambers refers, originated in John Payne Collier's *History of English Dramatic Poetry to the Time of Shakespeare* of 1831. This study was highly praised.[24] As Schoenbaum says, 'It deserved its warm welcome, for it is in truth a monument of early nineteenth-century scholarship, superseding Malone (as was evidently the aim) by reason of its greater comprehensiveness, new documentary information, and more sympathetic view of the non-Shakespearean drama'.[25] Collier would later earn opprobrium as a forger of documents who mixed his forgeries with authentic material, but this trait is not evident in this work, which won him a high scholarly reputation. Collier had read play-cycles in manuscript, and in 1836 published an edition of *Five Miracle Plays* which included Chester's penultimate play, 'Antichrist'.[26]

Collier picks up an undeveloped claim by J. H. Markland in 1818, that the English mystery plays show resemblances to the plays in France.[27] For Collier, France provided the most immediate model for a mystery cycle; earlier large-scale Anglo-Norman plays had been written in England. He linked this to the authorship traditions. The plays could have been performed first in Arneway's mayoralty of 1268 [*sic*], but in French. Then c.1338 Higden gained the pope's permission for him to make them into English, after which Francis won the Pardon for the audiences. Collier is the first to note five passages of textually corrupted French in the cycle, the longest being of nine lines, all spoken as introductions by secular rulers, which he regards as 'probably relics of the most ancient structure, retained in the current transcripts, although Higden might not think them necessary for the performance, and therefore did not include them in his version'.[28]

Collier's views were assimilated by Thomas Wright, whose two-volume edition of 1843–47 provided for the first time a printed text of all 24 plays. On the basis of collateral research on French play-cycles Wright affirmed that he has 'little doubt in my own mind that in the thirteenth century the Mysteries performed in England were composed in French, or Anglo-Norman' (pp. xiii–xiv). While doubting that English mysteries were direct translations of French originals, he nonetheless states that 'if any were, the Chester Mysteries appear to have the greatest claim to that distinction' (xiv), and quotes Collier's examples of parallels with French plays. The scattered passages of French, spoken by Herod, Octavian and Pilate in the cycle, he attributes to the desire to allude to an aristocratic register, 'when French was the language of courtiers in the English court' (xv), and would therefore date the original of the cycle to 'the early part of the fifteenth or the end of the fourteenth century' (xiv), aligning the plays again with early date.[29]

Wright's views on the French passages as a dramatic device, as a social or ethnic marker, have been generally endorsed, but the thesis of a French dramatic model has persisted beyond the evolutionary theories in which it originated, albeit in somewhat ambivalent formulation. Ward in 1875 referred to the 'remarkable coincidences' with plays in the *Mystere*, and says that if indeed the French passages relate to a period when French was spoken at court, 'it would have to be viewed as evidence of the antiquity of these Mysteries'.[30] Hardin Craig in 1955 says: 'On the basis … of agreement in unique matters of structure and contents, we may be sure that the Chester plays were translated and adapted from the French'.[31] In 1972 Rosemary Woolf suggested that the French *Mystere du Vieil Testament* might have provided a model for a fifteenth-century revision of the cycle.[32] What therefore began as an antiquarian attempt to make sense of conflicting authorship theories ultimately contributed to the wider critical debate of the evolutionary origins of the English drama.

Chester's Play-text

The Banns' claim that the plays mix with biblical material

> … onely to make sporte
> some thinges not warranted by anye wrytte
> which glad the hartes – he woulde men to take hit.

(11–13)

suggests a tension between the scriptural and the entertaining that predicates a medieval audience that required its religion admixed with fun, unlike the sophisticated Tudor audience. Such a view anticipates Warton's belief that the medieval playwright 'had no just idea of decorum'.

'The Shepherds Play', performed by the Painters' company, provides a good example. The shepherds were popular comic characters who also appeared walking on stilts in the Midsummer Show. They have come from Wales into Chester in search of their sheep lost in a storm, journeying from Conway to Clwyd. One is called Tudd, short for Tudor. They refer to leeks. They boast of their remedies for sheep-diseases. They compete in wrestling and singing. Their 'alien' status is underlined by their enthusiasm for such exotic English foods as ale from Halton, butter from Blacon and a Lancashire jannock-cake. These stereotypical features contribute a gentle caricature of Chester's Welsh neighbours as 'comons and contrye men'. At the manger they present the Christ-child with comically ordinary gifts: bell, cup and spoon, a cap, and an old pair of women's stockings, while greeting Him eloquently. On their return from Bethlehem, they announce an unexpected and anachronistic change of vocation. Henceforth they will cease to be shepherds, and become severally preachers, a hermit and an anchorite.

The local humour caused offence to some even in the time of the plays. In 1572 Goodman complained of 'the unreverent speaking of the shepherds who by the Scriptures seem to be honest men'.[33] Ward echoes Goodman's concerns. He praises the 'simple effectiveness' of the shepherds' gifts, but finds the play 'in its earlier and longer portion purely comic and exceedingly coarse'.[34] Even in 1961 Eleanor Prosser objected to the play's lack of decorum: 'Would even the God of medieval England chuckle at a travesty of the announcement of Salvation?'[35]

The Late Banns anticipate such objections:

The appearinge angell and starr upon Cristes birthe,
the shepperde poore of base and lowe degree,
you Paynters and Glaseers decke out with all myrthe
and see that 'Gloria in Excelsus' be songe merelye.
Fewe wordes in the pagiante make merthe trulye,
for all that the author had to stande uppon
was 'glorye to God on highe and peace on earthe to man'.

(96–102)

They distinguish the authenticated 'myrthe' of the angels' song from the unauthenticated 'merthe' of men 'of base and lowe degree' and seek to excuse the 'author' for including the latter. Recalling the 'comons and contrye men' of their comments on the plays, these lines suggest that the 'unreverent' speech is appropriate to the level of the characters, which would accord with the rhetorical precept of matching style to status.

The perceived indecorum of such moments is complemented by the absence of what nineteenth-century critics looked for in drama, a degree of verisimilitude, allied to the creation of character. In an introductory section in 1875 which was omitted from later editions, Ward attempted to define drama. Drama was 'an art whose method is imitation in the way of action' (p. viii). Chester was, for him, a work of primitive didacticism: 'A living Bible has thus in a sense been unrolled before the people; or, if the expression be preferred, a sermon has been preached of which the whole Scripture narrative is the text' (I, p. 52). Nearly sixty years later Karl Young, in his monumental two-volume study, *The Drama of the Medieval Church*, echoed Ward's priority, speaking of 'genuine drama itself, in which the essential element is … impersonation';[36] he employed this criterion to distinguish Latin liturgical drama from liturgical ritual.

For convincing imitation, the characters required an inner life which was lacking in Chester's plays. In 1909 S. B. Hemingway, commenting on the Chester 'author', says: 'He has no interest in his characters except from the outside, no vicarious ability, no power of portraying the feelings and inner motives of his men and women, and no deep feeling of his own'.[37] Such criticism originates in part from a comparison of Chester with York, the only other definitely locatable and complete extant cycle. York shows people how to behave, while Chester fulfils Newhall's description in teaching people what to believe. York draws upon the rituals and activities of contemporary society to structure relationships between its characters, and produces a strong sense of role and human interaction that is virtually absent in Chester. Critics therefore concluded that Chester's antiquity was further confirmed by its crude concept of drama, while York had developed further towards modern ideas of drama.

New Approaches

By the late nineteenth century Chester's early origins had become so entrenched as to be axiomatic. Ten Brink, sceptical of the authorship ascription, nevertheless affirmed in 1883 that 'although our accessible evidence and records are of much later date, it is indeed highly probable that the development of the dramatic cycle at Chester had begun, at the latest, by the middle of the fourteenth century... We cannot place their origin in this town later than 1350' (p. 271). This view was taken also by E. K Chambers, who in 1903 established the prevailing thesis of the dramatic development for the first half of the twentieth century. His punning title, *The Medieval Stage*, gave early theatre its own defined niche in that development, but also consolidated its role as 'pre-Shakespearean', a separate stage in the evolution of Shakespeare's theatre.

Since Chambers is often seen as putting a brake on the study of early drama, it is as well to recall the truth of his claim that 'The history of the mediaeval theatre has never, from an English point of view, been written' (I, p. i). He believed that the starting-point of such a history must be 'the social and economic facts upon which the mediaeval drama rested' (I, p. i). He set the drama within a spectrum of entertainment, rather than within the textually directed world of literature. His work brings together an enormous number of facts gleaned from wide reading and researches among original documents in the British Museum. The volumes range across minstrelsy, festivals, customs, sword dances and mummers' plays, fools, masks and lords of misrule, as well as Latin liturgical plays, guild plays, puppet plays, moralities, interludes and the like. From this diversity emerged embryonic drama, nurtured unwittingly by the Church within the liturgy, but escaping its restrictions by a process of 'secularization', by which the plays moved from Church to street, the vernacular replaced Latin, and guildsmen took over from clergy as performers. And within this process, and drawing upon the Tudor descriptions and French analogues, he consolidated Chester's role as the early example of a vernacular play-cycle.

Although noted by some earlier critics, the shortcomings of this approach were decisively exposed in 1965 in 'Darwin, Mutation, and the Origin of Medieval Drama', the opening chapter of O. B. Hardison's *Christian Rite and Christian Drama in the Middle Ages*. His main criticisms are, first, Chambers' flawed empirical approach to his material: 'the "main line" traced by Chambers does not emerge in classical empirical fashion "from the data themselves" but is assumed before the data are discovered and then serves as an unconscious criterion for selection' (p. 9); and, secondly, his anti-clerical attitude, which underpinned 'secularization': 'The clergy is consistently cast in the role of the villain who opposes the "mimetic instinct", which is associated with such terms as "healthy", "human" and "pagan"' (p. 15). Overall, Hardison demonstrates that for Chambers, 'History has become teleological, interpreted both intentionally and unconsciously in terms of what texts anticipate rather than what they are' (p. 33). The challenge now was to understand what the texts are.

The past forty years have therefore seen a return to the basic evidence of texts and documents. All the major medieval dramatic texts have been re-edited. The 1974 edition of Chester was the first to collate all five cyclic manuscripts: Wright had used only two manuscripts for his edition, saying that a full collation would be 'a work of so much labour that it would hardly be repaid by the result' (xx). Moreover, the 1974 edition was the first to abandon the quest for an *ur*-text and to look at the process reflected by the individual variants. From them, it seems that underlying the extant texts was a sixteenth-century master version, which over time had acquired many alternatives and obscurities through which individual scribes had navigated in their own characteristic ways. Our extant text cannot be traced back further than the sixteenth century.

Chambers' concern with the spectrum of entertainment, and his study of documentary evidence, continues in the mission of the Toronto-based *Records of Early English Drama* project, founded in 1974: 'to find, transcribe and publish external evidence of dramatic, ceremonial and minstrel activity in Great Britain before 1642'. This project differs from earlier studies, however, by extending its time-line to 1642, dissolving the traditional 'medieval/Renaissance' distinction. Moreover, it removes the focus on the theatre of Elizabethan London of earlier studies, examining records by town and county, and reveals the extent and diversity of activity in the provinces. It is now clear that there were significant regional differences in drama, and that the so-called 'mystery cycles' were exceptional rather than typical. REED's first volumes, published in 1979, covered York and Chester.

In 1955 Craig had said that 'this drama had no theory and aimed consciously at no dramatic effects'.[38] But as interest in theory grew, critical attention turned from the issue of dates and origins to reading the play-texts in the light of those new approaches. Such theories have linked the cycles more closely to their occasions and communities. In 1966 V. A. Kolve sought to define a cyclic structure that developed in relation to the traditional festive occasion of performance, the Feast of Corpus Christi, in which the cycles related 'the history of the world in seven ages' (p. 101).[39]

Returning to the 'Shepherds', their change of vocation reflects patristic commentaries on their visit as signifying spiritual pastoralism. The cue lies in Luke 2.17: 'And when they had seen it, they made known abroad the saying which was told them concerning the child'. In Play 13 Christ images himself as the good shepherd, quoting St John's Gospel. Kolve extends this symbolic reading back, giving an added level to the literal in the play. The shepherds' healing salves reflect Christ the healer; the wrestling where boy defeats masters, the putting down of the mighty from their seat; and the discord among the shepherds yields to harmony with the news of the Nativity.[40] While this is not a definitive reading, it suggests that the play acquires greater resonance once the priority of character and decorum is abandoned.

However, Chester's Banns imply that the plays' author/reviser had some idea of what a 'conventional' play cycle might be:

> And then dare I compare that, this lande throughout,
> none had the like, nor the like darste set out.
>
> (40–41)

'Compare' suggests an awareness of civic cycles elsewhere, such as York, which by the 1570s were being suppressed. The Banns claim Chester was unique. It may be that, just as the Banns resist comparisons with the contemporary professional theatre, so they imply that the cycle represents a different concept of dramatic form and function from that of other cycles. Possibly a sense of generic identity was also promoted by the positioning of the plays alongside both the Corpus Christi procession, which continued alongside the plays until the abolition of the Feast in 1548, and the Midsummer Show, which since 1498–99 could substitute for the plays, and which replaced them after 1575. So far from it being 'archetypical', the Banns claim the cycle as self-consciously *sui generis*.

There is support for this self-awareness in the play-text. The plays position themselves in relation to their authoritative (usually biblical) sources, making it clear they stand at one remove from them, alert to the illusory, and – in the case of the 'Antichrist' play, where Antichrist deceives by replicating Christ's miracles, potentially delusory – nature of mimesis. The didacticism taken as a sign of early origin by nineteenth-century critics now seems part of a defensive strategy of the sixteenth century against clerical opponents of the plays. For example, Play 4 opens with an announcement of the arrival of the players and a call for silence and room. A chorus-character, Expositor, intervenes several times in the play, stopping the action to explain its significance and direct audience response. At the end, in front of a tableau of God, Abraham, Isaac and the sacrificial lamb, he explains that the event prefigures the crucifixion. Then he kneels to pray to the player-God for Abraham-like obedience. Finally, a Messenger interrupts to demand time and space for the next play, thus exposing the 'contemporary' authoritative Expositor as an actor within the play. Framing the play by the practicality of performance sets clear limits to illusion: the plays are dramatic artifice that must run to a set timetable. David Rogers refers to just such a relay of messengers running between playing-stations to ensure that the carriages all move round at the same time.

A different kind of theorizing, theorizing the event itself, is represented by Mervyn James's 1983 essay 'Ritual, Drama and Social Body in the Late Medieval English Town',[41] which links the Corpus Christi of the feast with the social body of a town, seeing the celebration as social mechanism: 'a mythology and a ritual in terms of which the opposites of social whole-ness and social differentiation could be both offered and brought into creative tension'. Such theorizing of the event, which accords with concerns with the body as site and metaphor in literary theory, provides the ground on which literary critics and urban historians can meet. The various entertainment activities have become the touchstones for religio-political studies of the local community.

For Chester, this approach is partly anticipated in Newhall's Proclamation which presented the route from Abbey to Pentice as emblematic of the partnership of Church and town. The route may have further significance. Since the Corpus Christi procession travelled from St Mary's, by the castle of the earl, to St John's, the former cathedral, and still subsequently the church used by the bishop of Lichfield before Chester became a see in 1540, the route might also be seen as marking a shift in the power-base within the city in the sixteenth century.

In the Tudor period, the civic play-cycles had become for many an expression of local community and authority, and their suppression reflected a wider restriction of local autonomy. As Michael O'Connell says:

[The loss of the cycles] was a local and regional loss, an impoverish-ment of the life of provincial centers. In this, as in so many other elements of English Reformation culture, a centripetal force was at work, moving authority and control away from the regions and toward the capital.[42]

The stubborn insistence of Chester's mayors in the 1570s on staging the plays in the face of local and national opposition can therefore be read as a defence of Chester's administrative independence in the face of a centralist Tudor government.

Conclusion

The Banns author and antiquarians of Chester proved useful allies of the scholars of medieval drama up to the early 1960s, confirming their assumptions about the nature and development of early drama and about the tastes of those who watched it. While the goal-orientated epithet 'pre-Shakespearean' is now avoided, without the need to explain Shakespeare's achievement medieval drama would have received even less attention in the past. That the evolutionary thesis, with its implications for Chester, dominated into the 1960s testifies to the persuasive authority of Chambers' work. Although, with its abandonment, the subject has developed in new and revealing directions, the gathering of documentary evidence and the social and economic circumstances prioritized by Chambers still informs our modern critical enquiries.

Notes

1. H. Craig, *English Religious Drama of the Middle Ages* (Oxford, 1955), p. 166.
2. Banns quotations from R. M. Lumiansky and D. Mills, *The Chester Mystery Cycle: Essays and Documents* (Chapel Hill, NC, 1983).
3. Text of the Banns from Lumiansky and Mills, *Essays*, pp. 285–95.
4. See D. Mills, 'Where Have All the Players Gone? A Chester Problem', *Early Theatre*, 1 (1998), pp. 129–37.
5. C. Rinaker, *Thomas Warton: a Biographical and Critical Study*, University of Illinois Studies in Language and Literature 2:1 (Urbana, IL, 1916), pp. 86–87.
6. Quotations from R. M. Lumiansky and D. Mills, eds, *The Chester Mystery Cycle*, EETS ss 3 and 9 (London, 1974 and 1983).
7. T. Warton, *The History of English Poetry from the Close of the Eleventh to the Commencement of the Eighteenth Century*, 4 vols (rev. edn, 1824), II, pp. 76–78.
8. E. Malone, *An Historical Account of the Rise and Progress of the English Stage* (London, 1790); reissued in his posthumous *The Plays and Poems of William Shakespeare... A Life of the Poet and the Enlarged History of the Stage* (London, 1821). Quotations are from the latter. Malone acknowledges his debt to Warton in vol. III, p. 8.
9. J. H. Markland, *Chester Mysteries: De Deluvio Noe: De Occisione Innocentium* (London, 1818), p. xv.
10. E. K. Chambers, *The Mediaeval Stage*, 2 vols (Oxford, 1903), II, p. 147.
11. Texts of documents are taken, unless otherwise noted, from L. M. Clopper, *Records of Early English Drama: Chester* (Toronto, 1979), here pp. 27–28. Missing readings supplied from BL Harley 2013, f. 1 are indicated by boldface.
12. Denbigh Record Office, Ruthin, Plas Power MSS, DD/PP/839, p. 119.
13. See Clopper, *Records*, pp. 238–52 and xxvii–xxxvi.
14. F. M. Salter, *Mediaeval Drama in Chester* (Toronto, 1955), pp. 32–45.
15. R. Beadle and P. Meredith, eds, *The York Play: A facsimile of British Library MS*

Additional 35290 (Leeds, 1983), p. ix.

16 Clopper, *Records*, pp. 6–7.

17 Denbigh Record Office, Ruthin, Plas Power MSS, c1539-1601 CL: DD/PP/839, pp. 120-21.

18 Clopper, *Records*, p. 80.

19 Warton, *The History of English Poetry*, III, p. 16 footnote.

20 W. Roscoe, *The Life of Lorenzo de' Medici* (London, 1795), p. 299 footnote; Markland, *Chester Mysteries*, p. iv. Henry Hallam cites both Warton and Roscoe on the date in his *Introduction to the Literature of Europe in the Fifteenth, Sixteenth and Seventeenth Centuries* (London, 1837–39), concluding: 'I cannnot but consider the language in which we now read [the plays] not earlier, to say the least, than the middle of the [fifteenth century]' (I, p. 297).

21 B. ten Brink, *History of English Literature*, trans. W. Clarke Robinson (London, 1893), II, p. 274.

22 Chambers, *The Mediaeval Stage*, II, p. 146.

23 Salter, *Mediaeval Drama*, p. 42.

24 J. P. Collier, *The History of English Dramatic Poetry to the Time of Shakespeare: and Annals of the Stage to the Restoration* (London, 1831). Studies of French drama antedate Warton, who drew upon accounts such as Du Tilliot, *Memoirs por servir a l'Histoire de la Fete de Foux* (1741); see Warton's sources in Rinaker, *Thomas Warton*, pp. 179–232.

25 S. Schoenbaum, *Shakespeare's Lives* (Oxford, 2nd edn, 1993), p. 247.

26 J. P. Collier, ed., *Five Miracle Plays or Scriptural Dramas* (London, 1836). Collier published a separate edition of Chester's Antichrist play in the same year.

27 Markland, *Chester Mysteries*, pp. iii–iv.

28 Collier, ed., *History*, II, pp. 131–32.

29 T. Wright, ed., *The Chester Plays. A Collection of Mysteries Founded upon Scriptural Subjects and Formerly Represented by the Trades of Chester at Whitsuntide*, 2 vols (London, 1843 and 1847), I, p. xx.

30 A. W. Ward, *History of English Dramatic Literature* (London, 1875), I, p. 45 and n.

31 Craig, *English Religious Drama*, p. 176.

32 R. Woolf, *The English Mystery Plays* (London, 1972), p. 306.

33 Denbigh Record Office, Ruthin, Plas Power MSS, DD/PP/839, p. 122.

34 Ward, *History of English Dramatic Literature*, I, p. 48.

35 E. Prosser, *Drama and Religion in the English Mystery Plays*, Stanford Studies in Language and Literature 23 (Stanford, 1961), p. 81.

36 K. Young, *The Drama of the Medieval Church*, 2 vols (Oxford, 1933), I, p. 80.

37 S. B. Hemingway, *The English Nativity Plays* (New York, 1909), p. xxvii.

38 Craig, *English Religious Drama*, p. 9.

39 V. A. Kolve, *The Play Called Corpus Christi* (London, 1966).

40 Kolve, *Corpus Christi*, pp. 151–59. On a possible influence on Chester's structure and meaning, see P. W. Travis, *Dramatic Design in the Chester Cycle* (Chicago, 1982).

41 *Past and Present*, 98–101 (1983), pp. 5–29.

42 M. O'Connell, *The Idolatrous Eye: Iconoclasm and Theater in Early-Modern England* (New York, 2000), p. 92.

Making the Old North on Merseyside
A Tale of Three Ships

A N D R E W   W A W N

This essay seeks to bang the drum for three Victorian makers of the Viking middle ages, all sons of Merseyside. Their names are John Thomas Stanley (1766–1847), George Stephens (1813–95), and John Sephton (1835–1915), and their achievements have not perhaps yet enjoyed the recognition, either on their native heath or further afield, that they deserve. These scholars were strikingly different in vision and achievement. Stanley brooded unsystematically but persistently about the old north for half a century following his expedition to Iceland in 1789; Stephens preached his version of Anglo-Scandic values passionately for almost fifty years from Copenhagen; and Sephton patiently promoted a many-sided old northernism in the heart of Liverpool towards the end of the century. Temperamentally they were poles apart. Stanley was a laconic lord, Sephton a dignified divine, and Stephens a peppery professor, whose lifelong *furor philologicus* was of so volcanic an intensity that it more than makes up for the relative equanimity of the others.

Yet they had much in common. They were all Merseysiders – Stephens from Wallasey, Sephton from Rainford in the south-west of Lancashire, and Stanley from Alderley Edge (which just about counts, particularly when we factor in the family's summer retreat in Hoylake). They were all, by the standards of their day, pioneering philologists, devoted in some way to the pursuit of old northern languages and literatures. And they all contributed distinctively to the fascination with the Viking Age that developed in Victorian Britain. The present writer, born and bred in Wirral, seeks to celebrate the achievement of all three, as representatives of an emerging medieval consciousness on Merseyside during the nineteenth century.

The tale to be told may be thought of, like the Christmas carol, as one of three ships that came sailing in – three vessels that can serve as symbols by which each of our old northernists can be identified initially. The first ship is a 160-ton brig, the *John*, chartered by John Thomas Stanley of Alderley to take him and his party of Edinburgh University natural scientists to Iceland in 1789. Nicholas Pocock (1740–1821), one of two accomplished topographical artists chosen by Stanley to turn rough sketches from the expedition into a lasting record, depicts the vessel as it approaches the Vestmannaeyjar, off the south coast of Iceland.[1] The overall impression of Pocock's watercolour is one of thrusting modernity, energy, and confidence: the swell is up, the sky is bright, the sails are full, the pennants are flying, and the deck is crowded. Local fishing smacks are dwarfed by the bronze-coloured brig as it bustles into the foreground.

The sense of brisk imperiousness hinted at in this picture is sustained as the visitors interact with the natives, as in the scene outside an Icelandic farmstead painted by Edward Dayes (1763–1804).[2] The smartly clad and well-shod Britons tower over the deferential local women and children; Stanley's pointing finger suggests authority and command; and his companion's handful of flowers reminds us of the importance to the expedition of natural scientific research. There are also certain elements missing from the picture – dogs that fail to bark. Neither this picture nor any of the two dozen others from the expedition[3] includes anything specifically medieval, whether in terms of locations, objects, or atmosphere. There are hot springs, basalt crags, and eccentricities of animal husbandry aplenty, but no saga-steads, no medieval manuscripts being handed over to eager British purchasers, and no representations of *kvöldvökur*, evening gatherings at which the household would sit around, listening to saga tales about the settlement of Iceland, or the kings of Norway and their glittering courts, or Vikings near and far, or Norse gods and myths, or trolls, elves and other members of the ubiquitous community of 'hidden folk'. For Stanley's party and their official artists, the wild landscapes were a laboratory rather than a store of lore and legend.

When Stanley returned to Alderley Edge, he kept the Iceland experience largely to himself and his family. They employed an Icelandic *au pair*, and played with their Icelandic dogs, horses, and costumes.[4] Stanley was doubtless pleased when trade between Liverpool and Iceland developed early in the new century, with cargoes of mittens, skins and train oil arriving at the Pier Head.[5] And he must have been amused to learn that James Robb, agent for Horne and Stackhouse, the Liverpool merchants, settled and married in Iceland, establishing trading premises in Reykjavík. Until recently on that site there was a toy store rejoicing in the name of 'Liverpool'.[6]

But, unusually for the period, Stanley never published a travel journal. He confined himself to two short papers on the science of Icelandic geo-thermal springs.[7] How, then, on this evidence of modest scientific research and unstructured family enthusiasm, can John Thomas Stanley be thought of as a maker of the middle ages? The answer lies in evidence which points to another – more private and more literary – John Thomas Stanley.

Some twenty years ago, in a second-hand bookshop in Reykjavík, I stumbled across a volume from the pioneering series of late eighteenth-century editions of medieval Icelandic sagas, published in Copenhagen after 1770. Each volume features an edited Icelandic text and facing-page Latin translation. Enthusiasts all over Europe read the Eddic poems and prose sagas of Iceland in such editions; hardly anyone knew Icelandic, but everyone could read Latin. Enlightenment-Age antiquarianism and notions of the Romantic sublime created the will to engage with the old north;[8] and newly edited texts created the means. Sir Walter Scott's library in Abbotsford had many such volumes,[9] and local library societies often had individual items, as did a growing number of private household libraries in Middle England.[10] The volume I purchased in Reykjavík was *Viga-Glums saga* (1786),[11] and its bookplate confirmed that the original owner had been 'John Thomas Stanley Esqr of Alderley'.

That a young English natural scientist should be interested in Icelandic sagas need not surprise us, for this was the age of sense as well as sensi-bility, and Stanley had a foot in both camps. We have noted the public scientific sense, but there is also evidence of the private Romantic sensi-bility. This seems to have been hard-wired into his mind during teenage years spent being tutored in Germany, where he relished the local Braunschweig legends of the wild huntsman riding at night over the windswept hills.[12] Stanley duly created and had published his own version of Gottfried August Bürger's much-translated and famously macabre German ballad 'Leonora', with the title-page featuring a William Blake engraving and lines from the Old Icelandic Eddic poem *Hárbarðslióð*.[13] During his student years in Edinburgh there were opportunities to attend society meetings at which the young Walter Scott read papers on old northern mythology.[14] Moreover, Scott and Stanley had a mutual friend in Anna Seward, the 'Swan of Lichfield', who not only composed an orig-inal poem about Hoylake, but also a paraphrastic version of the Old Icelandic poem popularly known as 'The Waking of Angantýr', about the steely-minded and vengeful Viking heroine in *Hervarar saga*.[15]

In short, we may say that there was a resilient old northern popular sub-culture at the end of the eighteenth century linking Hoylake, Alderley

Edge, Lichfield, Abbotsford, Edinburgh and Reykjavík. This was the privately tilled soil in which Stanley and other early nineteenth-century Merseyside makers of the middle ages could sow their seed. One such individual deserves a passing mention: Henry Holland, an Alderley Edge protégé of Stanley. Holland was an Edinburgh medical graduate, who travelled in Iceland in 1810, devoted his 1811 Edinburgh MD dissertation to a study of Icelandic diseases,[16] and wrote an influential chapter on Old Icelandic literature for Sir George Mackenzie's *Travels in Iceland in the Summer of the Year 1810* (1811). That volume, based largely on Holland's own journal,[17] enjoyed further exposure a generation later via a revised edition.[18]

As for Holland's mentor, he would surely have been intrigued to know that the Wirral, where he spent his summers, had once been a Viking stronghold; that Meols had once been the special trading port of the local northmen, and perhaps the site of their local mint;[19] and that many local place-names were of Old Norse origin. But by the time of Stanley's death in 1847, such knowledge was in its infancy. In that same year Revd Abraham Hume, an accomplished local antiquarian (he was a Fellow of the Royal Society of Northern Antiquities in Copenhagen) identified Hoylake as 'a locality [...] which has seen the raven banner of the Dane, and the white horse of the Saxon'.[20] But no systematic archaeology or coherent place-name scholarship relating to the district had yet emerged, and thus few Wirralians would have understood the Viking tale waiting to be told.[21] Moreover, at this time very few people in Britain could read Old Icelandic texts: there was no easily accessible dictionary, no modern grammar book in English before 1843,[22] and no formalized instruction in any British university until much later in the century.

Yet there were individuals who mastered the old language, and others who dabbled in it – and among this latter group was John Thomas Stanley. In 1840s annotations to his fair copies of the 1789 Iceland expedition journals kept by his companions, we find the elderly baronet pondering the etymology of the word *geysir*, distinguishing it from *Laugar-* and *Reykja(r)-* place-names, and identifying 'gush' as an English cognate, when copying out and translating lines from *Kristni saga*.[23] At much the same time we find Stanley pondering the etymology of *niflheimr*, the Old Norse region of death, citing texts from the latest Copenhagen edition of the poetic *Edda*, a copy of which he probably owned.[24] He copies out and translates lines from *Vafþrúðnismál* and *Baldrs draumar*, and from Finnur Magnússon's glossary, with its philologically alert etymology involving Greek, Latin and Old High German cognates. Stanley's own less secure speculations recall the unsystematic impressionism of a celebrated earlier grammarian, John Horne Tooke (1736–1812): 'the negation of motion – *ne*, not; *fle*, flow, flight'. Here, then, was an amateur philologist stumbling painstakingly towards the creation of his own old northern cosmology, and marking out the ground for a later generation of more linguistically experienced Merseyside old northernists, even as he prepared for his own imminent journey to that same region of mist and death.

John Thomas Stanley lived and died in Cheshire, whereas our second maker of the old north on Merseyside left the district while young and never returned, save as a visitor. The mercurial George Stephens was born into a Merseyside clerical family touched by political radicalism. His brother Joseph, a firebrand Chartist in Warrington, was in jail when *Frithiof's Saga: A Legend of Norway* (1839),[25] the book which first made George's name, was published. After studying in London, George had made his way first to Stockholm, and then to Copenhagen, where for more than half a century he promoted tirelessly his idiosyncratic and politicized old northern vision.

Another ship, this time a Viking long-ship, can provide us with a suitably striking image for this philological son of Wirral. It appears in the *Frithiof's saga* volume, as one of the dozen or so illustrations that provide the mood music for Stephens's translation of two versions of the Sognefjord saga. The ship, fierce dragon-head at its prow and bizarre serpentine tail at the stern, may well owe something to the Danish artist Carl Peter Lehmann's 1826 depiction of the saga's famous monster-slaying scene.[26] These 1826 and 1839 depictions of Friðþjófr's magic ship *Elliði* are the product of vivid imaginations as yet unexposed to post-1860 archaeological realities. The 1839 volume itself undoubtedly helped George Stephens to become first lektor and eventually (in 1855) Professor of Old English and of English Language and Literature at (as Stephens would have it) the 'University of Cheapinghaven [Copenhagen]'. It also signalled his arrival on the Anglo-Scandinavian scene as a major and trenchant maker of the middle ages.

In deciding to translate *Friðþjófs saga* into English, Stephens certainly chose the right text at the right time. This tale of a Norwegian Viking chief, Friðþjófr the Bold, existed in a late medieval Icelandic saga version, and in Bishop Esaias Tegnér's 1825 virtuosic Swedish verse paraphrase. George Stephens's translation of both versions was a major factor in creating the almost Ossianic levels of popularity that the story came to enjoy in Britain, the British Empire, North America and Europe. My battered copy was purchased in a second-hand bookshop in Seattle, having done years of late nineteenth-century service with members of the Mercantile Library Association of Baltimore. The story itself, as we shall see, became familiar to members of the Liverpool Philosophical and Literary Society in 1894.

Frithiof, son of a great Viking hero Thorsten Vikingsson (to use Stephens's spellings), wishes to marry Princess Ingeborg, daughter of Thorsten's loyal friend, King Beli. With the death of the two patriarchs, Beli's sons object to the proposed match between their sister and a commoner, and send Frithiof on a tax-collecting expedition to the Orkneys, intending to have him killed en route by two gruesome sea-witches. These denizens of the deep duly conjure up a storm but are destroyed by our hero, who eventually returns with his crew to Sognefjord, where he learns that Ingeborg has been married to the aged King Ring, who had been threatening to attack the region. A disguised Frithiof seeks out the king, and serves him loyally, rejecting all temptation to do away with his host and run off with Ingeborg. When the king eventually dies, Frithiof is reunited with his bride-to-be, returns to Sogn, deals robustly with the royal brothers, and becomes leader of the region by popular acclaim. At the end of Bishop Tegnér's version of the story, the righteous pagan hero eagerly awaits the arrival of Christianity.

The most famous scene in the story is that in which the two sea-witches attack Frithiof on board his magic ship *Elliði*. The 1826 Lehmann canvas is full of fashionable *sturm und drang* elements: clouds scudding across the moonlit sky, waves lashing the aerodynamically problematic ship, manic witches flashing their fearsome fangs, despairing crew, and unflinching leader. Once the Lehmann version of *Elliði* had been adopted by Stephens's illustrator, it was in turn used as a front-cover image for at least two celebrated nineteenth-century books about the ancient and modern north.[27]

The values to which the Frithiof story gave expression are not difficult to define, and will have played as well on Merseyside as anywhere else. As accessed in Stephens's volume, *Frithiof's saga* presented a thoroughly civilized and 'family-values' old north with no unseemly elements of murder, rape or pillage; it was a senior service old north, with Frithiof as exemplary and inspirational sea-captain; it was a homosocial old north, with the Viking life made to seem like an extension of the male bonding with which Victorian gentlemen would have been familiar from their public schools, Oxbridge colleges, military regiments – and Liverpool clubs; it was a meritocratic old north, with yeoman birth no barrier to upward mobility; it was a sexually unthreatening old north, with the hero waiting patiently for his demure bride (the first ever translation of the poem was dedicated to Princess Victoria in 1833, and the translator was a royal chaplain at Windsor);[28] it was an articulate old north, with Frithiof showing himself to be a wittily laconic poet in times of stress; it was an old north favouring constitutional monarchy and mutual respect between leader and led; and, not least, it was a spiritual old north. In a modern age of growing scientific materialism, here was a medieval tale that valorized righteous pagan spirituality as it awaited fulfilment in the new faith.

The enterprisingly multi-media nature of George Stephens's volume also helped to popularize the old north. Along with the translations, we find parlour songs specially written by the translator, and illustrations that served to three-dimensionalize the real or imagined material culture of Sognefjord – its runic stones, halls, sledges, drinking horns, musical instruments, stave calendars, and burial mounds. Moreover, in his notes Stephens sometimes politicizes the old north unblushingly:

> The Kingship of the old North was originally, as it should be, – an Elective Presidency; though the history of the Scandinavian Kingdoms affords melancholy proof enough, how respect for the 'divine races' (as the families said to be descended from Oden are called) overwhelmed the land with destructive minorities or imbecile manhood. With the 'hereditary principle,' whether monarchic or aristocratic equally cementing Dynasties formed in Kingdoms gained by the sword, came in also 'hereditary degradation'.[29]

The waspish tone was to become as characteristic of Stephens's medieval making as the political radicalism.

We may say that even Stephens's style of translation had an ideological edge. Here is part of Frithiof's rousing response to the attack of the sea-witches:

> 'Weird witches see I,
> Two, on the wave there; —
> Helge has sent them,
> Hither to meet us:
> Ellida shall snap a-
> Sunder I' th' middest
> Their backs, — ere o'er billows
> Bounds she right onward.'

The translator seeks here to render the manner as well as the matter of the Old Icelandic *fornyrðislag* verse, with its interior and interlinear alliteration and staccato rhythms. His instinctive willingness, eagerness even, to challenge linguistic decorum encourages him to deploy archaism, contractions, paratactic syntax, flexible word order, unfamiliar word division, and non-standard idioms in the service of his spiky old northern original.

Deployment of these elements (along with compound forms and alliterative doublets) in his translations – and his own prose – needs to be viewed in the light of nineteenth-century philological politics. Stephens resisted the notion that the only respectable literary–linguistic–cultural reference points for Victorian England were ancient Athens and Rome. He had no sympathy for the eighteenth-century Lowthian parlour pieties about 'good grammar' which were, he believed, the melancholy result of imprisoning the rural 'folk-tungs' of England within an alien grammatical straitjacket. He sought to reinvigorate the word stock of modern English by reactivating resources that had (he claimed) once been at the heart of a common Anglo-Scandic language, whose residual elements could now best be identified in runic inscriptions, rural dialects, and Old English and Old Icelandic texts. Stephens was uncowed by the rigid morphological paradigms of the two old languages, regarding such grammar as having been derived from texts improperly standardized by scribes working in unhealthy monastic isolation from the rich inclusiveness of agrarian and nautical oral tradition.[30] In his translation style Stephens, with his Chartist family background, aimed to champion that orality and those vagaries.

There was a broader European political dimension to George Stephens's philological instincts. At one level he believed that the dawning of the golden age of comparative philology in the early nineteenth century represented a welcome challenge to complacent linguistic and cultural hierarchies that had survived unchallenged since the Renaissance.[31] How could medieval and modern European languages still be viewed with lofty disdain when compared with Greek and Latin, when Sanskrit was demonstrably older and more morphologically complex than, yet clearly linked to, both those prestigious tongues? The 'new philology' had created a new paradigm, whereby a common Indo-European language (and culture) could be reconstructed, with Sanskrit as its oldest extant expression. Greek and Latin could no longer legitimately assume the role of stern parents to unruly modern languages and cultures, but had instead to do battle for prestige as fellow siblings.

Yet, if George Stephens and Jacob Grimm and his philological followers could agree on the importance of cultivating the newly valorized medieval languages and literatures of northern Europe, and collecting and codifying folklore and non-standard linguistic forms, they differed sharply on the geo-political implications of the paradigm shift. Stephens rejected the Grimmean tendency to treat Scandinavian languages and cultures as part of some greater Germano-Saxon cultural entity. Stephens harboured an almost visceral dislike of Germans, despising the Hanoverian royal family, and despairing at the supine response of the British Foreign Office to the 1848 moves by Prussia against Slesvig-Holsten, and to the eventual German annexation of those regions. He regarded Slesvig and Holsten as integral parts of his adopted Danish homeland and as 'clan-lands of our forefathers',[32] whence had come the first Anglian settlers of England. As we have noted, Stephens saw early England as the heart of a common North Atlantic Anglo-Scandic, rather than Anglo-Saxon, culture. And it was grammar, he argued, that signalled the fundamental irreconcilability of the Anglo-Saxon (a term he loathed) and Old Icelandic languages, by virtue of their differing infinitive forms (OE *-an*, OI *-a*), and the absence in Old English of forms equivalent to the suffixed definite article and middle voice elements that characterize Old Icelandic.[33] For all George Stephens's suspicions concerning the artificiality of grammatical paradigms, he was more than happy to exploit their evidence when it suited him.

The *furor philologicus* which possessed George Stephens throughout his life generated the remarkable scholarly energy that he directed to the textual recreation of his idealized Anglo-Scandic old north. More and better editions were needed, and by the 1840s he had set the Swedes an excellent example by editing Swedish folktales and saints' lives,[34] and pioneering editions of important Old and Middle English texts followed.[35] Above all he produced his great catalogue of English and Scandinavian runic inscriptions,[36] whose texts were immune to the meddling of monastic scribes, and which therefore offered, he believed, the most authentic witness to the earliest Anglo-Scandic language.

In short, George Stephens's old north was dialectally diverse rather than standardized, oral as much as written, popular as much as learned, rural as much as urban, secular as much as sacred, individual as much as institutional, runic as much as Roman in script, and civilized as much as piratical – with the exception of Frithiof, he loathed Vikings. We might say that George Stephens was a 'new philologist' long before the re-invention of the breed at the end of the twentieth century. His agenda sounds eerily modern, with grammar linked to questions of ethnicity, nationality, regional identity, and social status. Stephens's idealized old north was to be accessed through better texts, sensitive to linguistic diversity; through runes, to which he often assigned improbably early dates; and through dialect study, which could facilitate re-engagement with marginalized modern voices and forgotten ancient ones. He found such voices all over rural Denmark and northern England, and he encouraged his English friends to collect, edit, and interpret the available data. No wonder that he regarded English language teaching in universities as so important. What a difference he could have made in England had his 1860s hopes for a Chair at Cambridge been fulfilled – but the call never came.[37]

It is said that owners end up looking like their dogs, and George Stephens's middle ages ended up looking (and sounding) very like George Stephens. It was excitingly international and interdisciplinary, with language, literature, archaeology, history, geography, geology, theology, mythology, folklore, naval architecture and much else besides all contributing to the cause. It was also, it has to be said, frequently wrong-headed, as with Stephens's explanation of the Brough Stone in Yorkshire. He confidently identified as runic an inscription which proved to be written in Greek hexameters! When this error was drawn to his attention, the Great Man noted cheerfully that 'I ought to be beaten', before moving unstoppably onwards.[38] George Stephens did not 'do' doubt. Yet it can truly be said of him, as it was later said affectionately of the great Icelandic scholar Finnur Jónsson, 'the trouble with Finnur is that he wasn't always wrong'.

And so to our last ship, and our third and final Merseyside philologist, who can be introduced with reference not to a picture, but to a passage from a late Victorian oratorio. In 1896, the year after George Stephens's death, the young pre-*Gerontius* Edward Elgar composed *Scenes from the Saga of King Olaf*, based on Longfellow's verse paraphrase (in *Tales from a Wayside Inn*) of Snorri Sturluson's early thirteenth-century saga about the life and death of Ólafr Tryggvason, the great Christianizing king who had brought the new faith to Scandinavia at the end of the tenth century. The first performance of *King Olaf* took place in the Victoria Hall, Hanley, and if it wasn't subsequently performed in Liverpool, it should have been. One scene, 'The Death of Olaf', tells of the king standing high on the deck of his famous 'Long Serpent' dragon ship, 'with war-axe grasped in both his hands'.[39] Any Victorian music lover preparing for a performance could have read about King Ólafr and his ship in popular novels, poems, or in Revd John Sephton's 500-page translation of *Óláfs saga Tryggvasonar en mesta.*[40]

At this time Sephton was best known in Liverpool as the much-respected former headmaster of Liverpool Institute, where he served for 23 years up to 1889. Born and raised in south-east Lancashire, he was educated at St John's College in Cambridge, lived in Huskisson Street for most of his long Liverpool life, and was eventually appointed to the position of Reader in Icelandic at the new University College of Liverpool from 1895–1910. Sephton had an excellent pedigree as a medieval scholar, for he became the middle-aged protégé of one of the greatest Icelandicists in Britain, Guðbrandur Vigfússon in Oxford, who used to visit Liverpool regularly, en route to examining the runes in the Isle of Man, and visiting scholarly friends in the north of England and in Scotland.[41]

Regular visits of this kind will have helped Guðbrandur to realize that John Sephton was not ploughing a lone philological furrow on Merseyside. Several papers delivered at the Liverpool Literary and Philosophical Society after 1850 confirm that there were plenty of potential makers of the middle ages among the membership:[42] Robert McLintock, 'The Nibelungenlied' (1882–23), Revd S. Fletcher Williams, 'Robin Hood: A History and Vindication' (1886–87), E. A. Wesley, 'The English Miracle Play' (1898–99), William Wortley, 'Aelfred the Great, King of England, 1000 years ago' (1900–01), and C. W. Stubbs, 'Cynewulf' (1904–05). An occasional evening was devoted to specifically Scandinavian matters: Sir Edward Read, 'An Explanation of the Geysers of Iceland' (1862–63), Joseph Boult, 'The Danish Intrusion into South Britain' (1873–74), Jessie MacGregor, 'Scandinavian Mythology from the Picturesque Side' (1883–84), and J. Linton Palmer, 'Notes on Runes' (1894–95).

Many other titles reveal how the new comparative philology, born and bred in north Europe, trickled down into Middle England. The data upon which the new theories were based may have been intricate, but the conclusions and implications were regarded as accessible and intriguing. Thus, we find Revd Arthur Ramsay, 'Comparative Philology: The Practical Application' (1852–53), E. M. Geldart, 'Illustrations of Grimm's Law' (1874–75), and R. J. Lloyd, 'The Aryan Cradle-Language' (1889–90). Above all, we might note the sequence of related lectures given by Sir James Picton, architect, antiquarian and pillar of Liverpool society: 'The Ancient Gothic Language and its Place in the Indo-European Family' (1859–60), 'On Sanskrit Roots and English Derivations' (1863–64), 'The South Lancashire Dialect' (1864–65), 'The Use of Proper Names in

Philological and Ethnological Enquiry' (1865–66), 'On Social Life among the Teutonic Races in Early Times' (1867–68), and 'Our Mother Tongue and its Congenors' (1868–69).

Along with painstaking explanations of the new theories, Picton's papers confirm that cultural triumphalism was not confined to Prussia. English, he claimed, may now be regarded simply as the best language in the world: it has 'a richness and fertility, which has never been surpassed in the world's history, and which render it unrivalled amongst modern languages as a vehicle for thought'.[43] And, as with English, so with England: '[English] may truly be called a world language, and seems, like England herself, destined to rule over all the corners of the earth'.[44] And Picton's study of early Germanic legal texts leads him to identify and celebrate those elements that had helped to make the English character 'that union of individual self-reliance and capability of combination, that self-denial, perseverance and energy which have enabled [us] to pioneer the world'.[45] Such sentiments were unlikely to have been challenged among an audience of the brightest and best in the British Empire's greatest port.

As we shall see, John Sephton was an active member of the Liverpool Literary and Philosophical Society, and there is good reason to suppose that he was in the audience for many of these papers. However, a tradition of lively medieval and philological scholarship at the 'Lit. and Phil.' was one thing; formalizing and promoting such interests within the new University College was quite another. Were there any potential makers of the middle ages among the faculty? Sephton, while still an outsider, sent a dispirited letter (6 January 1886) to Guðbrandur Vigfússon noting that 'I fear there is no-one [at the College] to represent Icelandic'.[46] In his reply two days later, Guðbrandur notes wryly that Picton and his circle were 'deserving of respect for having literary interests at all in Liverpool, where all the world rotates around bales of cotton'. Guðbrandur's cynicism was somewhat overstated, however, and Sephton's tune had certainly changed by 27 December 1888, when he was able to report that 'a new Icelandic scholar is rising in Liverpool (Dr Kuno Meyer, the Celtic Scholar), vigorous and energetic'. Meyer, an accomplished philologist from Germany who also taught Irish, Welsh and Anglo-Saxon, must have supported Sephton's appointment to the college. He will certainly have been aware of his reputation, and was probably wise to his plans.

Had mission statements been in vogue in 1895, that of the newly appointed Reader in Icelandic would have been easily definable: credibility, diversity, outreach, and localism. Sephton's credibility derived from his well-grounded linguistic and codicological expertise: that scholarly authority lent instant validity to his academic initiatives. As for diversity, Sephton was well aware of the seductive force of images of buccaneering Vikings in late Victorian popular culture. And he was happy enough to ride the wave, as when, like George Stephens, he too produced a translation of *Friðþjófs saga*. But, also like Stephens, he embraced a broader range of medieval Icelandic literature. He published a translation of *Sverrissaga*,[47] the kind of Norway-related biographical narrative in danger of being excluded from an emerging canon of *Íslendingasögur* ('sagas of Icelanders') dictated by the understandably nationalist agendas of Icelandic scholars. His 1895 *Óláfs saga Tryggvasonar* translation (dedicated to the memory of Guðbrandur Vigfússon, who had died in 1889) underlines the importance that Sephton attached to the Christian old north, as befitted a highly respected Liverpool clergyman. His translation of the comic Eddic poem *Þrymskviða* draws attention to Norse myth and pagan legend; and his version of *Eiríks saga rauða*, one of two celebrated saga narratives about the Norse discovery of America, was an ideal subject for an Icelandicist plying his trade in the principal British port of embarkation for the modern United States of America.

As for outreach, Sephton was a popular lecturer in Liverpool. Two of his papers make the point. First, over the winter of 1893–94 the Liverpool Literary and Philosophical Society were treated to papers on 'Gypsies' (28 members present), 'Mushroom Beds of South American Ants' (50), 'Recent Socialistic and Labour Legislation in New Zealand' (59), and 'Astrophotography' (75). Only two papers attracted larger audiences: 'Recent Discoveries as to the Origin and Early History of the Human Race' (95), and, on 19 March, 'The Saga of Frithiof' (79), when John Sephton read out and discussed his new translation. As ever at the society, medieval literature took its place confidently alongside cutting-edge social and natural science. The society's lecture programmes recall the traditions of humane culture in Enlightenment-Age Edinburgh that John Thomas Stanley had experienced a century earlier.

The second Sephton lecture was delivered, as he reports to Guðbrandur Vigfússon, 'at the request of the Senate [...] I had as fine an audience as Liverpool can furnish'. His chosen subject was the Norse god Þórr, as presented in *Þrymskviða*. The poem tells of attempts by Þórr to recover his hammer, one of the symbols and sources of his fabled strength, which has been stolen by the predatory frost giants. Its successful recovery depends on the beautiful goddess Freyja agreeing to marry the giant Þrymr. With Freyja unsurprisingly disinclined to enter into such an arrangement, a ruse is devised, whereby the equally reluctant Þórr will dress up as Freyja, make the bridal journey to Útgarðr, and recover the hammer himself. With the aid of his bridesmaid, the trickster figure of Loki, Þórr's mission is successful, as the conclusion of Sephton's version confirms:

> Thrym, stooping to kiss the bride, sprang back
>   The full length of the hall, with amaze;
> 'Oh! Why are the eyes of Freyia so fierce
>   With fire they are all ablaze?'
>
> The bridesmaid cleverly answer made,
>   ''Tis Freyia's joyous glee;
> For eight nights past has she eaten nought,
>   Eager thy land to see.'
>
> Then Thrym the giants' lord spake forth,
>   'We'll hallow the bride,' said he;
> 'Yea, hallow us both with wedlock's hand;
>   Lay the Hammer on her knee.'
>
> Thor's spirit laughed in his breast, as he felt
>   The hard hammer in his hand;
> He slew Thrym first, and after him
>   The race of the giant's land.[48]

The style is deftly judged. For an oral performance of a narrative poem Sephton chooses an *abcb* rhyme scheme and alternating four- and three-stress lines, features reminiscent of English popular balladic tradition, but he also deploys a dusting of interlinear alliteration as a gesture towards one of the distinguishing features of his Eddic source. We may note that Sephton again nods in the direction of balladic tradition when rendering the hero's rousing verse in the *Friðþjófs saga* passage, previously quoted in Stephens's version, though he winches up the level of formality by deploying an end-stopped *aabb* rhyme scheme and four-stress lines throughout:

> 'Lo there in front are witches twain,
> By Helgi sent across the main;
> Ellidi's prow the two shall slay,
> As swift she glides upon her way.'[49]

Sephton's subtle accommodation of Old Icelandic poetic forms within equally traditional English metrical forms will have helped his readers and listeners to identify with this initially unfamiliar medieval literary culture. In his 'Thor' lecture he seeks to extend this sense of involvement by offering his audience an immediately accessible meteorological explanation of the Thunderer god: he symbolizes the spring gales from the south Atlantic that cause thunder and lightning when clashing with colder winds from the north.[50] His audience may have had cause to appreciate this interpretation more fully at the end of the evening as they made their way down Brownlow Hill into the prevailing March wind. They will also have understood Sephton's claim that Þórr survives in popular British legend in the figure of Jack the Giant Slayer.[51]

In associating Old Icelandic literary tradition with modern English folklore, Sephton locates himself securely within the flourishing Victorian tradition of what we might call popular Grimmeanism. As we noted in respect of George Stephens, the example set by Jacob Grimm's three great (and linked) projects, *Kinder- und Hausmärchen* (1812), *Deutsche Grammatik* (1819) and *Deutsche Mythologie* (1842), helped to promote the idea that elements of local and national popular culture (dialect, place-names, local lore and legend) could be traced back to early Germanic, Scandinavian and, ultimately, Indo-European tradition. Sabine Baring-Gould (1832–1924), celebrated creator of 'Onward Christian Soldiers', was another accomplished English Old Icelandicist with a similarly Grimmean agenda.[52] Old Icelandic could thus be promoted, not as some marginal north Atlantic exoticism, but rather as an integral part of the culture of the British Isles, not least of proud regional communities such as Merseyside.

Sephton's work on local place-names was another aspect of that cultural contextualization. He was only too happy to identify a Viking-Age past for familiar locations such as Litherland (Hlíðarendi, home of the famed *Njáls saga* hero Gunnarr), and, I feel compelled to add, Everton (Yfir tún).[53] Nor did he shy away from identifying more shameful political parallels, as when noting that the cruel Norwegian Hákon jarl had favoured the slave trade, just like 'his descendants in Wirral and West Derby down to the present century'.[54]

The keys, then, for the successful promotion of Old Icelandic in late Victorian and Edwardian Merseyside were credibility, diversity, outreach, and localism. In the 10th annual lecture to commemorate the inauguration of Queen's College in Liverpool (founded by the directors of Liverpool Institute in 1857 as a centre for those studying for London

University qualifications), John Sephton noted that its professorships in the different subjects 'are regulated by the strict law of supply and demand'.[55] If the eventual operations of University College Liverpool, after its inauguration in the winter of 1882, were somewhat less market-driven, we may nevertheless say that Sephton's instincts towards the promotion of both Christianity and Icelandic studies on Merseyside never lost sight of the importance, in Victorian terms, of posteriors on pews.

His own example within Liverpool attracted two kinds of important support, academic and financial. Thus, for example, Oliver Elton came over to join him from Owens College in Manchester, and became a maker of the middle ages in his own right, through his pioneering translation of much of Saxo Grammaticus's twelfth-century compendium of old northern lore, legend, and history,[56] and his translation of *Lárentíus saga biskups*,[57] the fourteenth-century biography of an influential Icelandic bishop. And, as regards funding, members of at least two of Liverpool's wealthiest and most influential families had swallowed the Icelandic bait in a big way. Eager participants in a Liverpudlian expedition to Iceland in 1880 include Alfred, Robert, George and Emma Holt, and Oswald Rathbone, whose father and uncle had previously explored the Faroes in 1855. Mrs George Holt, another of the travellers, was the niece of Henry Holland's 1810 Iceland travelling companion, Dr James Bright.[58] The enthusiastic and well-informed nature of the privately published travelogue of the 'Argonauts' confirms that Icelandic culture had friends in high places in Liverpool thereafter.

This essay has sought to characterize the role of three men of Merseyside in the making of the middle ages. They were, as we have seen, a mixed bunch in terms of background, temperament, and achievement, but their distinctive witness to the medieval cause spans over 150 years, with some pleasing continuities. John Thomas Stanley discovered the old north in the 1780s, but lived long enough to read George Stephens's *Frithiof's saga* in 1839. George Stephens, born three years after Stanley's Cestrian protégé Henry Holland went to Iceland in 1810, lived just long enough to learn of John Sephton's installation as Reader in Icelandic at Liverpool's University College in 1895. Sephton, in turn, was to see his protégé Oliver Elton installed as King Alfred Professor of English in Liverpool in 1901.[59] And, on a minor note, the present writer was alive, just, when Elton died in Oxford in 1945. Those of us who sit on the shoulders of these formidable old northernists are aware that the middle ages they created was not for all time but of an age. But their witness reminds us, first, of the fundamental importance – and romance – of medieval

language learning and exploration; secondly, of the value of interdisciplinarity of spirit and informality of academic structure; and thirdly, of the
virtues of well-informed populism and unapologetic localism.

Notes

1 F. Ponzi, *Ísland á átjándu öld* (Reykjavík, 1987), pp. 31, 92–93.

2 Ibid. p. 115.

3 All reproduced handsomely in Steindór Steindórsson, trans., *Íslandsleiðangur Stanleys 1789: Ferðabók* (Reykjavík, 1979).

4 For detail see J. H. Adeane, *The Early Married Life of Maria Josepha […] Lady Stanley* (London, 1899), p. 368; Cheshire Record Office, MSS DSA 5/7, 127/1; A. Wawn, 'John Thomas Stanley and Iceland: The Sense and Sensibility of an Eighteenth-Century Explorer', *Scandinavian Studies*, 53.1 (1981), pp. 52–76, at 66–71; A. Wawn, 'Hundadagadrottningin', *Saga: Tímarit Sögufélagsins*, 23 (1985), pp. 97–133.

5 Representative glimpses of the early nineteenth-century Liverpool–Iceland trade can be found in *Liverpool Mercury*, 5 August 1814, p. 40; 9 August 1814, p. 64; 2 September 1814, p. 79. See also E. Henderson, *Iceland; or The Journal of a Residence in that Island During the Years 1814 and 1815* (Edinburgh, 1819), pp. 404–05.

6 Wawn, 'Hundadagadrottningin', p. 130 (note 3).

7 J. T. Stanley, 'An Account of the Hot Springs in Iceland with an Analysis of their Waters', *Transactions of the Royal Society of Edinburgh*, 3 (1794), pp. 127–37, 138–53.

8 See A. Wawn, 'The Post-Medieval Reception of Old Norse and Old Icelandic Literature', in R. McTurk, ed., *A Companion to Old Norse-Icelandic Literature and Culture* (Oxford, 2005), pp. 320–37.

9 See J. Cochrane, *Catalogue of the Library of Abbotsford* (Edinburgh, 1838).

10 The library of Revd Sabine Baring-Gould, now kept at Killerton House, Exeter, is a fine example of the phenomenon: it contains about a hundred volumes related to the ancient and modern north.

11 *Viga-Glums saga sive Vita Viga-Glumi* (Copenhagen, 1786) [various editors].

12 See Stanley's 1813 manuscript journal: MS JRL [John Rylands Library] 722, pp. 14, 18–19, quoted in A. Wawn, 'James Six and the Court of Brunswick, 1781–2. Unpublished Translations, Poems and Letters', *Archiv für das Studium der neueren Sprachen und Literaturen*, 220.135 (1983), pp. 241–67, at 243.

13 G. A. Bürger, *Leonora*, trans. J. T. Stanley (London, 1796).

14 J. G. Lockhart, ed., *Memoirs of the Life of Sir Walter Scott*, 4 vols (Paris, 1838), I, pp. 91, 105, 118–19.

15 Sir Walter Scott, ed., *The Collected Poems of Anna Seward*, 3 vols (Edinburgh, 1810), III, pp. 90–103. The poem existed in draft as early as the year of Stanley's Iceland expedition: see M. Clunies Ross, *The Norse Muse in England, 1750–1820* (Trieste, 1998), p. 250.

16 H. Holland, *Dissertatio medica inauguralis de morbis islandiæ* (Edinburgh, 1811).

17 A. Wawn, ed., *The Iceland Journal of Henry Holland 1810* (London, 1987).

18 H. Holland, 'Preliminary Dissertation on the History and Literature of Iceland', in Sir George Mackenzie, *Travels in the Island of Iceland in the Summer of the Year 1810* (Edinburgh, 1811).

19 P. Cavill, S. Harding and J. Jesch, eds, *Wirral and Its Viking Heritage* (Nottingham, 2000), p. 5.

20 A. Hume, *The Antiquities Found at Hoylake in Cheshire* (London, 1847), p. 20; see also his *Ancient Meols: or Some Account of the Antiquities Found near Dove Point, on the Sea-Coast of Cheshire* (London, 1863), pp. 392–93.

21 As told, for instance, in S. Harding, *Ingimund's Saga: Norwegian Wirral* (Birkenhead, 2000).

22 R. Rask, *A Grammar of the Icelandic or Old Norse Tongue*, trans. G. Webbe Dasent (London and Frankfurt, 1843).

23 Lbs. [Landsbókasafn Íslands] MS 3888 4to, p. 374; the verse is from P. F. Suhm, ed., *Kristni-Saga, sive Historia religionis Christianæ in Islandiam introductæ* (Copenhagen, 1773), p. 38. Lbs. MS 3888 4to, pp. 415–29, has a lengthier section from the same saga, translated from the 1773 Latin version, and in need of 'future correction' (p. 429).

24 Stanley's comments survive on a loose sheet in Cheshire Record Office, MS DSA 5/6; the edition he cites is *Edda Sæmundar hinns Fróda*, 3 vols (Copenhagen, 1787–1828).

25 G. Stephens, ed. and trans., *Frithiof's Saga: A Legend of Norway* (Stockholm and London, 1839).

26 In the Bergen Billedgalleri. The canvas is reproduced in D. M. Wilson, *Vikings and Gods in European Art* (Højbjerg, 1997), p. 36.

27 Lord Dufferin, *Letters from High Latitudes* (London, 1857); R. Anderson and Jón Bjarnason, trans., *Viking Tales of the North* (Chicago, 1877).

28 W. Strong, trans., *Frithiof's Saga: A Scandinavian Legend of Royal Love* (London, 1833).

29 Stephens, *Frithiof's Saga*, p. 228.

30 For a representative statement of such views, see G. Stephens, *Handbook of the Old-Northern Runic Monuments of Scandinavia and England* (Edinburgh and Cheapinghaven [Copenhagen], 1884), pp. vii–xxiv, 214–26. More generally, see A. Wawn, *The Vikings and the Victorians: Inventing the Old North in Nineteenth-Century Britain* (Cambridge, 2000), pp. 215–44.

31 On Grimmean philology and its influence, see H. Aarsleff, *The Study of Language in England, 1780–1860* (London, 1983), pp. 115–211; T. Shippey, 'A Revolution Reconsidered: Mythography and Mythology in the Nineteenth Century', in Shippey, ed., *The Shadow Walkers: Jacob Grimm's Mythology of the Monstrous* (Tempe, AZ, 2005), pp. 1–28.

32 Stephens, *Handbook*, p. 225.

33 G. Stephens, '"English" or "Anglo-Saxon"', *The Gentleman's Magazine*, 36 (1852), pp. 323–27, 472–76; G. Stephens, *Er Engelsk et tysk Sprog?* (Copenhagen, 1890).

34 For example, G. Stephens, ed., *Ett Forn-Svenskt Legendarium*, 2 vols (Stockholm, 1847–58).

35 G. Stephens, ed., *Two Leaves of King Waldere's Lay* (London and Cheapinghaven [Copenhagen], 1860); G. Stephens, ed., *Ghost Thanks, or The Grateful Unburied* [*Sir Amadace*] (London and Cheapinghaven [Copenhagen], 1860).

36 G. Stephens et al., eds, *The Old-Northern Runic Monuments of Scandinavia and England*, 4 vols (London and Cheapinghaven [Copenhagen], 1866–1901).

37 In an unpublished letter bound into the Bodleian Library copy of his *Two Leaves of Waldere's Lay* (1860) edition, Stephens writes: 'I am now advancing in years, and long – like a bird – to fly home again, and work in our own libraries. If some good men and true would follow the example of Oxford and found an O.E. Chair in Cambridge, and would honour me by calling me to fill it – how great would be my delight!'

38 T. Hodgkin, 'Professor George Stephens', *Archaeologia Aeliana*, 18 (1895), p. 53.

39 Edward Elgar, *Scenes from the Saga of King Olaf*, EMI Classics CMS 5 65104 2 (London: EMI Records, 1994), p. 21, Scene 11.

40 J. Sephton, trans., *The Saga of Olaf Tryggwason* (London, 1895).

41 For correspondence between Sephton and Guðbrandur Vigfússon, see Bodleian MS Eng. Misc. d.131, and Sidney Jones Library, University of Liverpool, MS 3.32.

42 Listed in A. W. Newton, *An Index to the Proceedings of the Liverpool Literary and*

Philosophical Society (Liverpool, 1912).

43 J. A. Picton, 'On Sanskrit Roots and English Derivations', *Proceedings of the Liverpool Literary and Philosophical Society*, 18 (1864), pp. 31–64, at 64.

44 J. A. Picton, 'Our Mother Tongue and Its Convenors', *Proceedings of the Liverpool Literary and Philosophical Society*, 23 (1869), pp. 52–84, at 83.

45 J. A. Picton, 'On Social Life among the Teutonic Races in Early Times', *Proceedings of the Liverpool Literary and Philosophical Society*, 22 (1868), pp. 68–98, at 84.

46 Sidney Jones Library, University of Liverpool, MS 3.33: the source of all three letters quoted in the paragraph.

47 J. Sephton, trans., *Sverrissaga. The Saga of King Sverri of Norway* (London, 1899).

48 J. Sephton, *Thor and His Sway* (Liverpool, 1887), p. 26.

49 J. Sephton, 'A Translation of The Saga of Frithiof the Fearless', *Proceedings of the Liverpool Literary and Philosophical Society*, 48 (1894), pp. 69–97, at p. 81.

50 Ibid., pp. 14–15.

51 Ibid., p. 32.

52 See S. Baring-Gould, *Iceland: Its Scenes and Sagas* (London, 1863); Baring-Gould, *A Book of Folklore* ([London, 1913]).

53 J. Sephton, 'Notes on the South Lancashire Place-Names in Domesday Book', *Otia Merseiana*, 4 (1904), pp. 65–74, at 68; Sephton, 'On the Study of Icelandic', *The Library*, 3rd series, 12.3 (1912), pp. 385–411, at 393.

54 J. Sephton, *The Religion of the Eddas and Sagas* (Liverpool, 1892), p. 19.

55 J. Sephton, *Queen's College, Liverpool. Inaugural Lecture of the Tenth Session, Delivered at the Conversazione, January 11, 1867* (Liverpool, 1867), p. 5. More generally, see D. R. Jones, *The Origins of Civic Universities: Manchester, Leeds, Liverpool* (London, 1988).

56 O. Elton, trans., *The First Nine Books of the Danish History of Saxo Grammaticus* (London, 1894).

57 O. Elton, trans., *The Life of Laurence Bishop of Hólar in Iceland* (London, 1890).

58 For the 1880 expedition journal, see Anon., *A Narrative of the Voyage of the Argonauts in 1880* (Edinburgh, 1881), pp. 1, 73, 109: a rare volume, consulted in Landsbókasafn Íslands.

59 On Elton, see L. C. Martin, 'Oliver Elton, 1861–1945', *Proceedings of the British Academy*, 31 (1945), pp. 317–34.

Early Nineteenth-Century Liverpool Collectors of Late Medieval Illuminated Manuscripts

EDWARD MORRIS

The collecting of medieval illuminated manuscripts was an unusual pursuit in late eighteenth- and early nineteenth-century Britain. They were appreciated principally by antiquarians, above all Francis Douce and Joseph Strutt, because, by the fourteenth century, they were rich (especially in their margins) in representations of contemporary everyday life, costumes, occupations, domestic work, local customs and architecture, painted with the ever-increasing descriptive naturalism of the late middle ages. The new patrons in this period were aristocratic – and often royal – laymen wanting romances, histories, didactic treatises and works of private devotion. Illumination had moved out of the church and cloister to a more secular environment. The development of heraldry and genealogy could be studied in these manuscripts by the eighteenth-century descendants of these noble and royal patrons and by their librarians and chroniclers. Realistic portraits of their remote ancestors could be found there. Horace Walpole carried his pioneering enthusiasm for Gothic art into making a small collection of illuminated books. His most important acquisition was a Psalter bought from the duchess of Portland and formerly owned by the earls of Arundel and Oxford; it eventually passed to the earl of Waldegrave, the son of his niece. It dated, however, from the sixteenth century and it was attributed to Giulio Clovio, the most fashionable illuminator of the period whose miniatures were effectively often small-scale easel paintings rather than book decoration.[1] There were so few British collectors of illuminated manuscripts that their prices, far below those of comparable rare printed books until about 1900, were actually falling in the early nineteenth century.[2]

These few collectors were generally concentrated in London, traditionally the centre of the book trade, but in Liverpool, 'a remote part of this remote kingdom',[3] there were three very remarkable enthusiasts for late medieval illuminated manuscripts who were neither antiquarians nor aristocrats. They were more or less exact contemporaries: William Roscoe was born in 1753, Sir John Tobin in 1763 and Charles Blundell in 1761. In their various fields each was pre-eminent – Roscoe as the epitome of Liverpool culture with an international reputation, Tobin as one of the most enterprising and successful merchants and shipowners in Liverpool, Blundell as the very wealthy owner of by far the most important art collection in Liverpool. In other respects they could not have been more different: Tobin the slave trader, the privateer during the Napoleonic Wars, the mayor, the Tory, the Anglican establishment insider; Roscoe the intellectual Unitarian, the ethical abolitionist of slavery, the Radical, the unrelenting opponent of the war with France; and lastly Blundell, the reclusive and eccentric Catholic landowner. Indeed they represented the three principal strands of Liverpool's highly polarized political, economic, cultural and religious elite. They certainly knew of each other – and Roscoe's books were famous – but they were emphatically not a group of Liverpool collectors with esoteric tastes learning from each other.

Roscoe was the oldest and much the most famous. Throughout his writings his main concern was to describe and analyse that improvement in the arts discernible both in Renaissance Italy and in eighteenth-century Liverpool. He would have liked to have identified one of the principal causes of artistic progress as political freedom but was aware that Hume and other Tory historians could point to the France of Louis XIV to disprove this idea, and that his own heroes, Lorenzo de' Medici and Leo X, were scarcely champions of civic liberties. He had to content himself with emphasizing the advantages for the arts provided by a stable and settled government and by commercial and agricultural prosperity. But even by these more basic criteria the middle ages, that 'long and feverish sleep of the human intellect' as he put it,[4] could not qualify as an artistic age:

> The circumstances in which all Europe was placed during the middle ages, when, for a long course of time, one species of desolation was followed by another in quick succession, and the world was thinned in its numbers by famine, by pestilence, and by the sword, or debilitated and exhausted by oppression in every variety of form, exhibit too certain a cause of the deep debasement of the human kind and of the almost total relinquishment of liberal studies. Even independent of the miseries occasioned by war, whether unsuccessful or successful, its long continuance is hostile and destructive to letters and to arts.[5]

However, for Roscoe medieval art required study if only to clarify the improvements on it achieved during the Renaissance. His collection of paintings included notable fourteenth- and fifteenth-century paintings acquired 'chiefly for the purpose of illustrating ... the rise and progress of the arts in modern times ... They are therefore not wholly to be judged of by their positive merits but by reference to the age in which they were produced.'[6] He considered writing a 'Historical Sketch of the State of the Arts in the Middle Ages' and was particularly interested in medieval illuminated manuscripts because, 'before the invention of printing, a stricter union subsisted between literature and the arts of design than has since been the case, and the artist and the scholar frequently combined their efforts to recommend their joint productions to the public favour'.[7] Thus illuminated manuscripts were particularly important for Roscoe's interdisciplinary approach, combining the history of Renaissance literature with the history of Renaissance art. In old age he devoted much time to the cataloguing of the manuscripts at Holkham, owned by his friend, Thomas Coke – a project which only failed because he was more interested in history than in paleography, understanding earlier than most historians that art history can be studied in manuscripts as well as in paintings.[8] Thus in his draft 'History of illumination in Italy from Cimabue to Clovio' he observed:

> The alterations and improvements which have successfully taken place with respect to the arts of design are no where more strikingly exemplified than in the MS copies of works before the invention of printing. From them we find an almost uninterrupted series of picturesque representations from the decline of ancient art ... No sooner was it perceived that the arts of design admitted of something beyond the meagre forms thus represented than a sudden change took place in the decoration of manuscripts – the unnatural figures formed in the Greek MSS were discarded, their prescriptive modes of representing the events recorded in the sacred writings corrected and improved, until a novel and superior style was formed, which from its merit as well as its antiquity is entitled to the approbation of the present day.[9]

His detailed account of the development of illuminated books is taken directly from those Italian historians, Lanzi, Baldinucci and Vasari, on whom he generally relied, but it gains interest when he discusses works in his own collection, noting the relationship between paintings and illumination and discussing his favourite subject, the historical development of style and technique. Thus he argues that his *Christ discovered in the Temple* by Simone Martini (Fig. 1), a narrative painting directly illustrating a Gospel text,[10] provides evidence that that artist's style 'if not derived from is well calculated for the illumination of MSS'. Similarly, in connection with some late fourteenth-century miniatures by Don Silvestro dei Gherarducci, of which he owned one (Fig. 2),[11] he observed that Leo X greatly admired them in the early sixteenth century. Roscoe's most celebrated illuminated manuscript was the Bible of Clement VII written and illuminated in Tuscany with about a hundred narrative miniatures around 1330–50 and later owned by the Anti-Pope Clement VII. Roscoe had acquired it from his friend William Ottley, undoubtedly the leading British pioneer scholar, dealer and collector in the appreciation of both medieval art and illuminated manuscripts.[12] Relying on Ottley's expertise he described it thus:

> The volume is decorated with historical designs from subjects of the Old and New Testaments, supposed to be executed by Giotto, or some artist of his school; he having been employed at Avignon under Clement V in 1305 about which time this MS was written. Independent of the value of this volume as exemplifying the state of art at a very early period, it is certainly one of the finest and most highly ornamented manuscripts of the Sacred Writings, which have been handed down to the present times.[13]

Roscoe's entire collection was sold in 1816 in an unsuccessful attempt to pay the debts incurred by his bank, but another collection reflecting his influence survived. Joseph Brooks Yates was the son of Revd John Yates, the Unitarian minister at the chapel where Roscoe and his friends worshipped. Both father and son belonged to Roscoe's radical, dissenting and anti-slavery literary and artistic circle, the son 'bearing with him the remembrance of its palmy days in the time of Roscoe, Currie, Traill and Shepherd' until his death in 1855, and it must have been the memory of Roscoe's great library that encouraged him to collect 'many curious manuscripts and early black-letter editions'.[14] At his death he bequeathed ten of these medieval manuscripts to his grandson, Henry Yates Thompson, then only eighteen years old. Yates Thompson became the foremost manuscript collector of his age and, although he eventually left Liverpool, the distant connection with Roscoe, whose prestige in Liverpool mounted throughout the century, must still have been a powerful element in his collecting.[15]

Fig 1. *Christ discovered in the Temple* by Simone Martini, panel, 1342
(National Museums, Liverpool, Walker Art Gallery)

Fig 2. *The Birth of St John the Baptist* by Don Silvestro Camaldolese (or dei Gherarducci), vellum, about 1375 (National Museums, Liverpool, Walker Art Gallery)

Sir John Tobin (Fig. 3), one of seventeen children of a modestly prosperous Manx merchant, went to sea as a boy from Liverpool. He and his brother, Thomas, were soon immensely successful as captains of slave trading ships and of privateers, capturing numerous French slave ships between 1793 and 1799. John retired from the sea in 1803 but his company, John Tobin and Co., remained active in the slave trade until its abolition in 1807. His marriage in 1798 into the Aspinall family, also very prominent in the slave trade, probably provided the capital required for the establishment of his company. Like most Liverpool shipowners the Tobins strongly opposed abolition, Thomas even arguing before an official inquiry that the African slaves begged to be taken to the West Indies.

Fig 3. *Bust of Sir John Tobin*, British School, marble, about 1820 (National Museums, Liverpool, Walker Art Gallery)

After abolition they survived as merchants by moving into the African palm oil trade, largely thanks to trading links already established with an infamous local chieftain and slave trader known as Duke Ephraim. John Tobin later diversified successfully into shipbuilding, dock development, passenger liners and railways on a considerable scale. He was active in the Liverpool Town Council where he was the most important of the strongly Anglican and Tory African merchants which dominated its affairs. He was elected mayor in 1819, paying, it was said, six shillings to each of the 3,000 electors in 'one of the most barefaced acts of bribery that ever disgraced even the electioneering annals of this venal rotten borough'. In 1828 he persuaded the council to buy land in Wallasey, just acquired by him, for building docks. From this transaction he apparently made a profit of over £60,000 in only four months. An inquiry suggested corruption but nothing was done. He did not retire from business until the early 1840s.[16]

Strong differences in religion, politics and ethical standards between Tobin and Roscoe need not have precluded artistic interchange and personal friendship, but the slavery issue was more fundamental. Roscoe and his friends believed that Tobin and the other Liverpool African traders, who controlled about four-fifths of the British slave trade, were simply engaged in kidnap and murder on a huge scale for enormous profits. James Currie, one of Roscoe's circle, wrote: 'The general discussion of the slavery of negroes has produced much unhappiness in Liverpool – men are awaking to their situation and the struggle between interest and humanity has made great havoc in the happiness of many families'.[17] A large, substantially working-class parliamentary and town council electorate, often violent and always highly partisan, further polarized and exacerbated these issues.

Perhaps it was because enthusiasm for art and culture was rarely to be found among Tobin's friends and associates that neither the compiler of his obituaries in 1851,[18] nor the author of the family history in 1940,[19] nor the writer of his life in the *Oxford Dictionary of National Biography* in 2004[20] even knew that Tobin was a collector at all. Roscoe's collection of books and works of art was an essential part of his public and private life and identity, but for Tobin these were a thing apart. Like some other early nineteenth-century Liverpool merchants Tobin acquired in middle age a group of old master paintings with a few British late eighteenth-century works. He was certainly buying seventeenth-century landscapes and one by Joseph Wright of Derby at the Liverpool sale of the well-known Ashton-under-Lyme collector Francis Dukinfield Astley in 1810.[21] Wright of Derby was popular in Liverpool through his personal connections with many Liverpool merchants whose portraits he painted there between 1768 and 1771. In 1823 Tobin lent eleven old master paintings to an exhibition at the Liverpool Royal Institution. His collection was sold in 1860 and by then it contained for the most part seventeenth- and eighteenth-century Italian and Netherlandish – and a few British – landscapes, views and genre paintings. It is very difficult to assess the quality of these early nineteenth-century collections because so few of the paintings can now be identified with any certainty. However, Tobin's *View of Eton College* by Canaletto is almost certainly the painting of that description now in the National Gallery – and it is of high quality.[22]

Good paintings, like good furniture, could easily impress a Liverpool merchant's visitors, friends and business associates. However, medieval miniatures are not suitable for ostentation and display, but can only serve for private admiration among specialist collectors or for personal contemplation – or even devotion. Tobin's motives in this area remain entirely unknown, but he certainly acquired between about 1823 and 1835 perhaps the most important small group of late medieval illuminated manuscripts ever assembled by a private individual. The most important was probably the Bedford Hours. This book of hours commemorated the dynastic marriage between the duke of Bedford, brother of Henry V and Regent of France after the king's death in 1422, and Anne of Burgundy, sister of Philip, duke of Burgundy who was England's most notable ally in the conquest of France. The Bedfords presented the book to the young Henry VI in 1430. Thus it was an icon of a very glorious phase of English history and appealed to British early nineteenth-century nationalism, especially perhaps to a veteran of the Napoleonic wars such as Tobin. Both Bedford himself, who commissioned the book, and Anne's family were ardent bibliophiles. It was made by an anonymous French artist known as the Master of the duke of Bedford between 1423 and 1430 and has his usual sense for soft and sensitive colour harmonies. Each page has a principal scene surrounded by marginal roundels showing related figures or events set in a richly decorated and very inventive background (Fig. 4). The exceptionally varied subject matter, the imaginative profusion of incident and image, the great scope of the iconographic programme and the sharply realistic portraits of the duke and duchess, probably taken from the life (Fig. 5) make it one of the most significant manuscripts of its period.[23] Second only to it is the Isabella Breviary presented around 1497 to Queen Isabella of Castile, the first Spanish ruler to be seriously interested in Flemish art. A breviary contains all the text required for the recitation of the eight services that together make up the usual daily

Fig 4. *The Visitation with Scenes from the Life of St John the Baptist* by the Master of the Duke of Bedford and his studio, vellum, from the *Bedford Hours*, f. 54b, about 1425 (Permission British Library, London Add. MS 18850)

Fig 5. *John, Duke of Bedford at prayer before St George with Scenes from the Martyrdom of the Saint* by the Master of the Duke of Bedford and his studio, vellum, from the *Bedford Hours*, f.256b, about 1425 (Permission British Library, London Add. MS 18850)

routine of the clergy. Thus it offers to the artist a greater range of texts and scenes than the more popular books of hours intended for the laity. This exceptionally lavish breviary, rich in very uncommon subjects, was begun in the 1480s in Bruges or Ghent principally by the Master of the Dresden Prayer Book but four large miniatures are by Gerard David, the last great artist of the Bruges school. Of these the famous *St John on Patmos*, 'conceivably the most beautiful miniature in Flemish illumination' (Fig. 6),[24] has both great poetic refinement and a strong sense of atmosphere and perspective rare in the late fifteenth century.[25] The Hours of Joanna of Castile, Isabella's daughter and wife of Philip the Handsome, son of the Emperor Maximilian of Austria, was commissioned for her between 1496, the date of the marriage, and 1506. Her portrait appears twice and some unusual didactic texts would have been seen as very appropriate for a young wife. It is generally attributed to the Master of the David Scenes in the Grimani Breviary, who was working in Bruges or Ghent. The architectural borders, which suggest a window into an interior, are an unusual feature sometimes used with great imaginative force as part of the narrative in, for example the *Temptation of Adam and Eve* (Fig. 7). The *Speculum Consciencie* (or Mirror of Conscience) (Fig. 8), a framed convex mirror showing a skull placed in the book opposite the *Temptation of Adam and Eve* and close to other moralizing scenes and texts, is a remarkable and very unusual combination of Flemish realism in execution and otherworldly meditation in subject matter.[26] Indeed it is the characteristically Flemish mixture of a rich and searching naturalism with a stiff and solemn gravity which makes this and the Isabella Breviary among the greatest achievements of the period immediately before the arrival of a new Italianate style in the Netherlands – just as the earlier Bedford Hours is a masterpiece of the more courtly International Gothic style.

In 1835 Gustav Waagen, director of the Picture Gallery at the Berlin Museum and then just beginning his great inventory of art in Britain, was better informed about Tobin's manuscripts than Tobin's later biographers, partly thanks to letters of introduction from William Ewart, son of a Liverpool merchant and the future founder of the British public library system. Waagen had just given evidence at a parliamentary select committee in support of Ewart's attack on the Royal Academy, and Ewart owed him a favour.[27] Waagen had a special interest in illuminated manuscripts and his first destination in Liverpool was Oakhill, Tobin's home just outside Liverpool. There, in Waagen's own words and despite his poor English, Tobin's daughter 'received me in a very friendly manner … and

Fig 6. *Saint John on Patmos* probably by Gerard David, vellum, from the
Isabella Breviary, f. 309, about 1490 (Permission British Library,
London Add. MS. 18851)

Fig 7. *Temptation of Adam and Eve with the Expulsion from Paradise* by the Master of the David Scenes in the Grimani Breviary, vellum, from the *Hours of Joanna of Castile*, f. 14v, about 1500 (Permission British Library, London, Add MS. 18852)

Fig 8. *Speculum Consciencie (Mirror of Conscience)* by the Master of the David Scenes in the Grimani Breviary, vellum, from the *Hours of Joanna of Castile*, f. 15, about 1500 (Permission British, Library, London, AddMS. 18852)

here again I found the freedom from constraint which I have before commended in the English ladies, united with much love of art, and a cultivated understanding'. Waagen then described in great detail the Bedford Hours (Figs 4–5). 'The splendour with which it is got up, the richness of the pictorial ornaments, render it one of the most important monuments of this kind, which that age, so fertile in works of art, produced', he wrote and after a long stylistic analysis concluded that it was Flemish in origin and partly by the Van Eyck brothers – and indeed there are some Flemish elements in its style. For him the portrait of the duke, 'entirely in the free, natural manner of Van Eyck' was probably by Jan Van Eyck himself. He then went on to describe the Isabella Breviary, correctly noting that this was the work of more than one artist and that the best, Gerard David, was 'an accomplished artist whose pictures are executed in a very refined taste of the later followers of Van Eyck, in an extremely delicate soft tone … The finest is St John in Patmos.' He praised especially the borders in which 'flowers, insects and fruits were painted with the greatest fidelity on coloured grounds' as 'among the most elegant and finished that I have ever seen, in this taste' (Fig. 6). Waagen then moved on to the Hours of Joanna of Castile. For him this was

> one of the most delicate and elegant remains of the School of Van Eyck. The representations of the Calendar … fill the whole borders, and are very simple and animated. The numerous pictures of Scriptural subjects are most beautifully executed … The little animals, birds, butterflies, three of which adorn the border of each page, are almost superior to all the rest; there is in them as much truth to nature as cheerful humour. (Fig 8).

He then went on to discuss a much less important illuminated manuscript, the Hours of Francis I, made for the king of France between 1515 and 1525.[28] Sadly, however, he did not describe Tobin's four full-page ambitious and dramatic calendar miniatures of the 1540s by Simon Bening, an artist much influenced by David, which well demonstrate the new Flemish feeling for realistic landscape and for atmospheric and spatial perspective of those years (Fig. 9)[29] – perhaps Tobin had not acquired them by 1835. Waagen also recorded the prices Tobin had paid for three of the manuscripts – £1,000 (in fact £1,100) in 1833 for the Bedford Hours 'perhaps the largest sum that was ever paid for a monument of this kind', £160 (in fact £645) in 1832 for the Breviary and £105 in 1833 for the Hours of Joanna of Castile.[30] Tobin paid £164 in 1824 for the Hours of Francis I.

Fig 9. *March* by Simon Bening, vellum, f. 108r, about 1545 (Permission British Library, London, Add MS. 18855)

Waagen was not the first critic to commend these manuscripts. Tobin's principal guide in the acquisition of his manuscripts was almost certainly the *Bibliographical Decameron* published in 1817 by the antiquary T. F. Dibdin. In 1836 Tobin and his family subscribed to three copies of Dibdin's *Reminiscences of a Literary Life*.[31] The *Bibliographical Decameron* was the first serious general survey in English on the history of illuminated manuscripts, although some of its language is extravagant almost to the point of absurdity. Dibdin devoted some fourteen pages to enthusiastic praise for the three of Tobin's manuscripts. For Dibdin the Bedford Hours was a supreme achievement: 'Even so, and after all that has been thought, said and written respecting the Missals in this country, give me the Bedford Volume'. The Isabella Breviary was so remarkable 'in point of variety, richness and number of embellishments I hardly know where or how to class it' while its border decoration was 'finished with a charming precision and in perfect tenderness of colouring'. Dibdin was sufficiently perceptive to reproduce its very fine *St John on Patmos*, 'the choicest illumination in the volume'. For him the miniatures in the Hours of Francis I combined 'the dignity of Poussin with the tenderness of Murillo'. Dibdin also relates that at the Edwards sale of 1815, at which the Bedford Hours were bought by the future duke of Marlborough, John Dent, the owner of the Isabella Breviary, accompanied by the duke of Gloucester, brought the Breviary into the sale room in order to compare it with the Bedford Hours, evidently believing it to be the only manuscript then in England able to compete in quality with the Bedford Hours.[32] Tobin was not present, but he would certainly have read about the incident in Dibdin's book, and it is a remarkable coincidence that his two most important manuscripts lay briefly side by side in R. H. Evans's sale rooms.

Tobin was an extremely active businessman in Liverpool at least until the early 1840s and, before the coming of the railways, cannot have easily followed the London book auctions even if he had the knowledge to do so. Most of the nineteenth-century northern merchants and manufacturers who acquired large art collections relied on dealers. In Manchester and Liverpool Thomas Agnew and Son advised them on paintings and continued to do so even after the firm moved to London in the 1860s. If they needed guidance in the purchase of paintings, they required it all the more with the more specialized and technical expertise involved in the assessment of medieval illuminated manuscripts. Frederic Madden, keeper of the Department of Manuscripts at the British Museum, visited Tobin only a few days before Waagen and described Tobin as 'not a man of polish or education – but a most generous open-hearted liberal-minded person'.[33] Tobin depended on the book dealer John Cochran. On 6 April 1832 the architect and collector John Soane bought the Isabella Breviary at the London auction of Philip Hurd's manuscripts for £520 through his dealer Thomas Boone.[34] On 12 April Cochran wrote to Soane:

> Permit me respectfully to trouble you with a few lines relative to Mr Hurd's Breviary now in your possession. I had an unlimited commission to buy it at the sale, but my customer, never having seen the volume, and leaving the whole affair in my hands, I went, as you know, as far as £515 for it; - above £100 more than I had intended; and was then satisfied to lose it. Mr Boone called at my house on Saturday last, and stated that you were dissatisfied with your purchase, and that, if my customer would have it, it was at his disposal ... I wrote by Saturday's post, strongly recommending the Breviary to my customer and urging him to purchase it.

Cochran's customer was Tobin, who immediately agreed to buy the Breviary from Soane through Cochran, and Soane after some hesitation relinquished it to Tobin for the cost to him plus an extra £125 making a total of £645.[35] The extra £125 scarcely seems gentlemanly, but Soane probably did not regard Tobin, the sharp Liverpool entrepreneur and former slave trader, as a gentleman, even if he was, by then, Sir John Tobin. Only about a year later Soane and Tobin fought again in Evans's sale room over a manuscript, the Bedford Hours, but on this occasion Tobin was successful. Tobin clearly had immense confidence in Cochran's judgment on illuminated manuscripts.

Little is known about Cochran.[36] As a junior partner in Ogles, Duncan and Cochran and in Rivington and Cochran he established and managed antiquarian bookshops in Holborn and at 148 The Strand between 1814 and 1826.[37] In 1824 Rivington and Cochran at The Strand published a huge catalogue of over 17,000 books; they were almost entirely printed books but included seven 'missals', some with illuminated miniatures and initial letters.[38] The partnership with the Rivington family, a well-known firm of London booksellers and publishers, ended due to heavy losses attributed to Cochran's poor commercial judgment.[39] Cochran then set up his own bookshop at 108 The Strand, now specializing in manuscripts rather than in valuable printed books, and he issued his own catalogues of manuscripts for sale in 1826, 1829 and 1837.[40] Although Cochran's preference seems to have been for post-medieval political and religious history, these catalogues, especially the last two, contained considerable numbers of medieval illuminated books – principally missals, breviaries, books of hours, bibles, psalters and theological works of the fourteenth, fifteenth and sixteenth centuries but a few dating back, according to Cochran, to the tenth century. In his 1829 catalogue he apologized for the length of the explanatory notes which he wrote for many of his manuscripts and which were then unusual in booksellers' catalogues. These notes generally seem scholarly and provide evidence that Cochran was more than a mere bookseller – although certainly not a Catholic since in 1837, in connection with a twelfth-century penitential, he used his notes to denounce 'the abominations of the confessional'.[41] In 1829 and 1831 he was acting on behalf of the great collector of books and manuscripts, Sir Thomas Phillipps, and by 1831 Phillipps owed Cochran over £5,500.[42]

In 1838 Tobin gave all his manuscripts to his only son, an Anglican priest whose Greek Revival church, built for him by 1832–33 by subscribers near his father's house in Liscard, does not suggest much interest on his part in medieval manuscripts. On Tobin's death in 1851 Boone hurried north and purchased all his manuscripts for about £1,500. Boone offered them to the British Museum for £3,000. Madden was worried by the price and by the indifference to manuscripts often displayed by the Museum Trustees, but on this occasion he recorded that 'to my great surprise they were all unanimous that they [Tobin's manuscripts] were at all events to be secured for the Museum'. The Trustees at the meeting included the great medievalist Henry Hallam as well as two other historians Lord Macaulay and Lord Mahon (later Stanhope).[43]

Of the three collectors Charles Blundell is much the most mysterious figure. The most useful biographical source for him is the trial at which his family attempted, after his death, to prove him both reclusive and insane.[44] He was the only son of the great collector Henry Blundell of Ince Blundell, about seven miles north of Liverpool. Like many of the other major landowners of south-west Lancashire, the family had always been Catholic but Henry Blundell in particular seems to have moved easily in both Catholic and non-Catholic circles. He was the most important patron and benefactor of the artists' societies formed in Liverpool in the late eighteenth century but he was also a trustee of the Catholic church in Liverpool and both his daughters married Catholics.[45] Charles Blundell was educated in the Catholic Academy at Liège between 1775 and 1781 just as his father had studied with the Jesuits at St Omer and Douai.[46] However, he did not fit as easily as his father into contemporary landed society. His father complained in 1799: 'The rambling life he has led for many years, living mostly at inns, not visiting families, without any employ, pursuit or taste for social amusements, usual at this time of life, renders him, I think, not so happy as I could wish him' but added that he would continue his son's allowance on a generous scale.[47] As a result of this bohemian lifestyle Charles Blundell never married, causing immense inheritance problems on his death. While the father concentrated on the extrovert arts of sculpture and painting, the son preferred the more private delights of drawings, prints and manuscripts. The father built a reduced replica of the Pantheon together with a garden temple for the display of his sculpture collections at Ince Blundell to friends and tourists, but the son, although at first welcoming to visitors, seems later to have refused access even to specialists.[48] Charles Blundell was a friend of the Liverpool merchant John Gladstone and left him two paintings by Richard Wilson in his will.[49] Gladstone's son, later the great prime minister, rode over to Ince Blundell to see Blundell in 1825 while on holiday from Eton.[50] Otherwise, however, Blundell seems to have had few friends and probably only knew Gladstone because their estates adjoined each other north of Liverpool. He was, however, a close friend of the eminent scientist T. S. Traill who, with Roscoe, played a considerable part in the foundation of the Liverpool Royal Institution.

Possibly Charles Blundell took his Catholic faith more seriously than did his father, reflecting the Catholic Revival of the early nineteenth century, which with Pugin in the 1830s had such a deep impact on English attitudes to the middle ages. He was 'intimately acquainted with the literature of the middle ages' and frequently conversed about early printed books and about paintings and sculpture 'matters with which he seemed perfectly familiar'. His library 'principally consisted of rare books and books on the arts and classics'. He had travelled in France and Italy as a young man. He had apparently added many sculptures to his father's collection.[51] Only about seven miles north of Ince Blundell another rather eccentric and reclusive Catholic landowner, Charles Scarisbrick, was assembling a large collection of late medieval sculpture and paintings in the 1820s and 1830s.[52] Pugin incorporated many of them into the new Scarisbrick Hall of 1836–45, his first and most important country house closely reflecting his idea of the Catholic middle ages.[53] Henry Blundell knew Scarisbrick's family[54] – the two families were by far the richest Catholic landowners in south-west Lancashire and had inter-married in the seventeenth century[55] – and his son certainly corresponded with Charles Scarisbrick.[56] Charles Blundell left well over £200,000 towards the costs of building and maintaining new Catholic churches in Britain, 'one of the largest sums of any in modern times' for this purpose.[57] In gratitude for money which helped to pay for his rigorously Gothic churches, Pugin included Blundell's arms in one of the windows of his Bishop's House in Birmingham of 1840.[58] In another clause of his will, also fiercely challenged by his immediate family and causing much litigation, Blundell bequeathed most of the rest of his estate to a distant relative Thomas Weld (later Weld-Blundell), a 'strong Catholic [who] lives almost exclusively among Catholics'.[59] The Welds were certainly fervent Catholics; Thomas's grandfather moved the Catholic Academy at Liège to Stonyhurst in 1794 and turned it into a Jesuit public school for Catholic boys, and his uncle was the first British cardinal since the seventeenth century. In France the Catholic Revival had a considerable influence on the growth of interest in the middle ages, the Age of Faith. British Catholicism was much less significant in this respect with the notable exception of Pugin – and perhaps, on a very modest scale, of Charles Blundell.

Henry Blundell's religion disqualified him from public office but provided him both with cosmopolitan contacts and with that easy access to the papal authorities that was so invaluable in securing the export of antiquities from Rome. Between about 1777 and his death in 1810 he acquired the largest, though not the best, collection of classical sculpture in England, now owned by National Museums Liverpool. He relied heavily on the advice of another Lancashire Catholic collector, Charles Townley, whose smaller but more judicious collection of ancient sculpture is now in the British Museum.[60] Blundell also acquired some 200 paintings. Following the taste of most Liverpool merchants of the period he concentrated on Italian and Netherlandish seventeenth- and early eighteenth-century artists with a few versions or copies of work by the great Italian masters of the High Renaissance and some very interesting paintings by late eighteenth-century British artists including Richard Wilson and George Stubbs.[61] The catalogue of his collection, which he published in 1803 at the age of 79, includes only three pictures which he described as pre-High Renaissance or late medieval, a *Holy Family* attributed to Pinturicchio, a *Virgin and Child* apparently in the style of Durer and an early sixteenth-century Flemish *Virgin and Child with St Louis and St Margaret* which he described as 'an admirable picture for the age'.[62] This attitude to late medieval art is very similar to that of Roscoe who may have been advising Blundell on his purchases at this time or rather later.[63] In 1850 Waagen visited Ince Blundell – having perhaps been deterred from seeing the collection on his earlier visit to Liverpool in 1835 by Charles Blundell's anti-social tendencies. He noted that 'by far the most important part of the collection consists' in 'a number of pictures of the early Netherlandish and German schools, as well as some of the early Italian school'.[64] The surviving documentation on the growth of the collection is not extensive – outside Blundell's published 1803 catalogue – but it seems very probable that most of these 'early' German and Netherlandish paintings dating from around the years 1450 to 1530 were bought by Charles Blundell between 1810, when he inherited Ince Blundell, and his death in 1837.[65] Two certain exceptions to this rule are the *Virgin and Child with St Louis and St Margaret* and the *Allegory of the Old and New Testaments* by Hans Holbein the younger of about 1532.[66] The former must have been acquired in about 1802 or 1803, since, unlike the others, it does appear in the 1803 catalogue but is listed there as bought 'since this catalogue was written'.[67] The latter was bought between 1803 and 1807 as it is listed in 1807 at Ince Blundell by John Britton, but Britton and presumably Blundell attributed it to Raphael.[68] However, although father and son were never on very good terms with each other, these acquisitions may still have reflected Charles Blundell's taste rather than his father's and it is even possible that Charles, who had corresponded with the Regius Professor of Divinity at Oxford on predestination, free will, foreknowledge and good works, understood the doctrine of redemption represented in Holbein's painting.[69] The *Virgin and Child with Angels* by Joos van Cleve of about 1520 was certainly bought by Charles Blundell between 1835 and 1837.[70] The *Virgin and Child*, formerly attributed to Jan van Eyck[71] and now thought to be the work of an immediate follower, is by far the most famous example of this group of German and Netherlandish paintings, which would certainly have been regarded as 'primitive' in the early nineteenth century.

However, in the context of illuminated manuscripts the most interesting of these paintings is the wing of a small German devotional altarpiece of about 1475, *The Meeting of the Three Kings with David and Isaiah* by the Master of the Saint Bartholomew Altarpiece (Fig. 10).[72] The Kings appear in the background on the summits of three mountains watching for the star that will lead them to Jesus, and then again in the foreground on their way to Bethlehem. David and Isaiah hold banners displaying Old Testament texts foretelling the Adoration of the Kings. Heralds with trumpets proclaim the great event. On the back of the panel is *The Assumption of the Virgin*. She is carried up to God the Father by musical angels, and yellow, pink and blue circles, ending in clouds, radiate from her. The small scale, minute detail, imaginative conception, fantastic accessories, ornate costumes, theatrical gestures, intense colours and

Fig 10. *The Meeting of the Three Kings with David and Isaiah* by the Master of the Saint Bartholomew Altarpiece, panel, about 1475 (J. Paul Getty Museum, Los Angeles)

expression all suggest late Gothic illumination and indeed the artist was well known as a manuscript illuminator as well as a painter.

An inventory of Charles Blundell's library was drawn up in 1841 in connection with the litigation over his will and Blundell was certainly an enthusiastic book collector.[73] Unfortunately the inventory was evidently the work of an ordinary provincial bookseller and its mention of at least one illuminated 'Missal' and one illuminated Bible does not contribute greatly to any assessment of Blundell's interest in illuminated manuscripts.[74] However, quite recently a superb book of hours, the so-called Ince-Blundell Hours, formerly owned by Thomas Weld-Blundell, to whom Charles Blundell bequeathed his entire collection, was discovered. It was almost certainly originally acquired by Charles Blundell.[75] It was made in Bruges or Ghent around 1510 by the Master of the David Scenes in the Grimani Breviary and thus fits well with the Netherlandish and German paintings of that period apparently acquired by Blundell. It contains the artist's longest series of half-length miniatures, many remarkable for their powerful expression of emotion and for their interest in human anatomy. The result is a strong sense of artistic unity within the book.[76] It is possible that the Catholic Weld family was the source of his enthusiasm for illuminated manuscripts, although Blundell does not seem to have known the family to whom he bequeathed his estates very well. The Welds had inherited a number of notable illuminated manuscripts including the famous *Luttrell Psalter*, which was widely reproduced and discussed from 1794 onwards.[77] Blundell may have also acquired his taste for illuminated manuscripts – and indeed for medieval art generally – from Roscoe, the Unitarian, from whom he bought a large number of old master drawings and prints, some of exceptional importance.[78] Blundell's father had indeed co-operated with Roscoe in the establishment of artists' societies in Liverpool, but Charles Blundell's behaviour towards him was worse than merely uncouth. On 22 July 1816 Roscoe's printer and close friend, John McCreery, spoke to Joseph Farington of the

> stoppage of Mr Roscoe's banking house, and of the great liberality of his creditors, excepting two persons viz. Mr Blundell of Ince and his old master in his profession, a solicitor, both of whom arrested him. His debt to the former, who possesses about £6,000 per annum is £8,000; he behaved brutally.[79]

On 18 June 1816 Roscoe had written to McCreery thanking him for trying to persuade Blundell to follow the rest of Roscoe's creditors in giving Roscoe time to repay his debts.[80] However, even if Blundell's relations with Roscoe himself were not good, he did know at least two members of Roscoe's literary circle, William Shepherd and the manuscripts collector J. B. Yates, with whom he used to discuss early printed books.[81] Books of hours, representing lay piety by means of their prayers and devotions appropriate to the eight canonical hours of the day, must have seemed more essentially and specifically Catholic than altarpieces and other medieval paintings to early nineteenth-century Protestant and Catholic collectors, who invariably described them as Missals – even if originally both books and paintings shared a common devotional purpose. The Bradyll family, also Lancashire Catholic landowners, owned in the later sixteenth and seventeenth centuries a book of hours. They seem to have regarded it as 'an interesting aesthetic object, an antiquarian curio, a prized family heirloom, an aid to private prayer and meditation and – perhaps most importantly – as a ... family icon of their persecuted Catholic faith'.[82] Perhaps over one hundred and fifty years later Charles Blundell's attitude was not dissimilar.

In 1856 William James and George Ashdown Audsley came to Liverpool and soon established a considerable reputation there as rather eclectic designers with a strong emphasis on oriental models. But their early interests were medieval and in 1860 Audsley lectured to the Liverpool Architectural and Archaeological Society on 'The Rise and Progress of the Art of Illuminating during the Middle Ages, and its Useful Application in the Nineteenth Century to Architecture and Art Manufactures'.[83] The brothers were leading members of the progressive Liverpool Art Club, which held in 1876 an 'Exhibition of Illuminated Manuscripts' with 177 items drawn almost entirely from Lancashire collections.[84] Audsley himself lent five manuscripts, the young Henry Yates Thompson lent nine and Stonyhurst College, maintaining the Lancashire Catholic tradition, lent fifteen. By then, however, the Gothic Revival was dominant in British architecture and design; its leading supporters, John Ruskin and William Morris, were forming important collections of illuminated manuscripts. Quite exceptionally the Bedford Hours had been partially reproduced in a detailed monograph by an eminent antiquary as early as 1794.[85] In the mid-nineteenth century the advent of new processes, especially chromolithography, permitted Henry Shaw, Noel Humphreys, Owen Jones and others to publish many well-illustrated and more popular books on illuminated manuscripts. The pioneering phase of the collecting of illuminated manuscripts was over.

Notes

1 A. N. L. Munby, *Connoisseurs and Medieval Miniatures* (Oxford, 1972), pp. 14–56.
2 G. Reitlinger, *The Economics of Taste*, 3 vols (London, 1961–70), II, pp. 71–73, 79.
3 W. Roscoe, *The Life of Lorenzo de' Medici* (London, 1836), p. lxxix.
4 W. Roscoe, *On the Origin and Vicissitudes of Literature, Science and Art and their Influence on the present State of Society: A discourse delivered at the Opening of the Liverpool Royal Institution* (Liverpool, 1817), p. 66.
5 Roscoe, *On the Origin and Vicissitudes*, p. 38.
6 *Catalogue of the ... Collection of Drawings and Pictures, the Property of William Roscoe which will be sold... by Mr Winstanley in his rooms, Liverpool, 23 September and five following days* (Liverpool, 1816).
7 J. E. Graham, 'The Cataloguing of the Holkham Manuscripts', *Transactions of the Cambridge Bibliographical Society*, 4 (1968), p. 137.
8 Graham, 'Cataloguing of the Holkham Manuscripts', pp. 125–54.
9 Liverpool Record Office, Roscoe Papers 5551.

10 Now in the Walker Art Gallery, Liverpool: see E. Morris and M. Hopkinson, *Foreign Catalogue, Walker Art Gallery, Liverpool* (Liverpool, 1977), *Text*, pp. 113–15, *Plates*, p. 140.

11 Now in the Walker Art Gallery, Liverpool; see Morris and Hopkinson, *Foreign Catalogue, Text*, pp. 275–76, *Plates*, p. 396.

12 Munby, *Connoisseurs and Medieval Miniatures*, pp. 62–71.

13 *Catalogue of the Library of William Roscoe which will be sold by Mr. Winstanley in his rooms Liverpool, 19 August to 3 September* (Liverpool, 1816), lot 1810. The Bible is now in the British Library, Add. MS. 47672.

14 *Liverpool Mercury*, 15 December 1855 quoted in S. A. Thompson Yates, *Memoirs of the Family of the Reverend John Yates* (Liverpool, 1890), pp. 11–12.

15 Peter Kidd kindly drew my attention to Yates Thompson.

16 R. C. Reid, *Annals of the Tobin Family of Liverpool and the Isle of Man* (1940), pp. 20–26, typescript, Liverpool Record Office; A. J. H. Latham, 'A Trading Alliance: Sir John Tobin and Duke Ephraim, *History Today*, 24 (1974), pp. 862–65; M. Lynn, 'Trade and Politics in Nineteenth-Century Liverpool: The Tobin and Horsfall Families and Liverpool's African Trade', *Transactions of the Historic Society of Lancashire and Cheshire*, 142 (1992), pp. 99–112.

17 R. D. Thornton, *James Currie, The Entire Stranger and Robert Burns* (Edinburgh, 1963), p. 198.

18 *Liverpool Mercury*, 4 March 1851; *Gentleman's Magazine*, April 1851, p. 434.

19 Reid, *Annals of the Tobin Family*, pp. 20–26.

20 *Oxford Dictionary of National Biography*, ed. H. C. G. Matthew and B. Harrison (Oxford, 2004), 54, pp. 862–63.

21 Winstanley, Liverpool Sale 2-3 August 1810, lots 74, 79 and 81. For Astley see C. P. Darcy, *The Encouragement of the Fine Arts in Lancashire* (Manchester, 1976), p. 133.

22 M. Levey, *National Gallery Catalogues: The Seventeenth and Eighteenth Century Italian Schools* (London, 1971), p. 28.

23 J. Backhouse, *The Bedford Hours* (London, 1990). Now in the British Library Add. MS. 18850.

24 Some scholars doubt the attribution of this miniature to David.

25 J. Backhouse, *The Isabella Breviary* (London, 1993); T. Kren, ed., *Renaissance Painting in Manuscripts: Treasures from the British Library* (New York, 1983), pp. 40–48; T. Kren and S. McKendrick, eds, *Illuminating the Renaissance* (J. Paul Getty Museum, Los Angeles, 2003), pp. 347–51. The Breviary is now in the British Library Add. MS. 18851.

26 Kren and McKendrick, *Illuminating the Renaissance*, pp. 385–86; Kren, *Renaissance Painting*, pp. 59–62. Now in the British Library Add. MS. 18852.

27 W. A. Munford, *William Ewart* (London, 1960), p. 80.

28 Now in the British Library Add. MS. 18853.

29 Kren and McKendrick, *Illuminating the Renaissance*, pp. 483–84; Kren, *Renaissance Painting*, pp. 79–85. Now in the British Library Add. MS. 18855.

30 G. Waagen, *Works of Art and Artists in England*, 3 vols (London, 1838), III, pp. 170–80; Munby, *Connoisseurs and Medieval Miniatures*, pp. 9–12.

31 T. F. Dibdin, *Reminiscences of a Literary Life* (London, 1836), p. xxxi.

32 T. F. Dibdin, *The Bibliographical Decameron or Ten Days Pleasant Discourse upon Illuminated Manuscripts and Subjects connected with Early Engraving and Bibliography*, 3 vols (London, 1817), I, pp. 177–80, 136–39, 163–68, III, p. 126.

33 Munby, *Connoisseurs and Medieval Miniatures*, p. 10.

34 Philip Hurd Sale, R. H. Evans, London, 29 March–6 April 1832, lot 1434.

35 Unpublished letters in Sir John Soane's Museum, Archive, Spiers Box, Books, MSS etc., Miscellaneous (10); I am most grateful to Stephen Massil for locating these letters

and sending photocopies of them to me; Backhouse, *Isabella Breviary*, p. 5 mentions the extra £125 paid apparently to Soane but Madden refers to an extra £105 'commission' paid to Boone (Journal of Frederic Madden, for 12 January 1852, photocopies in the British Library Department of Manuscripts, MSS Bodleian Library, Eng.hist.c.165). Tobin cannot surely have paid both amounts and it is unclear whether Soane or his agent received the money.

36 William Baker, who has worked extensively on John George Cochrane the first librarian of the London Library, thought that he and John Cochran might be the same man. Inez Lynn at the London Library tells me that their surviving records provide no proof or disproof of this theory, which seems, however, unlikely.

37 J. Cochran, *A Catalogue of Manuscripts in Different Languages* (108 The Strand, London, September 1826), pp. 2–3. However, the *Oxford Dictionary of National Biography* (2004), 47, p. 59 (under Rivington Family) gives the dates of the partnership with the Rivington family as 1820–27.

38 Rivington and Cochran, *A Catalogue of Books in Various Languages* (148 The Strand, London); the 'missals' are on p. 100, nos 1758–1764.

39 *Oxford Dictionary of National Biography*, 47, p. 59.

40 J. Cochran, *Catalogue of Manuscripts*; *A Catalogue of Manuscripts in Different Languages* (108 The Strand, London, June 1829), *A Second Catalogue of Manuscripts in Different Languages* (108 The Strand, London, 1837).

41 Cochran, *Catalogue of Manuscripts*, 1829, pp. v–vi.

42 A. N. L. Munby, *Phillipps Studies: The Formation of the Phillipps Library*, 5 vols (Cambridge, 1951–60), III, pp. 48–59.

43 Munby, *Connoisseurs and Medieval Miniatures*, pp. 12–13.

44 T.E. Gilson, *Lydiate Hall and its Associations* (London, 1876), pp. 134–44; *The Times*, 2–4 September 1840; *Liverpool Mercury*, 4 September 1840.

45 T. Burke, *Catholic History of Liverpool* (Liverpool, 1910), pp. 17–21.

46 R. Trappes-Lomax, 'Boys at Liège Academy 1773–91', *Catholic Record Society*, 13 (1913), p. 203. Pierce Walsh studied with Charles Blundell at Liège, and he may have been related to Thomas Walsh, later Catholic bishop and Vicar Apostolic of the Midland District, one of the two bishops to whom Blundell bequeathed his enormous legacy for the Catholic Church in England.

47 Letter to Charles Townley of 29 January 1799 now in the Townley Papers, British Museum, Department of Greek and Roman Antiquities quoted in X. Brooke, *Mantegna to Rubens: The Weld-Blundell Drawings Collection* (London, 1998), pp. 7, 146. However, the size of Charles Blundell's allowance caused ill feeling between him and his father.

48 S. H. Spiker, *Travels through England, Wales and Scotland in 1816* (London, 1820), pp. 313–14; Jones and Company, *Great Britain Illustrated: Views of the Seats, Mansions, Castles etc of the Noblemen and Gentlemen etc* (London, 1829), I; E. Southworth, 'The Ince Blundell Collection', *Journal of the History of Collections*, 3 (1991), p. 222; in its brief obituary of Blundell the *Liverpool Mercury*, 17 November 1837, commented that the collection was 'little visited', that Blundell himself was highly eccentric and that at his death £22,800 was found in cash in Ince Blundell Hall. I am indebted to John Edmondson for the first two references.

49 S. G. Checkland, *The Gladstones: a Family Biography 1764–1851* (Cambridge, 1971), pp. 92, 328; W. G. Constable, *Richard Wilson* (London, 1953), p. 164. Over 300 letters from Blundell to Gladstone survive (Glynne–Gladstone MSS, inv. 82–86, Flintshire Record Office). They date from November 1817 to June 1835 and relate to political, social, financial and local matters rather than to art. Xanthe Brooke kindly drew my attention to them.

50 *The Gladstone Diaries*, ed. M. R. D. Foot and H. C. G. Matthew, 14 vols (Oxford,

1968–94), I, p. 3.

51 *The Times* 2–4 September 1840.

52 Scarisbrick's early life is very obscure but he inherited the family's Wrightington estate in 1825 so he was certainly able to collect from that early date. The Scarisbrick Hall Sale, J. Hatch, Sons and Fielding, Southport, 16 July–27 July 1923, included as lot 2430: 'An early 16th. Century Missal of Dutch Work with numerous beautifully illuminated illustrations... bearing the Scarisbrickcrest'.

53 A. Wedgwood, 'Domestic Architecture', in *Pugin: A Gothic Passion*, ed. P. Atterbury and C. Wainwright (New Haven, 1994), p. 46.

54 Letters from Henry Blundell to Charles Townley, Townley Papers.

55 James Scarisbrick married Frances, daughter of Robert Blundell of Ince Blundell, in 1659.

56 *Liverpool Mercury*, 4 September 1840.

57 B. Walsh, *The Sequel to Catholic Emancipation*, 2 vols (London, 1915), I, pp. 187–91, 267–74; *Gladstone Diaries*, II, p. 564; *The Times*, 16 May 1838. Blundell's Catholic relatives challenged the bequest, relying on legal technicalities, and reduced the amount by over half to their own advantage. Pugin held that they had 'plundered the church': *The Collected Letters of A. W. N. Pugin*, ed. M. Belcher, 2 vols (Oxford, 2001–), I, p. 253. Fundraising for the huge and magnificent Gothic Revival Catholic Church of Our Lady and the English Martyrs in Cambridge began in 1841 with a 'substantial payment from the Blundell legacy': P. Wilkins, *The Church of Our Lady and the English Martyrs, Cambridge* (Cambridge, 1995), p. 37.

58 *Collected Letters of A. W. N. Pugin*, I, p. 172. The Bishop's House was demolished in the early 1960s.

59 *The Diaries of Edward Henry Stanley, fifteenth Earl of Derby, between 1869 and 1878*, ed. J. Vincent, Camden Fifth Series, 4 (1994), p. 158. The editor suggested that Derby was describing Nicholas Blundell of Crosby but Derby must have been referring to Thomas Weld-Blundell.

60 G. Vaughan, 'Henry Blundell's Sculpture Collection at Ince Hall', in *Patronage and Practice: Sculpture on Merseyside* (Tate Gallery, London, 1989), pp. 13–21.

61 Some of these paintings remain in the family collection; others have been dispersed by private treaty and in a series of sales at Christie's mostly in 1980–81 and in 1992. Most of them are listed in Walker Art Gallery, Liverpool, *Pictures from Ince Blundell Hall* (Liverpool, 1960) and in Russell-Cotes Art Gallery and Museum, Bournemouth, *Paintings from Lulworth Castle* (Bournemouth, 1967).

62 [Henry Blundell], *An Account of the Statues, Busts, Bass-Relieves, Cinerary Urns and other ancient Marbles and Paintings at Ince, Collected by H. B.* (Liverpool, 1803), nos 15, 116 and 190, pp. 216, 244 and 263. Only the last can now be identified with any certainty; it is in a private collection, see E. Dhanens, 'Het Raadselachtig van Ince Hall', *Medelingen van de Koninklijke Academie voor Wetenschappen, Letteren en Schone Kunsten van Belgie*, 46 (1985), pp. 26–59, repr. Fig. 3.

63 See John Jacob's introduction to *Pictures from Ince Blundell Hall*, pp. 7–8.

64 G. Waagen, *Treasures of Art in Great Britain*, 3 vols (London, 1854), III, p. 244.

65 Timothy Stevens in *George Bullock: Cabinet Maker*, ed. C. Wainwright and L. Wood (London, 1988), p. 152. Charles Blundell certainly bought paintings and works of art through Bullock and through the Liverpool auctioneer, art dealer and art historian Thomas Winstanley (*Liverpool Mercury*, 4 September 1840). However, Henry Blundell was still buying works of art on a considerable scale in 1806 using an adviser, probably Roscoe, as a result of his blindness and deafness: *The Diary of Joseph Farington*, ed. K. Garlick, A. Macintyre and K. Cave, 16 vols (New Haven, 1978–98), VII, p. 2796. John Jacob and Francis Russell therefore argue that the early paintings were probably acquired between 1803 and 1810 by Henry not by Charles Blundell,

that is 'during the last seven years of his life when he [Henry Blundell] was nearly blind'; see *Pictures from Ince Blundell Hall*, pp. 7–8, Christie's, London Fine Old Master Pictures Sale Catalogue of 19 April 1991 and National Gallery of Art, Washington, *The Treasure Houses of Britain* (New Haven, 1985), p. 366, no. 295.

66 Now in the National Gallery of Scotland, Edinburgh; see F. Grossman, 'A Religious Allegory by Hans Holbein the Younger', *Burlington Magazine*, 103 (1961), pp. 491–94.

67 See Blundell, *An Account*, p. 263.

68 J. Britton, *The Beauties of England and Wales*, 19 vols (London, 1801–16), IX, p. 312; the attribution was still accepted by the *Liverpool Mercury* of 17 November 1837 in its obituary of Charles Blundell, where the painting was clearly regarded as the most important picture in the collection.

69 *The Times*, 2–4 September 1840.

70 Now in the Walker Art Gallery, Liverpool: see E. Morris and M. Evans, *Supplementary Foreign Catalogue, Walker Art Gallery, Liverpool* (Liverpool, 1984), p. 10, repr. p. 74.

71 Now in the National Gallery of Victoria, Melbourne: see L. Baldass, *Jan van Eyck* (London, 1952), pp. 51–52, 277, pl. 104.

72 Now in the J. Paul Getty Museum, Los Angeles: see National Gallery, London, *Late Gothic Art from Cologne* (London, 1977), no 32, pp. 94–95.

73 Four letters to Blundell from Winstanley survive and they show that Winstanley was collecting rare books for him in 1823 (Lancashire Record Office, Preston DDIN 14/57).

74 Lancashire Record Office, box reference DDIN box 3740. John Edmondson kindly gave me a copy of his typescript made from the inventory.

75 See Christie's London Sale 23 November 1998, Valuable Illuminated Manuscripts, Printed Books etc., lot 11. Thomas Weld-Blundell was the second son of Joseph Weld of Lulworth and it is just possible that the book of hours came from the Weld family, who also collected illuminated manuscripts, but this seems very unlikely. The Weld-Blundells were not collectors – apart from their huge inheritance from Charles Blundell.

76 Kren and McKendrick, *Illuminating the Renaissance*, pp. 387–89. The book of hours was then owned by Heribert Tenschert

77 M. Camille, *Mirror in Parchment: the Luttrell Psalter and the Making of Medieval England* (London, 1998), pp. 16–28. The Psalter is now in the British Library (Add. MS. 42130).

78 Brooke, *Mantegna to Rubens*, p. 15.

79 *The Diary of Joseph Farington*, XIV, p. 4877. Published versions of the Diary have 'Creevey' not 'McCreery' but it is clear from the context that Farington meant 'McCreery'. Blundell's income from the Ince Blundell estate was estimated at £9,000 per year in 1840; see *The Times*, 2–4 September 1840.

80 Liverpool Record Office, Roscoe Papers 2525.

81 *Liverpool Mercury*, 4 September 1840.

82 M. G. Brennan, 'The Book of Hours of the Braddyll Family of Whalley Abbey', *Transactions of the Historic Society of Lancashire and Cheshire*, 146 (1997), p. 17.

83 *Proceedings of the Liverpool Architectural and Archaeological Society* (1860–61), pp. 32ff.

84 Joseph Sharples kindly mentioned this exhibition to me. There is a copy of the catalogue in the Liverpool Record Office. For the Club see D. Chun, 'Collecting Collectors: the Liverpool Art Club and its Exhibitions', *Transactions of the Historic Society of Lancashire and Cheshire*, 151 (2002), pp. 127–49.

85 R. Gough, *An Account of a Richly Illuminated Missal executed for the Duke of Bedford* (London, 1794).

Liverpool's Lorenzo de Medici

Arline Wilson

In his final volumes of *Decline and Fall* which appeared in 1788, Gibbon portrayed Italy as a centre of commercial activity that invigorated her cities and endowed them with sufficient material wealth to create an environment where not only business but also 'elegance and genius' could find fertile ground.[1] The Medici, it was suggested, were no longer responsible for the suppression of their country's liberty but, on the contrary, were responsible for its power and prestige. This interpretation of the Medici, according to John Hale, was not lost on some of the readers of Gibbon's work and the historian he particularly singles out as influenced by Gibbon is William Roscoe of Liverpool. Roscoe's stated ambition was to provide a bridge between the 'golden histories of Gibbon and Robertson'.[2] His championing of the Medici came at a time when the middle ages were still being criticized and the 'old prejudices' continued to be put forward in textbooks. In 1795, for example, the Revd John Adam's *View of Universal History* declared that 'till the sixteenth century, Europe exhibited a picture of the most melancholy barbarity'.[3] Roscoe's work was a vital factor in stimulating interest in the last part of the fifteenth century as a whole and in promoting the belief that it was a period of crucial significance. However, equally as important, it can be argued, was the effect of Roscoe's vision of the Medici on his native town.

Born on 8 March 1753, William Roscoe was the only son of a Liverpool innkeeper and market gardener. His formal schooling ending at the age of twelve, Roscoe valued education highly – a trait shared by many of the self–taught. The young William Roscoe was wide-ranging in his search for knowledge, taking lessons in painting and engraving from the workers in a neighbouring china works. His interest in botany began during the three years spent labouring on his father's market garden. Recognizing his son's love of reading, Roscoe senior apprenticed his son to a local book-seller, but the young William apparently found this little to his taste as he remained there only for a month. In 1769 he became an articled clerk of

Mr John Eyes, a local attorney (on whose death he transferred to Peter Ellames). Early mornings found Roscoe and a few like-minded friends, including Francis Holden, a young schoolmaster, and William Clarke, a banker, gathering before work to study literature, the classics and modern languages. It seems likely that it was from this period that the first stirrings of interest in the Italian Renaissance began, helping to mould his belief in the potentialities of the individual and the power of education to produce the complete man – a man of action (or man of business and commerce) who was also the master of all the culture of his age, later epitomized in his study of Lorenzo de Medici.

In 1774 Roscoe was admitted an attorney of the court of King's Bench and began the practice of law, but despite his business concerns he continued with his poetry and artistic interests while devoting the little leisure time remaining to reading historical works. For Roscoe, the more he studied the history of the Italian states, the more the Medici came to symbolize many of his most cherished beliefs and there came a growing conviction that their legacy should become more widely known and recognized. Throughout his life Roscoe remained convinced of the sudden progress of the fine arts 'after the middle ages – that long and feverish sleep of the human intellect', and that 'everything great and excellent in science and in art, revolved round Lorenzo de' Medici during the short but splendid era of his life'.[4] Spurred on by 'the real admiration I have of my hero', Roscoe believed it was his mission to make 'so extraordinary a man more generally known to my countrymen'[5] as 'certain it is that no man was ever more admired and venerated by his contemporaries or has been more defrauded of his just fame by posterity, than Lorenzo de' Medici'.[6] He declared that 'even in a remote part of this remote kingdom, and deprived of the many advantages peculiar to seats of learning, I saw no difficulty in giving a more full, and accurate idea of the subject than could be collected from any performance I had then met with'.[7] For Roscoe, Florence and its ruler came to symbolize the apotheosis of the union between commerce and culture: 'Earnest in the acquisition of wealth, indefatigable in improving their manufactures and extending their commerce, the Florentines seem not, however, to have lost sight of the true dignity of man, or of the proper objects of his regard'.[8] He proclaimed his interest as literary rather than political:

> It appeared to me, that the mere historical events of the fifteenth century, so far as they regarded Italy, could not deeply interest my countrymen in the eighteenth; but I conceived that the progress of

letters and of arts would be attended to with pleasure in every country where they were cultivated and protected.[9]

Roscoe's biography of Lorenzo was clearly a hagiographic work but it also displayed an enormous industry and a most skilful use of sources, despite his reluctance to travel abroad which meant relying on others for primary (none printed) sources. Roscoe did not appear to feel any regret at not visiting the country to which so much of his time was being devoted. As John Hale points out, Roscoe was not alone in feeling that there was no need to physically visit the home of his subject; it was a habit of English historians at least as late as Grote.[10] It was providential for Roscoe that, in 1789, one of his close friends, William Clarke, travelled to Fiesole for health reasons and readily complied with Roscoe's application for help with his research. Access to archives in Florence was granted freely and Clarke was able to consult material in the Riccardi and Laurentian libraries and in the Palazzo Vecchio. Anything he considered might prove helpful was copied or extracted and sent back to Liverpool, and the fact that it was Clarke's hand rather than Roscoe's that selected the material must be deemed to have had an influence on the work.[11]

Roscoe's biography tapped into a willing and ready market of readers and became an immediate success. The reception accorded to the book was helped by the fact that there was a lack of competition in this field of historical study. Existing Italian literature on Lorenzo was based on Valori's brief early life and was sparse. Roscoe felt that Valori, a friend and contemporary of Lorenzo, had failed to explore in sufficient depth the 'strength, extent, and versatility' of the mind and extraordinary talents of his subject.[12] The only books Roscoe had found to be of real value were a Latin life by Fabroni, printed in 1784 (sent to him by William Clarke) and Tenhove's *Memoires Genealogiques de la Maison de Medici*, which only appeared when the first few sheets of *Lorenzo* were already at the printers and in which Lorenzo did not play a major role. On receipt of Fabroni's work, Roscoe deliberated over whether he should give up his own work and concentrate on translating Fabroni's. However, Roscoe decided that the main focus of Fabroni's work was on political matters, whereas he intended to make 'the state and progress of letters and the arts'[13] the central theme of his book. He did, however, acknowledge the help that Fabroni's work gave to him, particularly in directing him to relevant primary sources. The lack of precedent was in Roscoe's favour as his critics had little for comparison and their reviews were overwhelmingly approving. Roscoe sold the copyright for £1200 and by 1799 the book had been translated into French, German and Italian, an edition appearing in the United States in 1803. Lord Lansdowne praised it in the House of Lords, while Fabroni, until now the greatest living authority on the Medici, cancelled the translation of his own work into Italian and arranged instead for the translation of Roscoe's.[14] William Roscoe now stood as a living symbol that humble origins, a remote northern birthplace and the pursuit of a business career were not incompatible with the highest intellectual improvement:

> I can scarcely conceive a greater miracle than Roscoe's history – that a man whose dialect was that of a barbarian and from whom in years of familiar conversation I have never heard an above average observation, whose parents were servants … that such a man should undertake and write the history of the 14th and 15th centuries, and the revival of Greek and Roman learning, that such a history should be to the full, as polished in style as that of Gibbon and much more simple and perspicuous … is really *too*![15]

Roscoe was now acknowledged as one of the greatest scholars of his era: 'within a generation, Roscoe's name was as internationally famous as Gibbons'.[16]

The book also brought some reappraisal of Liverpool's image. One critic marvelled that this 'model of literary endeavour' had been written and printed 'in the remote commercial town of Liverpool, where nothing is heard of but Guinea ships, slaves, blacks and merchandise'.[17] On Roscoe's insistence the book had been published in Liverpool, under his control.[18] He believed that 'the town which cannot produce books finely must remain a mere intellectual suburb of the town that can', and the printing of the book did much to prove 'to the world that London itself could not surpass this town in some kinds of elegant typography'.[19]

On the national scene Roscoe corresponded with, and in many cases became a personal friend of, many of the most notable personalities of his day, including Henry Brougham, Lord Lansdowne, Lord Holland, Sir Joshua Reynolds and Robert Burns. In addition to the renown gained from his historical studies Roscoe became a distinguished botanist, artist and art lover, minor poet, radical politician and MP and opponent of the slave trade. However, he was also a lawyer, a banker and a businessman, and throughout his life was concerned with and committed to the commercial success of Liverpool, sharing his fellow townsmen's keen eye for profit – even in the arts. An observer in 1844 remarked, 'The late Mr Roscoe had also spoken … of the benefits derivable from their pursuit, even in a commercial point of view, and referred to the late Benjamin West, who by his skill, and a few weeks industry, made a piece of canvas, which cost only a few shillings, sell for three thousand guineas'.[20]

Internationally, Roscoe was particularly admired in America. Although his ability to combine the literary and business world bemused the American author Washington Irving – 'To find therefore the elegant historian of the Medici mingling among the busy sons of traffic, at first shocked my poetic ideals'[21] – it was this very ability which appealed so strongly to many of America's aspiring businessmen. The fact that Roscoe was a self-made man made him an attractive role model for American merchants and professionals seeking to establish their civic and social position. For many Bostonians he symbolized 'the intellectual breadth and elegance which might lift a Boston businessman to a loftier social and cultural level'. Numerous Americans visited or corresponded with him and at least two Bostonians named their sons after him.[22]

The acclaim accorded to William Roscoe can scarcely have failed to impress Liverpool's elite. Looking to Renaissance Florence rather than to the metropolis would have been particularly appealing to Liverpool's merchants, who were vaunting their town as Britain's second city and seeking to rival rather than imitate London. For despite Roscoe's denial of any contemporary relevance, it was surely here that Roscoe looked for a role model for his native town. The more Roscoe studied Lorenzo, the more, it can be argued, he identified with his hero. Could he, as the town's cultural leader, emulate what Lorenzo had achieved in Florence over three hundred years earlier,[23] the efficacy of Lorenzo's academies, schools, libraries and associations providing him with the blueprint for the future construction of a similar infrastructure in Liverpool? Certainly the wide and lasting impression made by Roscoe's Italian vision is shown in the way it continued to be evoked after his death by men of all shades of political and religious opinions – in public speeches, lectures and in papers read at Liverpool scientific and literary societies. Although other provincial towns liked to draw comparisons with Italy, only Liverpool was in the fortunate position of having the country's acknowledged leading authority on the Medici as a native. For one historian of Liverpool, Roscoe's interpretation of Lorenzo de Medici was 'undoubtedly a turning point – if not the starting point of Liverpool's cultural life'.[24]

To some extent, however, this judgement is an overstatement and it would be wrong to dismiss Liverpool as a cultural wilderness prior to the publication of Roscoe's book. In common with other eighteenth-century provincial towns, growing civic pride accompanied increased prosperity, resulting in a number of initiatives which in timing and extent locate Liverpool within Borsay's urban renaissance.[25] Mid-century, the choice of John Wood, the architect of Bath, to design a new Exchange and Town Hall reflected a growing awareness of life outside the confines of Liverpool and its immediate environments. The need for a well-built theatre – a prerequisite for every town of any pretension – was met in 1749, with the new Theatre Royal on Williamson Square replacing the original theatre in 1772. Oratorios were performed in St Peter's church from 1766, and in 1786 a Music Hall was erected by public subscription. An increasing desire in Liverpool for the amenities of civilized life was reflected by a growing demand for books, periodicals and newspapers. In 1758 the Liverpool (later Lyceum) Library was founded, which survived until 1941. This was the first of the English gentlemen's subscription libraries, and was widely imitated in other provincial towns. Public lecturing began in the town from 1771 and debates in local coffee houses attracted a good response.

However, efforts to found formal cultural institutions and learned societies were less successful. At the age of nineteen (although it was not published until 1777) Roscoe wrote the poem 'Mount Pleasant', in which, although celebrating the increasing importance and prosperity of his native town, he condemned the slave trade and the Liverpool merchants' seemingly insatiable preoccupation with profit. Roscoe and his friends played an important role in initiating a number of cultural initiatives to ameliorate this situation. In 1773 he was instrumental in the foundation of the Society for the Encouragement of Designing, Drawing, Painting etc. He composed an ode, read before the society, in which he stressed in verse the influence that art could have on society at large – a proposition widely held and propagated throughout the eighteenth century in England as well as on the Continent.[26] Roscoe emphasized his view that the study of great works of art would enrich both the personalities and the lives of the businessmen of Liverpool and he was later to dedicate much time to this cause. The society held an exhibition in 1774 (the first of its kind outside London) at which Roscoe exhibited an Indian ink drawing entitled 'The Mother'. Although the society floundered, Roscoe was subsequently associated with every attempt made in Liverpool to establish an Academy and annual exhibitions. In 1783 he was vice-president and treasurer of the Society for Promoting the Arts in Liverpool which set out to make a deliberate appeal to the commercial men of the town, promising to provide 'a rational and liberal amusement for those few hours of leisure which an active and mercantile place affords its inhabitants'.[27] Exhibitions were held in 1784 and 1787 but in a few years the society was no more, one member claiming that in a mercantile town such as Liverpool it was extremely difficult to find gentlemen who had leisure to conduct such a society. In 1779 the Liverpool Philosophical and Literary Society was inaugurated but proved short-lived and was dissolved in 1783 due to 'the almost total want of zeal and attention in the larger number'.[28] In 1784 a new society was founded which eventually took the name of the Literary Society, but it lasted only until the early 1790s. If Liverpool's merchants opted to join a club in this period, it appears that they preferred it to be of the convivial rather than of the cultural variety.[29] It was the probably the failure of such early cultural initiatives that led one contemporary commentator of the 1790s to declare 'arts and sciences are inimical to the spot, absorbed in the nautical vortex, the only pursuit of the inhabitants is COMMERCE'.[30]

However, in the first decade of the new century the Bostonian Joseph Buckminster reported that:

> The City of Liverpool has now reached that point of wealth, at which societies, which have been hitherto merely mercenary and commercial, begin to turn their attention to learning and the fine arts, that is they perceive that something more than great riches is necessary to make a place worthy of being visited, and interesting enough to be admired.[31]

Although hyperbole played its part in both these judgements, they nevertheless indicate that there was a growing change in outside perceptions of Liverpool's cultural identity and a dawning recognition by Liverpool's merchants of the importance of cultural capital in enhancing their own status and in helping to shape the identity and reputation of their native town.

In part the motivation for redefinition can be explained by Liverpool's exponential rise to economic prominence towards the close of the eighteenth century and the desire of the elite for a matching cultural and social profile, but it can argued that added impetus came from the association of Liverpool's prosperity with the slave trade. Roscoe's book came at a time when the mercantile elite found itself facing not just a threat to its economic base but also to its cultural identity. For most of the century jealous eyes had been turned towards Liverpool's share of the slave trade but the inauguration of the abolitionist movement in 1787 saw public opinion begin to change, and Liverpool found itself subjected to public condemnation in Parliament and branded the metropolis of slavery. Although Liverpool merchants unceasingly fought against abolition, there is evidence to show that there was some disquiet about this stain on Liverpool's character. The *Liverpool Guide*, which just a few years before had had no qualms about justifying the trade, by 1799 was declaring that the trade was mainly conducted by outsiders – an obvious untruth.[32] Late eighteenth-century Liverpool, it could be argued, needed William Roscoe and his interpretation of the Medici more than most of its contemporaries.

The foresight and acumen of Liverpool's merchants had proved a major force in steering the town to economic prominence. When seeking to refashion their cultural profile, it seems likely that these same traits would be brought to bear. Although in many ways an outsider – a radical, a dissenter and an abolitionist – William Roscoe was now nationally and internationally revered as the leading historian of the Medici of his day. With his celebration of the mercantile elite of Renaissance Florence, Roscoe had rewritten history in a way that allowed the merchants to celebrate themselves. They were thus prepared to adopt William Roscoe as their cultural mentor despite their dislike of his views on the slave trade and his radical politics.

The first indication that the merchants were impressed by Roscoe's belief in the efficacy of Lorenzo's libraries and academies came in 1797 with the founding of the Liverpool Athenaeum, which still survives today. Although the Liverpool Library had existed in the town since 1758, it was considered 'not sufficiently select in its choice of books' and to have too many subscribers.[33] Roscoe had bemoaned the lack of a well-stocked library in his historical studies and felt that this must be remedied. The previous lack of response to cultural organizations was now reversed and despite the presence among the founders of men associated with reform and dissent the proposals met with an enthusiastic response. Civic pride overcame any reservations and the Common Council regarded it as a definite ornament to the town. The first president, George Case, was a member of the council and the mayor was elected as an honorary member. Membership of the Athenaeum quickly became an essential emblem of status for Liverpool's mercantile aristocracy.

The founding of the Athenaeum and its Roscoe connection helped to establish Liverpool as a cultural role model. The Boston Athenaeum, founded in 1807, based its laws on the Liverpool institution, with one of its founders claiming the intention 'to make ours as much like that as the different circumstances of the country will admit'.[34] For many Americans it appears that 'London and the Londoners were, in a sense, merely Liverpool and William Roscoe writ large'.[35]

In 1799 Roscoe purchased Allerton Hall, six miles from Liverpool, where he commenced writing his *Life and Pontificate of Leo the Tenth* and settled down to enjoy rural pursuits. His retirement from the business world, however, was to be short-lived. The bank of his old friend William Clarke experienced difficulties and Roscoe's assistance was requested to regularize the bank's legal affairs. With his friend's bankruptcy a real possibility, and conscious of the debt he owed him, Roscoe felt that he could not refuse. His intervention proved successful and the admission of the wealthy merchant Thomas Leyland as a partner in 1802 further secured the bank's position.

In the same year came the successful launch of a long-held ambition of Roscoe's, the opening of a botanic garden in Liverpool. He was again following the Italian example – the first botanic gardens were laid out in Pisa in 1543, Florence and Padua in 1545, and Bologna in 1567. In conjunction with his friends, Roscoe drew up a prospectus in which he made clear the importance he placed on the study of nature in man's artistic and cultural development. Roscoe's commercial instincts were also evident as he was careful in appealing to the business acumen of the town's wealthy townsmen as well as to their cultural aspirations. The garden would be a place of beauty and a source of 'elegant amusement', but it could also, through botanical experiments, contribute to advances in medicine, agriculture and manufacturing. Even the subscription might be recouped by the distribution of rare seeds and surplus plants among the subscribers. This two-pronged appeal, beauty allied to utility, proved successful and the shares in the garden were quickly appropriated, the list including wealthy men of all shades of political and religious opinion. Roscoe claimed that Liverpool's Botanic Garden quickly 'excited a spirit of emulation in some of the principal towns of the kingdom, where proposals have been published on a similar plan'.[36] This did not only apply to Britain – the botanic garden at Philadelphia, for example, was also based on the plan of the Liverpool institution.

In 1805 *The Life and Pontificate of Leo the Tenth* was published. Again Roscoe was reliant on the largesse of friends and acquaintances to inform his researches. A complete stranger, John Johnson, wrote from Rome and offered to collect material for him at the Vatican. Lord Holland paid the chaplain at the British Embassy at Florence to transcribe documents, resulting in two large folios.[37] Roscoe's established reputation ensured the book's success but reviews were less favourable. *The Edinburgh Review*, although praising Roscoe's industry and extensive research, criticized Roscoe's use and organization of his material –'the nice discrimination and selection of incidents, form no part of Mr Roscoe's ideas of historical excellence … the author … has no pretensions to the title of an historian'. However, the reviewer did concede that Roscoe's writings 'impress us with one uniform conviction, that he is a truly amiable and benevolent man', although by implication this was scarcely an adequate substitute for rigorous historical scholarship or likely to gain Roscoe literary immortality.[38] Roscoe was accused of inaccuracies and misrepresentations and of using the work as a vehicle to express his own beliefs and opinions. The *Christian Observer* declared that Roscoe was 'uniformly hostile to Christianity' and charged him with having 'received a retaining fee from the Pope'. The pope's opinion was demonstrated when he placed the Italian translation on his list of banned literature.[39] Roscoe answered his critics in a preface to the second edition but denied being perturbed by them – 'To malicious interpretations, ignorant cavills, and illiberal abuse, I entertain the most perfect indifference'. However, significantly, the hypersensitive Roscoe now turned his attention away from any further historical writings on Italy. Nevertheless, his writings on the Medici informed his thinking on the conjunction of commerce and culture throughout his entire adult life.

The public stature created through his work on the Medici secured Roscoe the opportunity to enter the arena of local and national politics, resulting in his election as MP for Liverpool in 1806. His election was not indicative of a sea change in attitudes among his fellow-townsmen towards his support for the abolition of slavery, his welcoming of the French Revolution and anti-war stance, but rather recognition of his worth to the town. References to the slave trade were minimal throughout the electoral campaign. With Roscoe now 'in the very zenith of his career', his standing in the eyes of his fellow-townsmen was such as to convince his supporters that any political prejudices of the voters would be outweighed by their respect for Roscoe the cultural and philanthropic icon.[40] The Liverpool freemen were urged to

View him as a HUSBAND, a FATHER, a FRIEND, a COUNSELLOR; the Votary of Science, the Promoter of the Arts! … Look at the School for the Blind, the ATHENAEUM, the LYCEUM, the BOTANIC GARDEN … Such is MR. ROSCOE; such FREEMEN OF LIVERPOOL! is the Man now offered to your choice. His Virtues and his Deeds have already immortalized his Name. It will be recorded and revered by your latest Posterity.[41]

Roscoe's success, however, probably owed much to the unpopularity of the other candidates and to extensive bribery. Roscoe is reputed to have spent over £12,000 in the election compared to Tarleton's £4,000 and Gasgoyne's £3,000. While in the Commons, Roscoe spoke and voted against the slave trade, advocated concessions to Catholics and in a debate on the Poor Law raised the question of a national system of education. On the fall of the government over Catholic emancipation in April 1807, Roscoe returned to Liverpool, which was now facing the effects of abolition. He was greeted by a hostile crowd (mainly seamen from the slaving ships) and in the ensuing mêlée one of Roscoe's supporters was killed, and Roscoe declined to stand again. In an address to the people of Liverpool he declared that if the representation of Liverpool could be obtained only by violence and bloodshed he would leave the honour of it to those who chose to contend it. Despite Roscoe's protestations, his supporters submitted his name, but the election resulted in a heavy defeat. This time the image of Roscoe the townsman was superseded by that of Roscoe the politician – one workman was said to have exclaimed, 'He is an ornament to the town, but what have we poor folk to do with ornaments?'[42] As he had retreated from his Italian writings, Roscoe now withdrew from active politics, although this did not signal an end to his interest and he continued his anti-war activities, his support for reform and his interest in promoting the cultural development of his native town.

Although support for the embryonic learned societies of the eighteenth century had been minimal, further confirmation of the Liverpool merchants' recognition of the importance of cultural endeavour in defining their image came in 1812 with the founding of the Liverpool Literary and Philosophical Society. Although Roscoe's name does not appear on the initial membership list (probably due to ill-health), a poem written by a founder member in 1812 indicates that the society considered him its mentor and the formative influence on its intellectual development:

> Long may attention's raptured ear
> Our Roscoe's tuneful numbers hear:
> The beauties of his native stream.
> At once his pleasure and his theme.[43]

The formation of literary and philosophical societies in provincial towns is testament to the recognition by commercial and industrial elites of the importance of culture in legitimizing their status. But whereas other early literary and philosophical societies such as Manchester and Newcastle chose science as their cultural mode of self-expression, the Liverpool society opted to define itself through a general intellectual and literary culture in which the arts and science were to be allotted equal attention. Many of the papers offered under generalized headings were used to stress the importance of both literary and scientific pursuits in enhancing personal worth. Presenters often invoked Roscoe's Florentine analogy and reiterated the motif of the compatibility of culture with commerce.

It was before the audience of the Liverpool Literary and Philosophical Society that the architect Thomas Rickman presented 13 papers. In 1817 the information that Rickman had transmitted to the gentlemen of Liverpool was spread abroad with the publication of his book, *An Attempt to discriminate the Styles of English Architecture, from the Conquest to the Reformation*, which became the cornerstone of the Gothic revival. Among his audience at the society would have been wealthy men on building committees for new public buildings and churches, and although they were not to repudiate the neo-classic form, it has been argued that Rickman's influence ensured that it was Liverpool which witnessed 'the birth ... of the Gothic Revival'.[44] Roscoe was president of the Liverpool Literary and Philosophical Society from 1817 until his death in 1831, presenting a number of papers before the society in which morality was a central theme.

In 1814, with the founding of the Royal Institution, came the culmination of Roscoe's dream of establishing a prestigious cultural centre that would exemplify the Liverpool conjunction of commerce and culture:

> An attempt to institute in the midst of a great trading city a place which should be a perpetual focus for every intellectual interest, a perpetual radiator of sane and lofty views of life, a perpetual reminder of the higher needs and aspirations of men in the midst of the fierce roar of commercial competition and the clangorous appeal of those surroundings to the vulgar lust of money.[45]

Roscoe was the chairman of the General Committee formed in 1814 and the first president in 1822, despite acute personal financial problems that culminated in bankruptcy in 1820. Although, as the choice of name suggests, it was partly inspired by its London namesake, it was never planned as purely a scientific establishment. From the beginning its stated aims were 'uncompromisingly cultural in character' – a reflection of Roscoe's generalist approach to the arts.[46] As with the Athenaeum and the Botanic Garden, the venture unified the town's elite and gained wide support. The plan of the Royal Institution was a reflection of Roscoe's broad intellectual interests in literature, art, science and education. As well as a comprehensive lecture programme it would provide a home for learned societies, a library and museum and academical schools where a new generation of scholar businessmen would be educated. There was also to be an exhibition room for an Academy of Artists. Roscoe firmly believed in a system of regional academies as the best means of promoting English art, his admiration and belief in the influence of the Florentine Academy of Lorenzo de Medici shaping this conviction. Throughout his life Roscoe continued as an avid collector of works of art and prints and, like his hero Lorenzo (according to the Roscoe interpretation), with a specifically pedagogical purpose. His collection, he claimed, was 'chiefly for the purpose of illustrating, by a reference to original and authentic sources, the rise and progress of the arts in modern times'.[47] It was to be an 'instructive and informative' collection rather than one 'to delight and move'.[48] To this end his paintings and prints were arranged in historical order in his home at Allerton Hall. Roscoe had portrayed Lorenzo as a generous patron of artists in Renaissance Florence and in emulation of his hero he became the most important single influence guiding art patronage in his native city in the first thirty years of the nineteenth century. He developed a close association with Henry Fuseli, giving him both practical and financial help. He imported at least 40 of Fuseli's paintings into Liverpool, owning 15 himself. Roscoe encouraged the sculptor John Gibson to visit Allerton Hall to study original drawings and engravings from his collection – inspired perhaps by Lorenzo's supposed patronage of the young Michelangelo. He was continually being requested to write a history of the rise and decline of Italian art – which he refused to do – but he was to remain preoccupied throughout his life with art. As Hale points out, his influence extended beyond Liverpool and his portrayal of the Medici could be used by artists as an example of the way patronage could be a tool in reinvigorating art in England.[49]

On 25 November 1817, at the opening of the Royal Institution, William Roscoe delivered an inaugural address before a large audience, including members of the Town Council. In this address he challenged the idea of 'art for art's sake', and attempted to justify his thesis that literature and the arts could not and should not be disassociated from commerce:

If you will protect the arts, the arts will, and ought to remunerate you. To suppose that they are to be encouraged upon some abstract and disinterested plan, from which all idea of utility shall be excluded, is to suppose that a building can be erected without a foundation. There is not a greater error, than to think that the arts can subsist upon the generosity of the public ... Utility and pleasure are thus bound together in an indissoluble chain, and what the author of nature has joined let no man put asunder.[50]

He traced a historical link between intellectual improvement and commerce, concluding that 'in every place where commerce has been culti-vated upon great and enlightened principles, a considerable proficiency has always been made in liberal studies and pursuits'.[51] He reiterated his belief in the significance of cultural associations, using Liverpool's Athenaeum and Lyceum as contemporary examples of the efficacy of such organizations. The Royal Institution, he claimed, would now confirm Liverpool as a cultural as well as a commercial centre of excellence and it was indeed to play a significant part, particularly in its early years, in enhancing Liverpool's status by gaining recognition as one of the major provincial organizations devoted to the diffusion of learning.

If Roscoe's celebration of commerce was pleasing to his merchant audi-ence, his contention that manufacturing was less suited to intellectual development would have also ensured him a warm reception. Manufacturing, he declared, tended to 'deaden the exertions of the intel-lect, and to reduce the powers both of body and mind to a machine'.[52] This may well have been rhetoric on Roscoe's part aimed at pleasing his merchant audience. In the printed version of the address Roscoe avoids giving offence to a wider readership by adding a footnote in which he states that recent improvements in manufacturing rendered his comments inapplicable to present-day circumstances. However, for the listening merchants here was confirmation of their status as Liverpool gentlemen, in contrast to their neighbours, Manchester's men.[53]

The printed version of the address received wide reviews. Roscoe was recognized as 'a living witness that in no situation is elegant literature irreconcilable with attention to the more active duties of life'.[54] For Washington Irving the identification of Roscoe with his hero was mani-fest: 'like his own Lorenzo de Medici ... he has interwoven the history of his life with the history of his native town, and has made the foundations of its fame the monuments of his virtues'.[55] The Liverpool merchants received equal praise as a reward for their investment, *Blackwood's Edinburgh Magazine* declaring 'of all examples of prompt and enlight-ened liberality among English merchants, we do not hesitate to say, that we consider this as by far the most remarkable'.[56] From America, too, came praise from Thomas Jefferson, who recognized the Institution as a prototype for the new university he was then establishing. Dr Aikin, writing to congratulate Roscoe on the address, was equally certain of the importance of the new Royal Institution, seeing its potential to 'one day convert Liverpool into an Athens or a Florence'.[57]

Although the Liverpool Royal Institution did not fulfil the expectations of its founders, floundering against the rising tide of public cultural enterprise from the mid-nineteenth century, Roscoe would have taken comfort not only in the knowledge of the formative role it had certainly played in initiating cultural and educational facilities in the town, but also from the fact that his dream of making Liverpool an example of the union of commerce and culture lived on. In 1877 the porch of the newly built Walker Art Gallery was surrounded by three statues, Raphael on one side, Michelangelo on the other, with Commerce on the top.

Roscoe's bankruptcy finally relieved him of his business commitments. The commercial panic at the end of the Napoleonic Wars in 1816 caused a run on the bank. After four years of struggling to realize his assets, he was finally declared bankrupt in 1820 and moved to a small house in Lodge Lane. He lived on an annuity purchased by his friends and a small pension. His last years were devoted to intellectual pursuits, writings on prison reform, the publication of a monograph on Monandrian Plants and the cataloguing of Thomas Coke of Holkham's collection of Italian manuscripts. His contribution to his native town was officially recognized by his fellow citizens in 1815 when he was granted the freedom of the town 'in testimony of the high sense entertained by the Council, not only of his great literary talents but of his private worth and value as a member of society'. He died from influenza at his home on 30 June 1831, eagerly looking forward to the anticipated Reform Bill. William Roscoe was buried in the grounds of Renshaw Street Unitarian Chapel, his life-long friend, the Revd William Shepherd, conducting the funeral service.

Although recent scholarship has seen the exact nature of Lorenzo's academies and patronage come under careful scrutiny, with Roscoe's interpretation being seen as myth rather than reality,[58] Roscoe's historical publications and art patronage did play a formative role in developing a new appreciation of the architectural and aesthetic importance of the Italian Renaissance across both British and international urban culture. Although his deep affection for his native town may have coloured his interpretation of Medici Florence, and though he identified too closely with its ruler, he gave Liverpool's elite 'the cultural confidence to celebrate their commercial pre-eminence',[59] and as merchant and patron he undoubtedly stands as a cultural linchpin in the town's development. A collection of his books remains in the Liverpool Athenaeum, part of his art collection is in the Walker Art gallery, and one hundred and seventy five years after his death his legacy has been revivified with Liverpool's selection as European Capital of Culture. The promoters of the Liverpool proposal insist that this accolade will prove pivotal in enhancing both the city's cultural life and its economy – not a new submission but rather a renewal of Roscoe's deeply held belief in the symbiotic relationship between commerce and culture.

Notes

1   J. Hale, *England and the Italian Renaissance* (London, 1954), p. 87.
2   H. Roscoe, *The Life of William Roscoe*, 2 vols (London, 1833), I, p. 178.
3   Hale, *England and the Italian Renaissance*, p. 106.
4   W. Roscoe, *The Life of Lorenzo de Medici called the Magnificent* (London, 10th edn, 1889), p. 14.
5   Liverpool Record Office, Roscoe Papers, 2322, 920 ROS, W. Roscoe to Lord Lansdowne, 23 December 1793.
6   Roscoe, *Life of Lorenzo de Medici*, p. 9.
7   Ibid., p. 13.
8   Ibid., p. 110.
9   Ibid., p.15.
10 Hale, *England and the Italian Renaissance*, p. 96.
11 D. Macnaughton, *Roscoe of Liverpool, his life, writings and treasures* (Birkenhead, 1996), p. 67.
12 Roscoe, *Life of Lorenzo de Medici*, p. 10.
13 Ibid., p. 15.
14 Hale, *England and the Italian Renaissance*, p. 93.
15 Sir Herbert Maxwell, ed., *The Creevey Papers. A Selection from the Correspondence and Diaries of Thomas Creevey, M.P. born 1768–died 1838*, 2 vols. (London, 1904), II, pp. 256–57.
16 Hale, *England and the Italian Renaissance*, p. 88.
17 H. Roscoe, *Life*, I, p. 169.
18 Roscoe had encouraged John M'Creery to establish a press in Liverpool. The two men developed a life-long friendship. M'Creery died in 1831, the same year as Roscoe: H. Roscoe, *Life*, I, p. 152.
19 G. Murphy, *William Roscoe: His early ideals and influence* (Liverpool, privately printed, 1981), p. 26. See also Roscoe Papers 2320; P. McIntyre, 'Historical Sketch of the Liverpool Library', *Transactions of the Historic Society of Lancashire and Cheshire*, 9 (1857), p. 238.
20 J. Rosson, 'On Ecclesiastical Architecture, particularly with reference to Liverpool', *Transactions of the Liverpool Polytechnic Society for the years 1844–46* (Liverpool, 1846), p. 22.
21 W. Irving, *Sketch of William Roscoe* (Liverpool, 1853), p. 6.
22 R. Story, 'Class and Culture in Boston: The Athenaeum, 1807–1860', *American Quarterly*, 27/2 (1975), p. 185.
23 Macnaughton, *Roscoe of Liverpool*, p. 17; Murphy, *William Roscoe*, p. 30. Checkland, however, accepts Roscoe's denial of any relevance: S. G. Checkland,

'Economic Attitudes in Liverpool, 1793–1807', *The Economic History Review*, new series, 5/1 (1952), p. 68.

24 C. Northcote Parkinson, *The Rise of the Port of Liverpool* (Liverpool, 1952), p. 3.

25 J. Stobart, 'Culture versus Commerce: societies and spaces for elites in eighteenth-century Liverpool', *Journal of Historical Geography*, 28 (2002), p. 474.

26 T. Fawcett, *The Rise of Provincial Art: Artists, Patrons and Institutions outside London, 1800–1830* (Oxford, 1974), pp. 4–5.

27 H. C. Marillier, *The Liverpool School of Painters; an account of the Liverpool Academy from 1810 to 1867, with memoirs of the principal artists* (London, 1904), pp. 5–6.

28 Liverpool Record Office, Holt and Gregson Papers, 942 HOL, 10 fq2091.

29 For example, The Ugly Face Club (1743), the Unanimous Club (1753), the Mock Corporation of Sefton (1753); see A. Wilson, 'The Cultural Identity of Liverpool, 1790–1850: the Early Learned Societies', *Transactions of the Historic Society of Lancashire and Cheshire*, 147 (1997), p. 57.

30 J. Wallace, *A General and Descriptive History of the Ancient and Present State of the Town of Liverpool* (Liverpool, 1797), p. 283.

31 Story, 'Class and Culture', p. 184.

32 The seminal article on the links between the slave trade and Liverpool's cultural redefinition is S. Drescher, 'The Slaving Capital of the World: Liverpool and national opinion in the age of abolition', *Slavery and Abolition*, 9/2 (1988), pp. 129–33.

33 Liverpool Record Office, Outlines of a plan for a library and newsroom, 942 HOL (8).

34 Outlines, p. 186.

35 Outlines, p. 184.

36 *An Address delivered before the Proprietors of the Botanic Garden in Liverpool, previous to the opening of the Garden, May 3rd, 1803* (Liverpool, 1802), p. 29.

37 Hale, *England and the Italian Renaissance*, p. 95.

38 *The Edinburgh Review*, 7/14 (1806), p. 336.

39 E. Baines, *The History of the County Palatine and Duchy of Lancaster*, 2 vols (London, 1870), II, p. 378.

40 J. Picton, *Memorials of Liverpool*, 2 vols (London, 1875), I, p. 271.

41 Liverpool University Library, Rathbone Family Papers, 11.4.16: 1806 Election handbill.

42 I. Sellers, 'William Roscoe, the Roscoe Circle and Radical Politics in Liverpool 1787–1807', *Transactions of the Historic Society of Lancashire and Cheshire*, 120 (1968), p. 61.

43 Liverpool Record Office, Liverpool Literary and Philosophical Society Minute Book, 1, 1 May 1812.

44 Q. Hughes, *Seaport; Architecture and Townscape in Liverpool* (London, 1964), p. 116. Hughes claims that Liverpool also saw the death of the Gothic Revival, citing the town's Anglican Cathedral as tolling its death knell – 'a final blaze of Gothic, in scale unprecedented – a fitting consummation of a great period'.

45 J. Ramsay Muir, *A History of Liverpool* (London, 1907), p. 293.

46 London's Royal Institution was established in 1799 with the aim (even though it did not in fact develop on such strictly technological lines) of diffusing a knowledge of applied science; T. Kelly, *A History of Adult Education in Great Britain* (Liverpool, 1970), pp. 113–14.

47 H. Roscoe, *Life*, II, p. 128.

48 Fawcett, *The Rise of Provincial Art*, p. 96.

49 Hale, *England and the Italian Renaissance*, p. 105.

50 W. Roscoe, *On the Origin and Vicissitudes of Literature, Science and Art and their*

Influence on the Present State of Society; A discourse delivered on the opening of the Liverpool Royal Institution, 25 November 1817 (Liverpool, 1817), p. 7.

51 Ibid., p. 46.

52 Ibid., p. 44.

53 A. Wilson, 'Culture and Commerce: Liverpool's merchant elite c.1790–1850', unpublished PhD thesis, University of Liverpool (1996), pp. 73–77.

54 M. Neve, 'Science in a Commercial City: Bristol 1820–60', in I. Inkster and J. Morrell, eds, *Metropolis and Province: Science in British Culture, 1780–1850,* (London, 1983), p. 202.

55 Irving, *Sketch,* p. 9.

56 *Blackwood's Edinburgh Magazine,* 2, February 1818, pp. 537, 535.

57 H. Roscoe, *Life,* p. 163.

58 C. Storey, 'Myths of the Medici: William Roscoe and Renaissance Historiography', unpublished Ph.D thesis, University of Oxford (2003), p. 18.

59 T. Hunt, *Building Jerusalem: The Rise and Fall of the Victorian City* (London, 2004). p. 155.

Secular Gothic Revival Architecture in Mid-Nineteenth-Century Liverpool

JOSEPH SHARPLES

The nineteenth century in Liverpool is neatly framed by two key events in the history of the Gothic Revival. It was while in Liverpool that Thomas Rickman (1776–1841) began the systematic study of old buildings that would result in his seminal 1817 book, *An Attempt to discriminate the Styles of English Architecture, from the Conquest to the Reformation*;[1] and it was in Liverpool, in 1904, that the foundation stone of the Anglican Cathedral designed by Giles Gilbert Scott (1880–1960) was laid. Rickman stands at the beginning of the scholarly revival of Gothic architecture, while Scott can be seen as marking its end. But what of the period in between? Victorian Liverpool has been regarded as essentially a Classical city, where the Greek Revival works of John Foster Junior (c.1787–1846), followed by the triumphantly Graeco-Roman St George's Hall of Harvey Lonsdale Elmes (1814–47) and Charles Robert Cockerell (1788–1863), set the architectural agenda for most of the rest of the century. It was a view expressed in 1874 by E. W. Godwin (1833–86), who remarked favourably on the difference in this respect between Liverpool and neighbouring Manchester: 'Fresh from Manchester oriels and plate-glass Gothic, the "Classic" buildings of Liverpool give quite a pleasing sensation, even to a Goth like me'.[2] But was early and mid-Victorian Liverpool really so single-mindedly Classical? That Gothic was the standard style for churches goes without saying, but what of the office buildings that made up the town's commercial core, and the suburban houses where the mercantile elite lived in almost rural seclusion?

In the commercial centre the 1840s and 50s were a period of comprehensive redevelopment, during which the streets around the Exchange were extensively rebuilt with speculative office blocks. These were modelled on Italian Renaissance *palazzi*, following the example set by the club houses of Charles Barry (1795–1860) in London's West End. They were largely the work of a generation of mature architects such as Cockerell, John Cunningham (1799–1873) and especially William Culshaw (c.1807–74) – heirs of late Georgian and Regency Classicism, to whom a restrained Italianate style came naturally. First used at Brunswick Buildings in about 1842 by Arthur (c.1809–53) and George Williams (1814–98), the *palazzo* style became the standard dress for business premises, the best surviving example being Cockerell's huge office complex for the Liverpool & London Insurance Co. at 1 Dale Street.

The prolific J. A. Picton (1805–89) designed over a dozen major Liverpool office buildings between 1843 and his retirement in 1866.[3] Some, such as the demolished Corn Exchange Buildings in Brunswick Street, were of the Barry type, but three of the handful that survive are markedly different. Commenting on the first of these, the Mercantile Bank in Castle Street, the Liverpool architect and critic T. Mellard Reade (1832–1909) considered 'the admixture of the Gothic and the Classic elements is the most noticeable feature',[4] while according to the *Building News*, in his machicolated block for the Queen Insurance Co. at 11 Dale Street, Picton appeared 'to have abandoned the usual idea in reference to harmony of style, and made a mixed composition of Italian, Greek and Gothic elements'.[5] The same mix can be seen at his Hargreaves Buildings in Chapel Street, possibly the best of the three, which is dated 1859. Just two years earlier George Gilbert Scott (1811–78) had advocated precisely this approach. He praised Barry for having revived the Italian Renaissance *palazzo*, but urged architects of the present generation to re-Gothicize it, reinstating medieval features that had been shed during its long evolution. 'We should adopt the horizontal cornice,' wrote Scott,

> though designing it with Gothic rather than classic details. We should have uniform ranges of arched windows subdivided into lights of considerable width by columns rather than mullions, the tracery, if any, being of the boldest and simplest form, – a mere circle being sufficient ... [and the] capitals, even if they resemble Corinthian in any degree in outline, should be founded on natural foliage of familiar types.[6]

Scott's recipe is so close to Hargreaves Buildings that it may have been a direct influence on Picton.

Picton was not the only architect to adopt the eclectic approach recommended by Scott. The Albany Building of 1856–58 by J. K. Colling (1816–1905), with its distinctive carved foliate decoration, was described

Fig 1 11 Dale Street, 1859, by J. A. Picton for William Brown (National Monuments Record)
Fig 2 (*opposite*) Hargreaves Buildings, Chapel Street, 1859, by J. A. Picton for William Brown (National Monuments Record)

by the *Builder* as 'a superior example ... of the application of many of the resources which are derivable from Gothic architecture, to a general Italian groundwork of style'.[7] An even grander attempt to reinvigorate Classicism with a transfusion of medievalism was the Municipal Buildings of 1862–67/8, begun by John Weightman (1798–1883) and completed by his successor as Corporation Surveyor, E. R. Robson (1835–1917). It has as its centerpiece a curiously hybrid spire, bristling with crockets but incorporating balustrades and pilasters, and its Corinthian capitals – each one different – are composed of lush English ferns rather than acanthus. Almost contemporary with Waterhouse's Manchester Town Hall, it embodies Liverpool's unwillingness to reject outright its allegiance to Classicism, while not being able to resist altogether the allure of Gothic. It is possible that the Gothic elements were due to Robson, who had been an assistant of Scott's before his appointment to Liverpool in 1864.[8]

Locally as well as nationally, the 'Battle of the Styles' (the conflict between Classicists and Gothicists that blew up around the 1857 competition for the Government offices in Whitehall) formed the background to architectural debate in the 1860s. By the middle of the decade, younger Liverpool architects had come to regard the Renaissance *palazzo* style as irredeemably old-fashioned, while the Gothic Revival appeared modern and full of novel possibilities. T. Mellard Reade, in a series of stinging articles published in the local satirical paper *Porcupine* in 1865–66, railed against the conformity and lack of imagination shown by his older colleagues – '[t]heir minds, so long accustomed to Classic properties, cannot grasp the picturesque'[9] – and pleaded for a new approach based on the 'diversified forms' and varied rooflines of Gothic architecture. Resistance to a move in this direction had been demonstrated not long before in the 1863 competition for the new Liverpool Exchange buildings. Reviewing the contest, the *Builder* noted that out of 44 sets of designs submitted only three were Gothic, showing clearly that 'the influence of the style of the present and surrounding buildings has been too strong even for Medieval talent to overcome'.[10]

And yet there is nothing to suggest that Liverpool architects were constitutionally anti-Gothic. Successive presidents of the Liverpool Architectural and Archaeological Society refused to come down on one side or the other in the 'Battle', each advocating a pluralistic approach to the architecture of the past. 'It is only the mind which is thoroughly imbued with principles and characteristics of all styles, and who draws his inspiration from every source', declared J. M. Hay (1823–1915), 'that is capable of producing great and original works.'[11] This doctrine must lie behind his firm's extraordinary, hybrid design of 1886 for a projected Liverpool Cathedral, in which Gothic spires and a Byzantine dome rise above Renaissance porticoes.[12] F. Horner similarly believed that '[t]he researches of the archaeologist and our intercourse with foreign countries have legitimately placed [the] acquired experience of generations within the grasp of the practitioner of the nineteenth century, to be interpreted and adapted freely by him'.[13] A later president, H. H. Vale (1830/1–75), urged architectural students to 'take that style or even that admixture of

styles which is the best suited to the particular ends [they have] in view ...
13th, 14th, or 15th century, Gothic, Grecian, Roman, Renaissance,
Victorian, or what you will, in the hands of the true architect they will all
yield forms of grace and beauty'.[14] The partisan note struck by G. A.
Audsley (1838–1925) was unusual, when he chided fellow members of
the society for 'watching, though not assisting in the great work of taste,
namely, the revival of Christian Architecture and Art; the noblest triumph
of the nineteenth century'.[15] A more mainstream view was expressed by
H. P. Horner (fl.1840–75) in a paper read before the society in 1869, in
which he gave historical arguments in favour of using Classical styles for
legal and commercial buildings and Gothic for ecclesiastical and educational commissions. 'Our legal system,' he told his audience,

> is in a great measure derived from the ancient Roman, guided and
> tempered by the Mosaic, and our fiscal and commercial arrangements
> nearly resemble those of medieval, or, as we might say cinquecento,
> Italy, and in neither is there any such exclusive reference to our own
> middle-age policy as to afford any strong argument for adopting such
> a style as then prevailed, a ground for which, on the other hand, as
> certainly does apply to what relates to religion and education.[16]

But as well as churches and schools, a significant number of Gothic
commercial buildings *were* erected in Liverpool from the mid-1860s. The
most notable survivor is Seel's Building of 1870–71 by E. W. Pugin
(1834–75), for the Catholic landowner T. Molyneux Seel;[17] another is
Imperial Chambers, Dale Street, of c.1873. The appropriately named
Lombard Chambers in Bixteth Street, of c.1869, is a rare Liverpool
example of Ruskinian polychrome brick construction, with vigorously
carved label stops. The architect is unknown, but it seems the client was
Thomas Price Jones, a former house agent from Wrexham.[18] Berey's
Buildings, next door, is a much bigger polychrome block of 1864. It shows
only a few hints of Gothic in its details, but the original drawings have a
more strongly medieval flavour, and though they are signed by William
Culshaw, they are almost certainly the work of his younger assistant and
future partner, Henry Sumners (c.1826–95).[19] Despite his commitment to
eclecticism, H. H. Vale did not favour Gothic for office buildings, considering it 'a mistake to design blocks of offices, as some have done recently,
so as to have the question asked whether the building be a "grammar
school" or "church institute"'.[20] It therefore comes as a surprise that he
was responsible for the decidedly medieval 42 Whitechapel of c.1875,[21]

Fig 3 42 Whitechapel, by H. H. Vale (*The British Architect*, 26 March 1875)

Fig 4 Musker's Buildings, Stanley Street, 1881–82, by Thomas E. Murray (*The British Architect*, 16 September 1881)

and the very large Oxford and Cambridge Chambers, Lord Street, now demolished, which was described by the *Building News* as 'Gothicised Italian'.[22] Later examples are Westminster Chambers, Crosshall Street, of 1879–80 by Richard Owens (1831–91); Musker's Buildings, Stanley Street, of 1881–82 by Thomas E. Murray (1847–1918), a former pupil of E.W. Pugin; and Bennett's Buildings, Whitechapel, of the same date by John Clarke (1852–1936).

The younger generation's rejection of the Renaissance *palazzo* style is nicely illustrated by G. E. Grayson (c.1834–1912), who in the 1860s and 70s designed a cluster of Gothic offices in Preeson's Row and James Street, just west of Derby Square. The site is significant, since Derby Square is where Liverpool's long-demolished thirteenth-century castle once stood. The *Building News* wrote in 1868: 'Mr. G.E. Grayson, who some little time since built a very dignified and palatial-looking block of offices in the Italian style in James-street, has, with true modern eclecticism, faced about, and is going in "heavily," in more senses than one, for Gothic.'[23] The journal objected to his Redcross Buildings on the grounds that 'the placing of dragons and griffins as dripstone terminations is really an absurdity in a modern building for business purposes', and described his Old Castle-buildings unfavourably as 'another grim and heavy structure, with trefoil-headed windows'; but a few years later it thought well enough of his Gothic block at 31 James Street to give it a full-page illustration.[24] By the later 1870s, when the prolific and successful Grayson began rebuilding much of Castle Street, the wheel of taste had turned again and he adopted a variety of exuberant Northern Renaissance styles, which allowed at least as much scope for carved decoration, sculpture and poly-chromy as Ruskinian Gothic had done.

Does the choice of Gothic or Classical show the taste of client or archi-tect? Barry's *palazzo* manner had successfully established itself as 'the style proper to modern Europe ... the style of the merchant, not of the priest or baron',[25] and it is easy to imagine how the connotations of Italian Renaissance palaces – mercantile rather than patrician, opulent but also cultured – would have attracted Liverpool's Victorian businessmen. However, much the same could be said of medieval Italian palaces, and those of maritime, imperial Venice might have been expected to appeal particularly strongly. Unfortunately, there is very little written evidence for the architectural tastes of these Liverpool merchants. The most prolific builder of speculative offices, the banker Sir William Brown (1784–1864), seems to have been chiefly concerned with keeping the cost of his build-ings down, arguing against holding an architectural competition for the

Fig 5 31 James Street, by G. Hamilton and G. E. Grayson, 1872 (*The Building News*, 2 January 1874)

new Exchange because it might result in 'a very florid scheme and an expensive one', whereas his own wish was for 'good, substantial buildings, without extraneous ornaments'. With regard to style he apparently had no particular view, and gave Picton *carte blanche* in designing Brown's Buildings.[26]

Functional requirements probably weighed much more heavily with such clients. The single most important consideration was good natural lighting, both for clerical work and for the examination of merchandise, especially cotton samples. In Classical architecture, tradition militated against very large windows, but architects were prepared to bend the rules to achieve better lighting.[27] In Gothic buildings, on the other hand, though there were medieval precedents for generous glazing, and though lancets could be combined in continuous arcades, pointed windows inevitably let in less light than square-headed ones, and larger openings had to be subdivided by stone tracery. It was perhaps such practical considerations that favoured the wider adoption of Classicism. At 31 James Street, Grayson tried to achieve good lighting within a Gothic idiom by using very large windows, many of which were almost square-headed, with the merest suggestion of ogee tops, but each opening was still heavily encumbered with mullions and transoms. At Bennett's Buildings in Whitechapel, John Clarke tried a similar approach, and gave his windows very shallow, splayed reveals to maximize the amount of light admitted.[28]

Turning to domestic architecture, Gothic in early nineteenth-century Liverpool was generally a minimal kind of Tudor, usually stuccoed, sometimes barge-boarded, with hood moulds over sash windows and perhaps a four-centred arch over the front door. Early examples, such as the demolished houses built from c.1823 by the Cropper family at the Dingle, were barely distinguishable from Classical Regency villas.[29] More decorative and varied, though scarcely more archaeologically correct, are the houses built c.1815 by John Cragg (1767–1854) in St Michael's Hamlet, with their lacy cast-iron window tracery and verandahs. Examples on a grander scale are Greenbank, the Rathbone family home extended c.1812–16, and John Nash's Childwall Hall, completed in 1813 for Bamber Gascoyne.[30] Gothic houses were almost invariably suburban – that is to say picturesquely semi-rural.[31] A particularly ambitious example of the mid-1840s is the superbly sited Holmestead, on the brow of Mossley Hill, built for the contractor Samuel Holme (c.1800–72) and probably designed by his brother, Arthur Hill Holme (1814–57).[32] Another was the demolished Elmswood, just south of Holmestead, with spectacular views to the river and north Wales, built in 1840 for the merchant, shipowner and future mayor, Thomas Sands (1790–1867).[33] Dingle Cottage, erected in 1838 from the designs of Arthur Williams, and nearby Otterspool were two more Gothic houses, situated close to the water's edge in Aigburth.[34] Across the Mersey, the development of New Brighton as an affluent seaside resort from the late 1830s provided similarly attractive sites for Gothic houses, as A. B. Granville noted in 1841: 'Smaller as well as larger marine villas … rest on some romantic and rugged rocks that project into the sea … The pointed Gothic, the cottage, and Lombard styles prevail.'[35] In 1845 Harvey Lonsdale Elmes, architect of St George's Hall, designed the grandest of these seaside Gothic houses – Redcliffe – for Daniel Neilson, with a loggia and terrace commanding magnificent views of the Mersey estuary.[36]

Well into the 1840s William Culshaw was still designing simple, stuccoed Tudor houses on the fringes of Liverpool. The superficiality of their styling is clear from his 1847 drawings for T. F. Bennett's house on Aigburth Road, for which he produced two alternative elevations to the same basic plan, one Classical, the other Tudor.[37] Exactly the same approach characterizes Holmestead, which is essentially a Georgian box with decorative Tudor trimmings. More or less contemporary with these, however, is a profoundly different building, and a landmark of national significance in the development of the Gothic Revival. This is Oswaldcroft at Childwall, designed by A. W. N. Pugin (1812–52) for the Roman Catholic timber merchant Henry Sharples (c.1809–74) and built in 1844–45. Here Pugin put into practice the views he had recently published in his *True Principles*, that in a truly Gothic building the exterior should not be a screen masking the asymmetry of the interior, and the irregular elevations should not be contrived artificially, but generated naturally by the plan.[38] The external appearance of Oswaldcroft is largely determined by its internal arrangement. On the entrance front, the big, asymmetrically placed stair window, the off-centre porch and the blank gables with their massive chimney breasts express rather than hide the varied spaces within. Oswaldcroft is a world away from Holmestead and its skin-deep Gothic facades. It is also remarkable as an example of adventurous patronage on the part of Pugin's client, in contrast to the conservatism so often associated with the merchant class. Frustratingly little is known about Sharples, but there is some evidence that his previous residence at Broad Green was a genuine sixteenth-century house.[39] It is possible, therefore, that a first-hand knowledge of late medieval architecture may have played a part in his decision to employ Pugin, as well as their shared Catholicism.

Fig 6 Oswaldcroft, Woolton Road, Childwall, 1844–45, by A. W. N. Pugin for Henry Sharples

Oswaldcroft long remained an isolated example of 'organic' Gothic design in Liverpool. The typical merchant's house of the 1840s and 50s, so far as the story can be pieced together from surviving examples, was usually Classical, and when it was Gothic it was of a kind still essentially picturesque, an ornament in the landscape. Around Prince's Park, and in the private estates of Fulwood and Grassendale parks, there are a few unremarkable Tudor houses of this type – for example, Eastbourne, in Sefton Park Road, built for the engineer Henry Booth (1789–1869) in 1853. Across the Mersey, Rock Park, Clifton Park and Birkenhead Park have further examples, though they tend to be more richly detailed and more substantially built in ashlar. Some are by Walter Scott (fl.1843–71), who also designed the grandest Liverpool Gothic house of the 1850s, Broughton Hall at West Derby. Built in 1858–59 for the merchant Gustav C. Schwabe (1813–97), Broughton only highlights the extraordinary novelty of Oswaldcroft, fifteen years earlier. Excluding the service wing, its entrance front is symmetrical except for minor variations in the fenestration, and the big window that lights the stairs is relegated to the equally balanced garden front. Inside, just one feature of the plan suggests that

Scott was aiming to evoke a genuine medieval house: the front door leads into a narrow vestibule, separated from the neighbouring hall by a wall with timber Gothic arcading on its inner face, an arrangement surely intended to recall a medieval screens passage.

Just as the 1860s and 70s saw Gothic making an appearance in the commercial centre, so in the affluent suburbs to the south-east a number of Gothic mansions of unprecedented ambition were built at this time, in some cases by the same architects. Henry Sumners designed Quarry Bank, Allerton, in 1866 for James Bland (c.1819–84), a prosperous timber merchant,[40] while St Clare in Sandfield Park was begun in 1865 for the corn merchant William Makin (c.1809–87), perhaps to the designs of G. E. Grayson.[41] Earlier houses were also extended. Holmestead was doubled in size in 1869–70 for the 'opulent cotton merchant' Michael Belcher (c.1816–88), with a boldly asymmetrical wing including a tower and a billiard room; nearby Elmswood House (as distinct from Elmswood) in Mossley Hill Road was extended in 1878 for another cotton merchant, Nicholas Duckworth (c.1817–89); and Kelton, a bland, early nineteenth-century Classical villa in Woodlands Road, was given a wildly disparate polychrome brick extension in 1864 for the merchant George Martin.[42] The leading local Goths, the brothers W. J. and G. A. Audsley, designed a number of important houses, two of which survive. Streatlam Tower near the north end of Princes Road dates from 1871, which is exceptionally late for a grand residence so close to the town centre. It was built for the wool broker James Lord Bowes (c.1835–99), and its style – 'Scotch Gothic' according to a contemporary description – was said to be an allusion to the Bowes family's historic seat in Northumberland.[43] The Towers, Ullet Road,[44] of 1874, was one of the earliest and largest villas to be built on the fringes of the newly created Sefton Park, and its style contrasts sharply with its mostly Classical, stuccoed neighbours. It was commissioned from the Audsleys by the American-born merchant John Newton Beach (c.1830–90), speculatively it seems, because he never lived there and the house was occupied instead by a succession of tenants.

Builders of the largest Gothic houses turned to architects of national standing, perhaps as a sign of status, or perhaps because they perceived a lack of expertise among local practitioners of the style. No less a figure than George Gilbert Scott designed Cleveley, Allerton, in 1865 for the cotton broker Joseph Leather, while London-based Alfred Waterhouse (1830–1905) carried out several important domestic commissions in and around his native Liverpool. First in 1856–57 came Hinderton Hall on the Wirral, for the wine merchant Christopher Bushell (1810–87),

Fig 7 The Towers, Ullet Road, 1874, by W. J. and G. A. Audsley for John
Newton Beach (National Monuments Record)

Fig 8 Cleveley, Allerton Road, Allerton, 1865, by George Gilbert Scott for Joseph Leather (National Monuments Record)

followed in 1861–65 by New Heys on Allerton Road, for the solicitor W. G. Bateson; in 1862–64 came Gisburn, next to Prince's Park, for the dock engineer George Fosbery Lyster (1821–99); then Allerton Priory of 1866–75, for the colliery owner John Grant Morris (1811–97); and finally Mossley House, Park Avenue, of 1869–71, for the produce broker Lloyd Rayner (c.1822–76).[45] Appropriate furniture was needed to complete the interiors of such houses. Both Allerton Priory and Mossley House were supplied with purpose-designed Gothic pieces by Gillow & Co.,[46] while the cotton broker John Swainson (1814–79), who lived at Thomas Sand's Elmswood in the 1860s, surrounded himself with Tudor bedsteads, a suit of armour and a billiard table 'in medieval style', which he purchased from the 1862 International Exhibition.[47]

Did they have anything in common, these clients with a shared taste

Fig 9 Hinderton Hall, Cheshire, 1856–57, by Alfred Waterhouse for
Christopher Bushell (*The Builder*, 15 January 1859)

for the Gothic Revival? With its connotations of national identity, feudal
tradition and the established Church, mid-nineteenth-century Gothic
might be seen as the natural choice of Anglican Tories, and a high propor-
tion of Liverpool patrons of the style fit this description. James Bland,
Michael Belcher, Nicholas Duckworth, John Grant Morris, Lloyd Rayner,
Christopher Bushell, John Swainson and, apparently, G. F. Lyster were
all Conservatives.[48] Morris and Bushell were also ardent churchmen,[49] and
it seems most of the rest were Anglicans too: Bland presented the east
window of All Hallows, Allerton, while Rayner and Belcher helped
purchase the site of St Matthew and St James, Mossley Hill.[50] A notable
exception is Joseph Leather. His politics are not recorded, but he was a
leading Methodist who 'never was beguiled by the temptation to join the
Establishment and so enter a social circle more refined and dignified';[51]
and yet as well as building himself an exceptionally grand Gothic house,
he paid for a Gothic Wesleyan Methodist chapel in Laurel Road, Fairfield,
complete with the church-like accoutrements of stained glass and a
reredos.[52]

The links between Conservatism, High Church Anglicanism and
Gothic Revival architecture are well illustrated in the case of the

immensely rich Conservative brewer, Andrew Barclay Walker (1824–93). In 1866 he employed Cornelius Sherlock (c.1824–88) to build him a Tudor Gothic house, Gateacre Grange, and in 1868 proposed building a church nearby. To gather ideas for this project, Walker's architect H. H. Vale visited ritualistic Gothic Revival churches in London, such as St Alban's, Holborn, and All Saints, Margaret Street, sending his patron a detailed account of their liturgical practices as well as comments on their architecture and furnishing: 'You could have a nice altar & cross', he told Walker, '& frescoed reredos & stained glass windows & some serpentine polished pillars, with a groined brick chancel ... and would be thoroughly up to "the tune of the times"'.[53] The church project did not materialize, but when St Stephen's, Gateacre, was built in 1872–74, Walker was a major donor, paying for the font and pulpit as well as the magnificent west window, designed by Burne-Jones and made by Morris & Co.[54] In 1874 Walker commissioned Vale to design a projected Conservative Club for Liverpool, on a site at the corner of Victoria Street and North John Street. The resulting perspective published in the *British Architect* shows an intensely Gothic building, richly crocketted and pinnacled.[55] Had it been carried out, it would have made a very telling contrast with the rival Reform Club, a sober Classical palazzo in Dale Street designed by Edmund Kirby (1838–1920), which opened in 1879.

That Gothic was the preferred choice of the self-made *nouveaux riches*, because by dressing up in borrowed old clothes they could acquire a veneer of ancestral respectability, is a view that has been discredited recently.[56] In Liverpool, however, where all money was more or less new, it comes as no surprise that these patrons of Gothic made their fortunes through trade, many as first-generation in-migrants to the town. The foundations of Walker's wealth were laid by his father, but he was 'the architect of his own prosperity' and learned the brewing business practically, at first hand;[57] John Grant Morris rose from 'exceedingly humble circumstances into the position of one of the wealthiest citizens of Liverpool';[58] Christopher Bushell, born the son of a civil engineer in Kent, moved north at the age of twenty and prospered in the wholesale wine and spirit trade;[59] while James Bland came from rural Scotland as a youth and made a fortune in the Liverpool timber trade on the back of the railway boom.[60] Quarry Bank alludes discreetly to the commercial source of Bland's wealth in its use of elaborate panelling inlaid with various woods, but more importantly it features the traditional aristocratic trappings of a carved coat of arms on the entrance front and heraldic stained glass on the stairs. And yet in Liverpool such architectural statements would not immediately

Fig 10 Proposed Conservative Club, Liverpool, by H. H. Vale (*The British Architect*, 9 January 1874)

have invited comparison with the local landed aristocracy, the seats of the two dominant, ancient families – the Stanleys' Knowsley Hall and the Molyneuxs' Croxteth Hall – being largely Classical (though Knowsley has a substantial wing of medieval origin, remodelled in castellated Tudor style between 1810 and 1821 by John Foster Junior, and Croxteth received major Jacobethan additions by T. H. Wyatt in 1874–77). The area does boast one particularly important late medieval house, and in 1867 this became the home of Liverpool's archetypal self-made man, the shipping magnate F. R. Leyland (1831–92). The son of an eating-house propri-etress, Leyland rose by hard work and natural ability to take control of the company in which he had begun as a humble clerk. While Bland and Morris employed Sumners and Waterhouse to realize their feudal fantasies, Leyland opted for the real thing, moving into the sixteenth-century timber-framed manor house Speke Hall.[61]

If Gothic was tinged with a Conservative, Anglican flavour, did those on the other side of the religious and political divide shun it? There is not much documentary evidence for the architectural tastes of nineteenth-century Liverpool businessmen, but it may be significant that two who expressed a dislike of Gothic and a preference for Classicism were both Liberals, and both committed to or sympathetic with Nonconformity. In 1848 the Unitarian cotton merchant George Holt (1790–1861) wrote regretfully in his diary about the Gothic design of the new Unitarian Church in Hope Street:

I had not previously seen the Elevation which appears to be in the elab-orated early English with a high Spire, & much broken details, not at all pleasing to my ideas of what would have been most suitable & Elegant, & inappropriate to the Town situation, besides which it must prove a costly structure. There is a great rage even down to the Unitarians in favor of this Monastic or Ecclesiastic style of Architecture, & like other manias [it] will have its course. An entirely different style wod. in my judgement have been more convenient, cheerful, elegant & less costly, some chaste & well considered adap-tation of the Grecian, using the beautiful stone lately brought from Derbyshire for constructing St George's Hall.[62]

For Holt, it seems, Gothic architecture was fundamentally at odds with Nonconformity. Sobriety and dignity, without undue expense, seem to have been the architectural qualities which he admired, and which he found in Classicism. His own pioneering office block, India Buildings, was

Classical, and so apparently was his house in Rake Lane.[63] If his attitude to the Gothic Revival shows an older man's distaste for modern fashions, it was a distaste shared by his sons George, Alfred and Robert, each of whom employed James Rhind to design or extend a Classical house.[64]

In the second half of the century, comparable views were expressed by Andrew G. Kurtz (1824–90), chemical manufacturer, art collector and amateur musician, who lived at Grove House, Wavertree, a late Georgian mansion which he enlarged in a fancifully Italianate style. He was a supporter of Gladstone. He was also an Anglican, but disapproved of Ritualism, and was at ease with the preaching of the Revd T. W. M. Lund at the church of the School for the Blind, which veered in the direction of Unitarianism.[65] Kurtz could admire modern Gothic churches such as All Hallows, Allerton (except for its Burne-Jones stained glass, which he described as 'queer'), and St Dunstan's, Earle Road,[66] but he thought that modern domestic Gothic architecture, though sometimes impressive, was essentially irrational, uncomfortable and antithetical to 'homeliness', his highest ideal. He disliked Cleveley, 'an imposing edifice by (I think) Sir Gilbert Scott – of a quasi ecclesiastic style – not altogether satisfactory to my architectural ideas'.[67] He considered James Lord Bowes's 'medieval house', Streatlam Tower, magnificent, but 'to modern notions ... somewhat fantastic',[68] while the music room of a Mr Coltart, 'got up in medieval style,' struck him as 'inconsistent and ill-balanced'.[69] On finishing Charles Eastlake's influential pro-Gothic Revival book *Hints on Household Taste* (1868) he wrote defiantly:

> It is not worth reading. Furniture & house building is a matter of personal taste, & tho' some tastes are good enough – for instance that things should not be 'shams' – yet, I should not like to return to the heavy medieval style here recommended. Such things were good in their day, & if I had such furniture in my house descended from a long line of ancestry I no doubt should be vy. proud of it, but that's a vy. different thing from having chairs & tables so manufactured nowadays.[70]

And yet it is impossible to predict an individual's taste in architecture on the basis of religious and political affiliations alone. The case of Joseph Leather, the Methodist employer of George Gilbert Scott, has already been mentioned. The Rathbones and Mellys – leading Liberal Unitarians – lived respectively at 'Gothick' Greenbank and at Riversley in Mossley Hill, a house for which William Culshaw designed a castellated Tudor extension in 1862.[71] The Quaker Waterhouses occupied a Tudor Gothic mansion near Riversley called Oakwood, close to which, in 1844, Culshaw designed a pair of semi-detached houses for them in the same style,[72] while Henry Bright (1830–84), another Unitarian, built himself Ashfield at Knotty Ash in a mildly Tudor style. 'Though a Liberal,' wrote Mrs Nathaniel Hawthorne of Bright, he was 'very loyal to his Queen and very admiring of the aristocracy.'[73] His uncle, the banker John Pemberton Heywood (1803–77),[74] had similarly mixed loyalties and was also a patron of Gothic architecture, but on an altogether grander scale. He was a large contributor to the building of Hope Street Unitarian church, which George Holt so disliked, before transferring from Unitarianism to the Church of England. In 1858 Holt noted that Heywood was attending the Unitarian Renshaw Street chapel less and less, and worshipping instead at the parish church of St Mary the Virgin, West Derby, and he attributed this to Heywood's affluence and position in society, such changes of allegiance being 'frequently the case where *large* wealth & more aristocratic association obtain'.[75] Holt was no doubt thinking of Heywood's friendship with the earl of Sefton, on the edge of whose Croxteth estate West Derby village lies, and of the mansions that had grown up in its vicinity from the 1820s, including Heywood's own Norris Green. Heywood also transferred his architectural patronage from Unitarianism to the established Church, he and his wife paying for the mighty crossing tower of St Mary's, designed like the rest of the church by George Gilbert Scott.[76] In addition they funded the elaborately Gothic village cross designed by W. E. Nesfield (1835–88), which marks the site of the medieval predecessor of Scott's church, and a nearby group of charity cottages dated 1863 which bear their initials. These combine with H. P. Horner's parochial schools of 1860 (the foundation stone of which was laid by Heywood),[77] further cottages by Nesfield and the lodge and gates of Croxteth Hall itself to give West Derby the feel of a feudal estate village. It might be a setting from one of Disraeli's novels, and yet in politics Heywood was a lifelong and active Liberal, and his friend the earl was a Whig.[78]

Norris Green was an unremarkable Classical villa dating from 1830,[79] but in 1864–70 the extremely wealthy Heywood employed Nesfield to build him a very ambitious and stylistically innovative country house, the now demolished Cloverley in Shropshire.[80] While Cloverley included pointed arches here and there, its mullioned-and-transomed oriel windows owed more to sixteenth- and seventeenth-century models than Gothic ones, and Nesfield's design can be seen as signalling the fragmentation of the Gothic Revival and the start of its long decline. It is closer to the nascent 'Old English' style of Richard Norman Shaw (1831–1912), and incorporates decorative elements such as sunflower motifs that were to become staples of the Queen Anne and Aesthetic movements in the 1870s.

In and around Liverpool, this transition from the Gothic Revival to a more eclectic and inventive domestic architecture, still drawing on the medieval past for some of its details, but much less weighed-down by considerations of archaeological accuracy, can be seen in many large houses from the 1870s. Before 1876, for example, G. E. Grayson designed High Meadow, Claughton, for his shipbuilder-brother H. H. Grayson, with half-timbering, pargetting, tile-hanging, leaded lights and mullioned windows.[81] Edmund Kirby built numerous red-brick mansions in Birkenhead, combining the same ingredients with a sprinkling of Tudor arches and clusters of soaring chimneys.[82] The studied informality of their elevations and internal planning is matched by Gledhill in Mossley Hill Drive, Liverpool, designed by J. F. Doyle (1840–1913) for the stockbroker R. W. Elliston: A. G. Kurtz saw it under construction in 1882 and described it disapprovingly as 'a curiously arranged straggling kind of mansion, with an infinity of odd corners & unsymmetrical rooms'.[83] A little later Doyle designed Gilcruce in Birkenhead for the shipowner John Sealby,[84] and Eddesbury at West Derby for the produce merchant James Latham,[85] the latter predominantly Classical, but still with a few gargoyle-like carvings. Doyle was associated with Norman Shaw on the grandest Merseyside house of the 1880s, and one of the grandest anywhere, Dawpool, at Thurstaston on the Wirral, for the head of the White Star Line, T. H. Ismay (1837–99). Like Cloverley (one of many modern houses Mr and Mrs Ismay visited when planning their new home), Dawpool's main antecedents were Elizabethan rather than Gothic, while the Ismays' taste in interior decoration ranged widely, embracing eighteenth-century furniture, oriental porcelain and modern British paintings.[86]

William Makin's 1865 Gothic house in Sandfield Park, St Clare, was altered by G. E. Grayson in 1881 for the merchant Robert Brocklehurst (c.1827–1916), when it received the refined Aesthetic Movement wood-work by Messrs Gillow that survives there today.[87] But the 1880s shift in taste away from medievalism is probably best illustrated at Gateacre Grange, where in 1882–84 Sir Andrew Barclay Walker employed the fashionable London architects Ernest George (1839–1922) and Harold Peto (1854–1933) to alter and extend his 1860s Tudor house. They added bay windows of the eighteenth-century 'Sparrowe's House' type popularized by Shaw, and sumptuously refitted the interior in an eclectic manner flavoured with Aestheticism. In the hall they installed a superb

Fig 11 Dawpool, Cheshire, 1882–84, by Norman Shaw and J. F. Doyle for
T. H. Ismay (*The Architect*, 25 October 1884)

alabaster chimneypiece, with caryatids and Ionic columns carved by James
Forsyth, and gave the drawing room a moulded plaster ceiling with
Renaissance-style grotesques. Their de-Gothicizing of the original house
is seen most clearly on the landing at the top of the main stairs, where
George and Peto reshaped Cornelius Sherlock's trio of four-centred Tudor
arches into simple, Classical curves.[88]

By the end of the century the Gothic Revival was largely a spent force
in secular architecture, though some of its underlying principles continued
to have an influence. In house design, it fed into the Domestic Revival and
the Arts and Crafts movement, and its descendants can be found among
the villas of Hoylake, West Kirby and Crosby, and the cottages of Port
Sunlight. In commercial architecture, overt medievalism lived on a little
longer, in Waterhouse's Pearl Life Assurance building of 1896–98, for
instance, and in the idiosyncratic works of Walter Aubrey Thomas
(1859–1934) such as the Lord Street arcade of 1901 and the State
Insurance office of 1903–05. Widespread demolitions in the twentieth
century have obscured the achievements of the Gothic Revival in the
middle decades of the nineteenth, but it is clear that despite the visual
dominance of St George's Hall and the 'forum' of public buildings in

William Brown Street, Liverpool in this period was more than just a Classical city. Its architecture reflected to some degree the range of Victorian eclecticism, and the Gothic style, though it never achieved the status it enjoyed in Manchester, did have a significant impact in Liverpool's central business district and in its residential suburbs.

Notes

This essay is an outcome of the Mercantile Liverpool Project funded by the Leverhulme Trust, English Heritage, the Philip Holt Trust, and Liverpool City Council's World Heritage Site. The author is grateful to all the project staff for their advice and assistance.

1   For Rickman, see A. T. Brown, *How Gothic came back to Liverpool* (Liverpool, 1937); J. L. Baily, 'Thomas Rickman, Architect and Quaker: the early years to 1818', unpublished PhD thesis, University of Leeds (1977); and H. Colvin, *A Biographical Dictionary of British Architects 1600–1840* (New Haven and London, 3rd edn, 1995).

2   E. W. Godwin, 'What I noticed in passing through Manchester and Liverpool', *Building News*, 10 (July 1874), p. 55.

3   For a list, see J. A. Picton, *Sir James A. Picton, A Biography* (London, 1891), pp. 113–15.

4   *Porcupine*, 20 January 1866, p. 404.

5   *Building News*, 20 May 1859, p. 463.

6   G. G. Scott, *Remarks on Secular & Domestic Architecture, Present & Future* (London, 2nd edn, 1858), pp. 196–97.

7   *Builder*, 7 November 1857, p. 636.

8   According to the *Builder*, 9 November 1867, p. 819, Weightman was the architect of the building, but Robson 'made such modifications in the first design as seemed desirable'.

9   *Porcupine*, 24 February 1866, p. 465.

10 *Builder*, 30 May 1863, pp. 381–82.

11 *Proceedings of the Liverpool Architectural and Archaeological Society, Thirteenth Session* (3 October 1860), p. 5.

12 *Builder*, 9 October 1886, pp. 518 and 520–21.

13 *Proceedings of the Liverpool Architectural and Archaeological Society, Twenty-First Session* (7 October 1868), p. 21.

14 *Proceedings of the Liverpool Architectural and Archaeological Society, Twenty-Fourth Session* (1 May 1872), p. 106.

15 *Proceedings of the Liverpool Architectural and Archaeological Society, Thirteenth Session* (28 November 1860), p. 33.

16 *Proceedings of the Liverpool Architectural and Archaeological Society, Twenty-First Session* (13 January 1869), p. 105.

17 See J. Sharples, 'Seel's Building, Church Street, Liverpool', *True Principles, The Journal of The Pugin Society*, 3 (2004), pp. 34–36.

18 An advert in the *Liverpool Mercury*, 12 July 1869, p. 2, invites those wishing to rent offices in the building to apply to T. P. Jones 'on the premises'. The initials 'T. P. J.' are carved on the façade in a monogram.

19 Lancashire Record Office, Culshaw & Sumners papers, DDX 162, Box 88/95–100.

20 *Proceedings of the Liverpool Architectural and Archaeological Society, Twenty-Fourth Session* (1 May 1872), p. 107.

21 *British Architect*, 26 March 1875, p. 177.

22 *Building News*, 27 September 1867, p. 666, and 14 February 1868, p. 106.

23 Ibid., 14 February 1868, p. 105.

24 Ibid., 14 February 1868, p. 106 and 2 January 1874, p. 8.

25 R. Kerr, 'The Battle of the Styles', *Builder*, 12 May 1860, pp. 292–94.

26 *Liverpool Courier*, 7 January 1863, p. 6.

27 For instance at the Albany Building, Old Hall Street. See *Porcupine*, 6 January 1866, p. 380.

28 The most radical solution to the lighting problem was devised by Peter Ellis at his Oriel Chambers, Water Street, of 1864. The *Building News*, 7 February 1868, p. 90, described its style as 'lunar Gothic', but despite the dogtooth ornament on its stone piers, its projecting plate-glass bays look like nothing in medieval architecture.

29 For the Dingle houses see F. A. Conybeare, *Dingle Bank, The Home of the Croppers* (Cambridge, 1925). A photograph album of the houses is in the Liverpool Record Office, 920 MD 440/1.

30 For Childwall Hall, see E. Twycross, *The Mansions of England and Wales ... The County Palatine of Lancaster, Vol. III, Southern Division, The Hundreds of West Derby and Salford* (London, 1847), pp. 22–23.

31 An exception is the pair of houses dated 1835 at Nos. 2 and 4 Percy Street, oddly contrasting with the neighbouring Grecian terraces.

32 Lancashire Record Office, Culshaw & Sumners papers, DDX 162, Box 46/1–18.

33 Twycross, *Mansions of England and Wales*, p. 60; for Sands, see Walker Art Gallery, Liverpool, *Merseyside – Painters, People & Places* (Liverpool, 1978), II, p. 166.

34 Twycross, *Mansions of England and Wales*, pp. 55, 62.

35 A. B. Granville, *The Spas of England and Principal Sea-bathing Places – Midland Spas* (London, 1841), pp. 10ff.

36 Royal Institute of British Architects, *Catalogue of the Drawings Collection of the Royal Institute of British Architect: C-F* (Farnborough, 1972), p. 108.

37 Lancashire Record Office, Culshaw & Sumners papers, DDX 162, Box 35/55–60. The house does not appear to survive.

38 A. W. Pugin, *The True Principles of Pointed or Christian Architecture* (Oxford, 1969), pp. 51–52.

39 An undated drawing and lithograph by J. R. Isaac in the Liverpool Record Office, Hf 942.7214 ISA, are inscribed 'The residence of H. Sharples Esq, Broad Green'. They show a partly timber-framed building with mullioned windows, some with hood moulds. I am grateful to Dr Jennifer Lewis for confirming the possibility that this was a genuine sixteenth-century house.

40 Drawings in Lancashire Record Office, Culshaw & Sumners papers, DDX 162, Box 26/77–92.

41 Liverpool Record Office, 352 BUI/3/9, West Derby Urban District Council, Register of Building Plans, house in Sandfield Park for William Makin approved 13 June 1865. Additions by G. E. Grayson were approved 8 November 1881, and he may have designed the first phase too.

42 Liverpool Record Office, 352 BUI/3/2, Garston Urban District Council, Register of Building Plans, entry No. 276.

43 *Liverpool Daily Post*, 28 October 1899, p. 6.

44 *Building News*, 7 March 1890, p. 336.

45 See C. Cunningham and P. Waterhouse, *Alfred Waterhouse, 1830–1905: Biography of a Practice* (Oxford, 1992).

46 See L. Microulis, 'Gillow and Company's Furniture for a Liverpool Maecenas: John Grant Morris of Allerton Priory', *Furniture History*, 41 (2005), pp. 189–216.

47 Liverpool Record Office, *Catalogue of ... household furniture ... the property of John Swainson Esq, which will be sold by auction by Mr. Branch ... at the Mansion known as 'Elmswood', Mossley Hill, near Liverpool*, 9–14 October 1867.

48 For Bland, see *Liverpool Courier*, 9 April 1884, p. 5; for Duckworth, see *Liverpool Courier*, 29 October 1889, p. 8; for Morris, see *Liverpool Courier*, 24 June 1897, p. 4; for Bushell, see *Liverpool Courier*, 19 February 1887, p. 5; for Rayner, see *Liverpool Daily Post*, 13 January 1876, p. 5; for Swainson, see *Liverpool Daily Post*, 24 May 1879, p. 6. Belcher was a member of the Liverpool Conservative Club: see *Proceedings in Connection with the Ceremony of Laying the Corner Stone of the Liverpool Conservative Club*, 1882, p. v. In retirement in north Wales, Lyster was vice-president of the Ruthin Constitutional Club: see *Liverpool Courier*, 17 May 1899, p. 7.

49 *Liverpool Daily Post*, 24 June 1897, p. 2; *Liverpool Courier*, 21 February 1887, p. 4.

50 J. P. Baker, *The Story of Mosslake Hill* (Garston, 1935), p. 13.

51 B. G. Orchard, *A Liverpool Exchange Portrait Gallery: First Series* (Liverpool, 1884), p. 64.

52 *Builder*, 27 July 1867, p. 556.

53 Liverpool Record Office, 380 PWK/1/1/6, Vale to Walker, 25 February 1868.

54 St Stephen's, Gateacre, parish magazine, vol. LVI, no. 9, September 1949 and vol. LVII, no. 1, January 1950.

55 *British Architect*, 9 January 1874, p. 24. A little later, the Liverpool Conservatives arranged to establish a club in part of New City Hall Buildings (now Garland's night-club), a Gothic restaurant in Eberle Street designed by Edmund Kirby in 1876 (see obituary of Philip Eberle from the *Porcupine*, 3 March 1906, in Liverpool Record Office, *Biographical Notices of Liverpool Worthies 1879–1923*, vol. 5, pp. 10–12). A purpose-built Conservative Club in Dale Street eventually opened in 1883, designed by F. & G. Holme.

56 J. Mordaunt Crook, *The Rise of the* Nouveaux Riches: *Style and Status in Victorian and Edwardian Architecture* (London, 1999), pp. 40ff.

57 B. G. Orchard, *Liverpool's Legion of Honour* (Birkenhead, 1893), p. 688.

58 Unidentified obituary in Liverpool Record Office, *Biographical Notices of Liverpool Worthies 1879–1923*, vol. 14, p. 160.

59 *Liverpool Courier*, 21 February 1887, p. 4.

60 *Liverpool Courier*, 9 April 1884, p. 5.

61 *Oxford Dictionary of National Biography*, ed. H. C. G. Matthew and B. Harrison (Oxford, 2004).

62 Liverpool Record Office, 920 DUR 1/2, Holt family diary, 14 May 1848.

63 For India Buildings, see *A Brief Memoir of George Holt, Esquire, of Liverpool*, privately printed (1861), pp. 70–72. Designed by Joseph Franklin and built 1833–34, it was demolished in the 1920s to make way for the present India Buildings. Plans and elevations survive in Liverpool Record Office, Hf 942.7213 IND.

64 Alfred Holt (1829–1911) built Crofton in Sudley Road; Robert Holt (1832–1908) built 54 Ullet Road; and George Holt (1825–96) extended Sudley in Mossley Hill Road.

65 Liverpool Record Office, 920 KUR 1/1–30, diary of A. G. Kurtz, 23 April and 5 December 1886, and 15 April 1888.

66 Ibid., 6 March 1876, 10 February 1886 and 27 January 1890.

67 Ibid., 3 November 1882.

68 Ibid., 16 December 1876.

69 Ibid., 15 March 1878.

70 Ibid., 9 January 1869.

71 Lancashire Record Office, Culshaw & Sumners papers, DDX 162, Box 46/29–36.

72 Lancashire Record Office, Culshaw & Sumners papers, DDX 162, Box 41/30-50.

73 R. Hawthorne Lathrop, *Memories of Hawthorne* (London and Cambridge, MA, 1897), p. 228.

74 For Heywood, see *Liverpool Mercury*, 10 May 1877, p. 6.

75 Liverpool Record Office, 920 DUR 1/3, Holt family diary, 3 October 1858.

76 *The Parish Church of St Mary the Virgin ... A Souvenir Booklet to commemorate the 125th Anniversary of the Consecration of the present building in 1856* (1979), p. 2. The tower cost £4000, a third of the cost of the entire church.

77 *Builder*, 12 May 1860, p. 302.

78 P. Searby, 'Gladstone in West Derby Hundred: The Liberal Campaign in South-west Lancashire in 1868', *Transactions of the Historic Society of Lancashire and Cheshire*, 111 (1960), pp. 139–65.

79 Twycross, *Mansions of England and Wales*, p. 61, where the house is illustrated and described as being in 'the modern style'.

80 C. L Eastlake, *A History of the Gothic Revival*, ed. with an introduction by J. Mordaunt Crook (Leicester, 1970), pp. 340–42; H. M. Colvin and J. Harris, eds, *The Country Seat: Studies presented to Sir John Summerson* (London, 1970), pp. 252–61.

81 Illustrated in *Building News*, 13 October 1876, p. 368.

82 For example Rathmore and Mere Hall in Noctorum Lane. Drawings for these and similar houses are among the Edmund Kirby papers, Liverpool Record Office.

83 Liverpool Record Office, 920 KUR 1/1–30, diary of A.G. Kurtz, 7 February 1882.

84 *Building News*, 24 October 1884, p. 664.

85 Ibid., 15 May 1885, pp. 784–85.

86 Margaret Ismay's diaries in the National Maritime Museum contain much information about the design and furnishing of the house.

87 See note 41, above. I am grateful to Laura Microulis for confirming the date of Gillows' involvement

88 One of the original arches was revealed during building work in 2004.

Bibliography

A Brief Memoir of George Holt, Esquire, of Liverpool, privately printed (1861)

Aarsleff, H., *The Study of Language in England, 1780–1860* (London, 1983)

Ackerman, G. P., 'J.M. Kemble and Sir Frederic Madden: "Conceit and too much Germanism"?', in C. T. Berkhout and M. Mc. Gatch, eds., *Anglo-Saxon Scholarship: the first three centuries* (Boston, MA, 1982), pp. 167–81

Adeane, J. H., *The Early Married Life of Maria Josepha* [. . .] *Lady Stanley* (London, 1899)

Allott, M., ed., *Keats, The Complete Poems* (London and New York, 1970)

Anderson, R. and Bjarnason, J., trans., *Viking Tales of the North* (Chicago, 1877)

[Anon.], *A Narrative of the Voyage of the Argonauts in 1880* (Edinburgh, 1881)

[Anon.], 'Chaucer', *North British Review* 20 (1849), pp. 293–328

Backhouse, J., *The Bedford Hours* (London, 1990)

Backhouse, J., *The Isabella Breviary* (London, 1993)

Baily, J. L., 'Thomas Rickman, Architect and Quaker: the early years to 1818', unpublished PhD thesis, University of Leeds (1977)

Baines, E.,*The History of the County Palatine and Duchy of Lancaster*, 2 vols (London, 1870)

Baker, J. P., *The Story of Mosslake Hill* (Garston, 1935)

Baldass, L., *Jan van Eyck* (London, 1952)

Banham, J. and Harris, J., *William Morris and the Middle Ages*, Catalogue, Whitworth Art Gallery (Manchester, 1984)

Baring-Gould, S., *Iceland: Its Scenes and Sagas* (London, 1863)

Baring-Gould, S., *A Book of Folklore* (London, 1913)

Bates, D., '1066: does the debate still matter?' *Historical Research*, 78 (2005), pp. 443–64

Beadle, R., ed., *The York Plays* (London, 1984)

Beadle, R. and Meredith, P., eds, *The York Plays: A facsimile of British Library MS*

Additional 35290 (Leeds, 1983)

Bennett, J. Waters, *The Rediscovery of Sir John Mandeville* (New York, repr. 1971)

Benson, L. D., ed., *The Riverside Chaucer* (New York and Oxford, 3rd edn, 1987)

Berger, S., Donovan, M. and Passmore, K., eds, *Writing National Histories, Western Europe since 1800* (London, 1999)

Bergeron, D. M., ed., *Pageants and Entertainments of Anthony Munday: A Critical Edition* (New York, 1985)

Bergeron, D. M., *English Civic Pageantry 1558–1642* (London, 1971)

Biddick, K., *The Shock of Medievalism* (Durham, NC, 1998)

Bjork, R. E., 'Nineteenth-century Scandinavia and the birth of Anglo-Saxon Studies', in A. J. Frantzen and J. D. Niles, eds, *Anglo-Saxonism and the Construction of Social Identity* (Gainesville, FL, 1997), pp. 111–32

Bloch, R. Howard and Nichols, S. G., eds, *Medievalism and the Modernist Temper* (Baltimore, MD, 1996)

Blundell, H., *An Account of the Statues, Busts, Bass-Relieves, Cinerary Urns and other ancient Marbles and Paintings at Ince, Collected by H. B.* (Liverpool, 1803)

Boos, F., 'Victorian Response to *Earthly Paradise Tales*', *The Journal of the William Morris Society*, 5/4 (1983–84), pp. 16–29

Boullainvilliers, Henri comte de, *Essai sur la noblesse de France* (Rouen, 1732)

Braunfels, W., 'Vorwort', in W. Braunfels, ed., *Karl Der Große: Werk und Wirkung* (Aachen, 1965)

Brennan, M. G., 'The Book of Hours of the Braddyll Family of Whalley Abbey', *Transactions of the Historic Society of Lancashire and Cheshire*, 146 (1997)

Bresslau, H., *Geschichte der Monumenta Germaniae Historica* (Hannover, 1921)

Brethe de la Gressaye, J., ed., *Montesquieu, De l'Esprit des Loix*, vol. 4 (Paris, 1961)

Brewer, D., *Chaucer: The Critical Heritage*, 2 vols (London, 1978)

Briggs, A., *Saxons, Normans and Victorians*, Historical Association, Hastings and Bexhill Branch (1966); reprinted in idem, *The Collected Essays of Asa Briggs* (Brighton, 1985–91), vol. II, pp. 215–35

Brink, B. ten, *History of English Literature*, trans. W. Clarke Robinson (London, 1893), vol. 2

Britton, J., *The Beauties of England and Wales*, 19 vols (London, 1801–16)

Brizard, Abbé G., 'Éloge historique de l'abbé de Mably', in *Collection complete des Oeuvres de l'Abbé de Mably*, ed. l'abbé G. Brizzard (Paris, 1794–95), pp. 1–120

Brooke, X., *Mantegna to Rubens: The Weld-Blundell Drawings Collection* (London, 1998)

Brown Price, A., *Pierre Puvis de Chavannes, Catalogue, Van Gogh Museum, Amsterdam* (Zwolle, 1994)

Brown, A. T., *How Gothic came back to Liverpool* (Liverpool, 1937)

Bürger, G. A., *Leonora*, trans. J. T. Stanley(London, 1796)

Burke, T., *Catholic History of Liverpool* (Liverpool, 1910)

Butterfield, H., *Man on His Past* (Cambridge, 1955)

Callander Murray, A., 'Reinhard Wenskus on "Ethnogenesis", Ethnicity and the Origin of the Franks', in A. Gillett, ed., *On Barbarian Identity: Critical Approaches to Ethnicity in the Early Middle Ages* (Turnhout, 2002), pp. 39–68

Camille, M., *Mirror in Parchment: the Luttrell Psalter and the Making of Medieval England* (London, 1998)

Cantor, N., *Inventing the Middle Ages* (New York, 1991)

Cavill, P., Harding, S. and J. Jesch, J., eds, *Wirral and its Viking Heritage* (Nottingham, 2000)

Chambers, E. K., *The Medieval Stage*, 2 vols (Oxford, 1903)

Checkland, S. G., 'Economic Attitudes in Liverpool, 1793–1807', *The Economic History Review*, new series, 5/1 (1952)

Checkland, S. G., *The Gladstones: a Family Biography 1764–1851* (Cambridge, 1971)

Child, F. J., ed., *The English and Scottish Popular Ballads*, 5 vols (Boston, 1882–98)

Christensen, A. S., Cassiodorus, Jordanes and the History of the Goths (Copenhagen, 2002)

Chun, D., 'Collecting Collectors: the Liverpool Art Club and its Exhibitions', *Transactions of the Historic Society of Lancashire and Cheshire*, 151 (2002), pp. 127–49

Clopper, L. M., Records of Early English Drama: Chester (Toronto, 1979)

Colley, L., *Britons: Forging the Nation 1707–1837* (New Haven and London, 1992)

Cook, E. T. and Wedderburn, A., eds., *The Works of John Ruskin*, 39 vols (London, 1903–12)

Collier, J. P., *The History of English Dramatic Poetry to the Time of Shakespeare: and Annals of the Stage to the Restoration* (London, 1831)

Collier, J. P., ed., *Five Miracle Plays or Scriptural Dramas* (London, 1836)

Colvin, H. M. and Harris, J., eds, *The Country Seat: Studies presented to Sir John Summerson* (London, 1970)

Colvin, H. M., *A Biographical Dictionary of British Architects 1600–1840* (New Haven and London, 3rd edn, 1995).

Conklin Hays, R., McGee, C. E., Joyce, S. L. and Newlyn, E. S., eds, *Dorset/Cornwall*, Records of Early English Drama (Toronto, 1999)

Constable, W. G., *Richard Wilson* (London, 1953)

Conybeare, F. A., *Dingle Bank, The Home of the Croppers* (Cambridge, 1925)

Cook, M., *London and the Culture of Homosexuality, 1885–1914* (Cambridge, 2003)

Craig, H., *English Religious Drama of the Middle Ages* (Oxford, 1955)

Crane, R. S., 'The Vogue of *Guy of Warwick* from the Close of the Middle Ages to the Romantic Revival', *PMLA*, 30 (1915), pp. 125–94

Cunningham, C. and Waterhouse, P., *Alfred Waterhouse, 1830–1905: Biography of a Practice* (Oxford, 1992)

Darcy, C. P., *The Encouragement of the Fine Arts in Lancashire* (Manchester, 1976)

de Jong, M., 'Johann Friedrich Böhmer (1795–1863). Romanticus en rijkspatriot', in *Die Middeleeuwen in de negentiende eeuw* (Hilversum, 1996), pp. 63–72

de Lollis, C., *Alessandro Manzoni e gli storici liberali francesi della restaurazione* (Bari, 1926)

Dearing, V. A., ed., *The Works of John Dryden*, 7 vols (Berkeley, 2000)

Delany, S., 'Women, Nature, and Language', in S. Delaney, *Medieval Literary Politics: Shapes of Ideology* (Manchester, 1990), pp. 151–77

Dewing, H. B., ed., Procopius, *De Bello Gothico*, 7 vols (Cambridge, MA, 1914–28)

Dhanens, E., 'Het Raadselachtig van Ince Hall', *Medelingen van de Koninklijke Academie voor Wetenschappen, Letteren en Schone Kunsten van Belgie*, 46 (1985), pp. 26–59

Dibdin, T. F., *Reminiscences of a Literary Life* (London, 1836)

Dibdin, T. F., *The Bibliographical Decameron or Ten Days Pleasant Discourse upon Illuminated Manuscripts and Subjects connected with Early Engraving and Bibliography*, 3 vols (London, 1817)

Dillon, J., *Performance and Spectacle in Hall's Chronicle* (London, 2002)

Dobson, R. B. and Taylor, J., *Rymes of Robyn Hood: an introduction to the English outlaw* (Stroud, 1997), pp. 289–90

Dopsch, A., *The Economic and Social Foundations of European Civilization* (London, 1937)

Drescher, S., 'The Slaving Capital of the World: Liverpool and national opinion in the age of abolition', *Slavery and Abolition*, 9/2 (1988)

Dressen, W., 'Aufklärung, Sichtbarkeit: ex Oriente Lux: ein Werkstattbericht', in *Ex Oriente: Isaak und der Weisse Elefant: Bagdad-Jerusalem-Aachen: Eine Reise durch drei Kulturen um 800 bis heute*, 3 vols (Aachen, 2003), I, pp. 18–21

Dubos, J.-B. *Histoire critique de l'établissement de la monarchie françoise dans les Gaules*, 3 vols (Amsterdam, 1735)

Dufferin, Lord, *Letters from High Latitudes* (London, 1857)

During, S., *Foucault and Literature: Towards a Genealogy of Writing* (London and New York, 1992)

Eagleton, T., 'Tennyson: Poetry and Sexuality in *The Princess* and *In Memoriam*', repr. in R. Stott, ed., *Tennyson* (Harlow, 1996), pp. 76–86

Eastlake, C. L., *A History of the Gothic Revival*, ed. with an introduction by J. Mordaunt Crook (Leicester, 1970)

Edda Sæmundar hinns Fróda, 3 vols (Copenhagen, 1787–1828)

Edelman, N., Attitudes of seventeenth-century France towards the Middle Ages (New York, 1946)

Edwards, P. and Gibson, C., eds, *The Plays and Poems of Philip Massinger*, vol. 3 (Oxford, 1976)

Ellis, S., *Chaucer at Large: The Poet in the Modern World* (Minneapolis, 2000)

Elton, O., trans., *The Life of Laurence Bishop of Hólar in Iceland* (London, 1890)

Elton, O., trans., *The First Nine Books of the Danish History of Saxo Grammaticus* (London, 1894)

Ex Oriente: Isaak und der Weisse Elefant: Bagdad-Jerusalem-Aachen: Eine Reise durch drei Kulturen um 800 bis heute, 3 vols (Aachen, 2003)

Fabion, J. D., ed., *Power: The Essential Works of Michel Foucault* (Harmondsworth, 2002)

Falco, G., 'La questione longobarda e la moderna storiografia italiana', *Atti del primo congresso internazionale di studi Longobardi* (Spoleto, 1952), pp. 153–66

Fawcett, T., *The Rise of Provincial Art: Artists, Patrons and Institutions outside London, 1800–1830* (Oxford, 1974)

Fellows, J., '*Bevis redivivus*: The Printed Editions of *Sir Bevis of Hampton*', in J. Fellows, R. Field, G. Rogers and J. Weiss, eds, *Romance Reading on the Book: Essays on Medieval Narrative presented to Maldwyn Mills* (Cardiff, 1996), pp. 251–68

Ferris, D'Arcy, 'A Review of ye Pageant', in W. Harrison, ed., *Ripon Millenary (1886). A record of the Festival* (Ripon, 1892), p. 160

Finlay, W. and Rosenblum, J., eds, *Chaucer Illustrated: Five Hundred Years of the Canterbury Tales in Pictures* (New Castle, DE, and London, 2003)

Fisher, J. L. and Allen, M., 'Victorian Illustrations to Chaucer's *Canterbury Tales*', in W. Finlay and J. Rosenblum, eds, *Chaucer Illustrated: Five Hundred Years of the Canterbury Tales in Pictures* (New Castle, DE, and London, 2003), pp. 233–74

Fitzgerald, E., *Euphranor, A Dialogue of Youth*, in G. Bentham, ed., *Poetical and Prose Writings*, 7 vols (New York, 1967)

Foakes, R. A. et al., eds, *Coleridge, Collected Works* (Princeton, 1971–2001), vols 5 and 7

Foot, M. R. D. and Matthew, H. C. G., eds, *The Gladstone Diaries*, 14 vols (Oxford, 1968–94)

Foucault, M., *The History of Sexuality, Volume One: An Introduction*, trans. R. Hurley (London, 1981)

Fourquin, G., 'Éloge funèbre de Christian Courtois', in *Caratteri del saecolo VII in Occidente*, Settimane di Studio del Centro Italiano di Studi sull'Alto Medioevo 5 (Spoleto, 1958), pp. 61–72

Fowler, J., *Medieval Sherborne* (Dorchester, 1951)

Frantzen, A. J., 'Prologue: Documents and monuments: difference and interdisciplinarity in the study of medieval culture', in A. J. Frantzen, ed., *Speaking Two Languages: Traditional Disciplines and Contemporary Theory in Medieval Studies* (Albany, NY, 1991), pp. 1–33

Frantzen, A. J., *Desire for Origins: New Language, Old English, and Teaching the Tradition* (New Brunswick, NJ, 1990)

Freud, S., *On Narcissism, An Introduction*, Standard Edition, vol. 14 (1914)

Fuhrmann, H., *'Sind eben alles Menschen gewesen'. Gelehrtenleben im 19. und 20. Jahrhundert. Dargestellt am Beispiel der Monumenta Germaniae Historica und ihrer Mitarbeiter* (Munich, 1996)

Furnivall, F. J., ed., *Robert Mannyng: Handlynge Synne*, Roxburghe Club 61 (London, 1862)

Fustel de Coulanges, Numa Denis, 'De la manière d'écrire l'histoire en France et en Allemagne', *Revue des Deux Mondes* (1 September 1872), trans. A. Brown Price, *Pierre Puvis de Chavannes, Catalogue, Van Gogh Museum, Amsterdam* (Zwolle, 1994)

Fustel de Coulanges, Numa Denis, *Histoire des Institutions Politiques de l'Ancienne France*, vol. 2, *L'invasion franque et la fin de l'Empire*, ed. Camille Jullian (Paris, 1891)

Galbraith, V. H., ed., *The Anonimalle Chronicle 1333 to 1381* (Manchester, 1927)

Garlick, K., Macintyre, A. and Cave, K., eds, *The Diary of Joseph Farington*, 16 vols (New Haven, 1978–98)

Gasparri, S., 'I Germani immaginari e la realità del regno. Cinquant'anni di studi sui Longobardi', *Atti del 160 congresso internazionale di studi sull'alto medioevo* (Spoleto, 2003), I, pp. 3–28

Gasparri, S., 'L'Europa del Medioevo. Etnie e Nazione', in *Lo Spazio Letterario del Medioevo, 2. Il Medioevo Volgare*, ed. P. Boitani, M. Mancini and A. Varvaro, vol. I, *La Produzione del Testo* (Rome, 1999), pp. 17–56

Geary, P. J., The Myth of Nations: The Medieval Origins of Europe (Princeton, NJ, 2002)

Gentry, F. G. and Müller, U., 'The reception of the middle ages in Germany: an overview', *Studies in Medievalism*, 3/4 (1991)

Gillett, A., ed., *On Barbarian Identity: Critical Approaches to Ethnicity in the Early Middle Ages* (Turnhout, 2002)

Giornata Lincei per il centenario della nascita di Claudio Sánchez-Albornoz (Rome, 1995)

Godwin, E. W., 'What I noticed in passing through Manchester and Liverpool', *Building News*, 10 (July 1874)

Goffart, W., *Barbarians and Romans, A.D. 418–584: the Techniques of Accommodation* (Princeton, NJ, 1980)

Gomont, H., trans., *Geoffrey Chaucer: Poète anglais du XIVe siècle. Analyses et fragments* (Paris, 1847)

Gossman, L., *Medievalism and the ideologies of the Enlightenment: The world and work of La Curne de Sainte-Palaye* (Baltimore, MD, 1968)

Gough Nichols, J., *The Diary of Henry Machyn*, Camden Society OS 42 (1848)

Gough, R., *An Account of a Richly Illuminated Missal executed for the Duke of*

Bedford (London, 1794)

Graham, J. E., 'The Cataloguing of the Holkham Manuscripts', *Transactions of the Cambridge Bibliographical Society*, 4 (1968)

Granville, A. B., *The Spas of England and Principal Sea-bathing Places – Midland Spas* (London, 1841)

Graver, B. E., ed., *William Wordsworth, Translations of Chaucer and Virgil* (Ithaca, NY, and London, 1998)

Grierson, H. J. C., ed., *The Letters of Sir Walter Scott*, 12 vols (London, 1932–37)

Grossman, F., 'A Religious Allegory by Hans Holbein the Younger', *Burlington Magazine*, 103 (1961)

Hale, J., *England and the Italian Renaissance* (London, 1954)

Hallam, H., *Introduction to the Literature of Europe in the Fifteenth, Sixteenth and Seventeenth Centuries* (London, 1837–39)

Harding, S., *Ingimund's Saga: Norwegian Wirral* (Birkenhead, 2000)

Hardison, O. B. Jr, *Christian Rite and Christian Drama in the Middle Ages: Essays in the Origin and Early History of Modern Drama* (Baltimore, MD, 1965)

Härke, H., '"The Hun is a methodical chap." Reflections on the German tradition of pre- and protohistory', in Peter J. Ucko, ed., *Theory in Archaeology: a world perspective* (London, 1995), pp. 46–60

Härke, H., 'All Quiet on the Western Front? Paradigms, methods and approaches in West German archaeology', in I. Hodder, ed., *Archaeological Theory in Europe* (London, 1991), pp. 187–222

Harrison, W., ed., *Ripon Millenary (1886). A record of the Festival* (Ripon, 1892)

Hawthorne Lathrop, R., *Memories of Hawthorne* (London and Cambridge, MA, 1897)

Hazlitt, W., *Lectures on the English Poets, The Spirit of the Age* (1818; London, 1910)

Heinzle, J., *Modernes Mittelalter. Neue Bilder einer populären Epoche* (Frankfurt am Main, 1994)

Hemingway, S. B., *The English Nativity Plays* (1909)

Henderson, E, *Iceland; or The Journal of a Residence in that Island During the Years 1814 and 1815* (Edinburgh, 1819)

Herzman, R. B., Drake, G. and Salisbury, E., eds, *Four Romances of England: King Horn, Havelok the Dane, Bevis of Hampton, Athelston* (Kalamazoo, 1999)

Hill, C., 'The Norman Yoke', in C. Hill, *Puritanism and Revolution* (London, 1958), pp. 46–111

Hill, T., *Anthony Munday and civic culture: theatre, history and power in early modern London 1580–1633* (Manchester, 2004)

Hodder, K., 'Elizabeth Barratt and the Middle Ages' Woeful Queens', in L. J. Workman and K. Verduin, eds, *Medievalism in England* II, Studies in Medievalism 7 (1995), pp. 105–30

Hodgkin, T., 'Professor George Stephens', *Archaeologica Aeliana*, 18 (1895)

Holland, H., *Dissertatio medica inauguralis de morbis islandiæ* (Edinburgh, 1811)

Holland, H., 'Preliminary Dissertation on the History and Literature of Iceland', in Sir George Mackenzie, *Travels in the Island of Iceland in the Summer of the Year* 1810 (Edinburgh 1811)

Horne, R. H., ed., *The Poems of Geoffrey Chaucer Modernized* (London, 1941)

Hughes, Q., *Seaport; Architecture and Townscape in Liverpool* (London, 1964)

Hume, A., *The Antiquities Found at Hoylake in Cheshire* (London, 1847)

Hume, A., *Ancient Meols: or Some Account of the Antiquities Found near Dove Point, on the Sea-Coast of Cheshire* (London, 1863)

Hunt, T., *Building Jerusalem: The Rise and Fall of the Victorian City* (London, 2004)

Hunter, W. B., ed., *The Complete Poetry of Ben Jonson* (New York, 1963)

Irving, W., *Sketch of William Roscoe* (Liverpool, 1853)

James, M., 'Ritual, Drama and the Social Body in the Late Medieval English Town', *Past and Present*, 98–101 (1983), pp. 3–29

Jones and Company, *Great Britain Illustrated: Views of the Seats, Mansions, Castles etc of the Noblemen and Gentlemen etc* (London, 1829)

Jones, D. R., *The Origins of Civic Universities: Manchester, Leeds, Liverpool* (London, 1988)

Jones, S., *The Archaeology of Ethnicity* (London, 1997)

Jorgensen, L., Storgaard, B. and Gebauer Thomsen, L., *The Spoils of Victory: the North in the Shadow of the Roman Empire* (Copenhagen, 2003)

Judge, R., 'D'Arcy Ferris and the Bidford Morris', *Folk Music Journal*, 4/5 (1984), pp. 443–80

Judge, R., 'Ferrars, Ernest Richard D'Arcy de', *Oxford Dictionary of National Biography*, ed. H. C. G. Matthew and Brian Harrison (Oxford, 2004), s.n.

Kaiser, T. E., 'The abbé Dubos and the historical defence of the monarchy in early eighteenth-century France', *Studies on Voltaire and the Eighteenth Century* 267, ed. H. T. Mason (Oxford, 1989), pp. 77–102

Kelly, T., *A History of Adult Education in Great Britain* (Liverpool, 1970)

Kerr, R., 'The Battle of the Styles', *Builder*, 12 May 1860

Kittredge, G., *Chaucer and his Poetry* (Cambridge, MA, 1970)

Knowles, D., *Great Historical Enterprises* (London, 1962)

Kolve, V. A., *The Play Called Corpus Christi* (London, 1966)

Krapf, L., *Germanenmythos und Reichsideologie. Frühhumanistische Receptionsweisen der taciteischen "Germania"* (Tubingen, 1979)

Kren, T. and McKendrick, S., eds, *Illuminating the Renaissance* (J. Paul Getty Museum, Los Angeles, 2003)

Kren, T., ed., *Renaissance Painting in Manuscripts: Treasures from the British Library* (New York, 1983)

Kulikowski, M., 'Nation versus army: a necessary contrast?', in A. Gillett, ed.,

On Barbarian Identity: Critical Approaches to Ethnicity in the Early Middle Ages (Turnhout, 2002), pp. 69–84

Lancashire, A., London Civic Theatre: City Drama and Pageantry from Roman Times to 1558 (Cambridge, 2002)

Langland, William, *The Vision of Piers Plowman: A Critical Edition of the B-Text Based on Trinity College Cambridge MS B.15.17*, ed. A.V.C. Schmidt (London, 1995)

Latham, A. J. H., 'A Trading Alliance: Sir John Tobin and Duke Ephraim', *History Today*, 24 (1974)

Lawrance, H., *Historical Memoirs of the Queens of England*, 2 vols (London, 1838)

Levey, M., *National Gallery Catalogues: The Seventeenth and Eighteenth Century Italian Schools* (London, 1971)

Lockhart, J. G., ed., *Memoirs of the Life of Sir Walter Scott*, 4 vols (Paris, 1838)

Lombard, A., *L'abbé Du Bos: un initiateur de la pensée moderne (1670–1742)* (Paris, 1913)

Longfellow, H. W., *The Poetical Works of Longfellow* (London, 1904)

Lot, F., *Les invasions barbares et le peuplement de l'Europe. Introduction à l'intelligence des derniers traités de paix*: vol. 1, *Arabes et Maures – Scandinaves – Slavs du Sud et du Centre* (Paris, 1942))

Lot, F., *Les invasions barbares et le peuplement de l'Europe. Introduction à l'intelligence des derniers traités de paix*. Vol. 2, *Slaves de l'Est. – Finno-Ougriens. – Turcs et Mongols. – États issus de la décomposition des Empire du Centre et de l'Est* (Paris, 1937)

Lot, F., *Les invasions germaniques: La pénétration mutuelle du monde barbare et du monde romain* (Paris, 1935)

Love Peacock, T., *Maid Marian* (London, 1822)

Loyen, A., 'Resistants et collaborateurs en Gaule', *Bulletin de l'Association Guillaume Budé*, 23 (1963), pp. 437–50

Lumiansky, R. M. and Mills, D., eds, *The Chester Mystery Cycle*, Early English Text Society, ss 3 and 9 (London, 1974 and 1983)

Lumiansky, R. M. and Mills, D., *The Chester Mystery Cycle: Essays and Documents* (Chapel Hill, NC, 1983)

Lynn, M., 'Trade and Politics in Nineteenth-Century Liverpool: The Tobin and Horsfall Families and Liverpool's African Trade', *Transactions of the Historic Society of Lancashire and Cheshire*, 142 (1992), pp. 99–112

Mably, Abbé Bonnot de, *Observations sur l'histoire de France*, in *Collection complete des Oeuvres de l'Abbé de Mably*, ed. l'abbé G. Brizzard (Paris, 1794–95)

MacDougall, H. A., *Racial Myth in English History: Trojans, Teutons and Anglo-Saxons* (Montreal, 1982)

Malone, E., *An Historical Account of the Rise and Progress of the English Stage* (London, 1790)

Malone, E., *The Plays and Poems of William Shakespeare... A Life of the Poet and the Enlarged History of the Stage* (London, 1821), vol. 3

Marillier, H. C., *The Liverpool School of Painters; an account of the Liverpool Academy from 1810 to 1867, with memoirs of the principal artists* (London, 1904)

Markland, J. H., *Chester Mysteries: De Deluvio Noe: De Occisione Innocentium* (London, 1818)

Markland, J. H., *A Dissertation on the Chester Mysteries* (London, 1818)

Martin, L. C., 'Oliver Elton, 1861-1945', *Proceedings of the British Academy*, 31 (1945), pp. 317–34

Matthew, H. C. G. and Harrison, B., eds, *Oxford Dictionary of National Biography* (Oxford, 2004)

Matthews, D., 'What was Medievalism?: Medieval Studies, Medievalism, and Cultural Studies', in R. Evans et al., eds, *Medieval Cultural Studies: Essays to Celebrate the Work of Stephen Knight* (Cardiff, 2006), pp. 9–22

Maurer, O. Jr, 'William Morris and the Poetry of Escape', in H. Davis, W. C. Devane and R. C. Bald, eds, *Nineteenth-Century Studies* (Ithaca, NY, 1940), pp. 246–76

Maurice, F. D., *Chapters from English History on the Representation and Education of the People* (London, 1866)

Maxwell, Sir H., ed., *The Creevey Papers. A Selection from the Correspondence and Diaries of Thomas Creevey, M.P. born 1768- died 1838*, 2 vols (London, 1904)

McIntyre, P., 'Historical Sketch of the Liverpool Library', *Transactions of the Historic Society of Lancashire and Cheshire*, 9 (1857)

McKisack, M., *Medieval History in the Tudor Age* (London, 1971)

McMullan, G., ed., William Shakespeare and John Fletcher, *Henry VIII (All is True)* (London, 2000)

Macnaughton, D., *Roscoe of Liverpool, his life, writings and treasures* (Birkenhead, 1996)

Metzger, D., Verduin, K. and Workman, L. J., 'Editorial', *Studies in Medievalism* 9.1 (1997)

Microulis, L., 'Gillow and Company's Furniture for a Liverpool Maecenas: John Grant Morris of Allerton Priory', *Furniture History*, 41 (2005), pp. 189–216

Milford, H. S., ed., *Poetical Works of Leigh Hunt* (London, 1923)

Mills, D., 'Where Have All the Players Gone? A Chester Problem', *Early Theatre*, 1 (1998), pp. 129–37

Montesquieu, Charles de Secondat, baron de, *De l'Esprit des Loix*, ed. J. Brethe de la Gressaye, 4 vols (Paris, 1950–61)

Mordaunt Crook, J., *The Rise of the Nouveaux Riches: Style and Status in Victorian and Edwardian Architecture* (London, 1999)

Morris, M., ed., *William Morris, Collected Works*, 24 vols (London, 1910)

Morris, E. and Evans, M., *Supplementary Foreign Catalogue, Walker Art*

Gallery, Liverpool (Liverpool, 1984)

Morris, E. and Hopkinson, M., *Foreign Catalogue, Walker Art Gallery, Liverpool* (Liverpool, 1977)

Munby, A. N. L., *Connoisseurs and Medieval Miniatures* (Oxford, 1972)

Munby, A. N. L., *Phillipps Studies: The Formation of the Phillipps Library*, 5 vols (Cambridge, 1951–60)

Munday, A., et al., *The First Part of the True and Honorable Historie, of the Life of Sir Iohn Old-castle, the good Lord Cobham* (London, 1600)

Munday, A., *Metropolis Coronata, The Triumph of Ancient Drapery* (London, 1615)

Munford, W. A., *William Ewart* (London, 1960)

Muratori, L. A., *Antiquitates Italicæ medii ævi*, 6 vols (Milan, 1738–42)

Muratori, L. A., *Rerum Italicarum scriptores ab anno 500 ad 1500*, ed. F. Argellati, 25 vols (Milan, 1723–51)

Murphy, G., *William Roscoe: His early ideals and influence* (Liverpool, privately printed, 1981)

Murphy, M., 'Antiquary to Academic: the progress of Anglo-Saxon scholarship', in C. T. Berkhout and M. Mc. Gatch, eds, *Anglo-Saxon Scholarship: the first three centuries* (Boston, MA, 1982), pp. 1–17

Murray, E. K. M., *Caught in the Web of Words, James A. H. Murray and the Oxford English Dictionary* (Oxford, 1979)

Nashe, T., *The Anatomie of Absurditie* (London, 1589)

National Gallery of Art, Washington, *The Treasure Houses of Britain* (New Haven, 1985)

National Gallery, London, *Late Gothic Art from Cologne* (London, 1977)

Neumeyer, H., 'Geschichte der archäologischen Erforschung der Franken in Frankreich', in *Die Franken: Wegbereiter Europas* (Mainz, 1996), pp. 35–42

Neve, M., 'Science in a Commercial City: Bristol 1820–60', in I. Inkster and J. Morrell, eds, *Metropolis and Province: Science in British Culture, 1780–1850*, (London, 1983)

Newton, A. W., *An Index to the Proceedings of the Liverpool Literary and Philosophical Society* (Liverpool, 1912)

Nicolet, C., *La fabrique d'une nation: La France entre Rome et les Germains* (Paris, 2003)

Northcote Parkinson, C., *The Rise of the Port of Liverpool* (Liverpool, 1952)

O'Connell, M., *The Idolatrous Eye: Iconoclasm and Theater in Early Modern England* (London, 2000)

Oergel, M., 'The redeeming Teuton: nineteenth-century notions of the "Germanic" in England and Germany', in G. Cubitt, ed., *Imagining Nations* (Manchester, 1998), pp. 75–91

Orchard, B. G., *A Liverpool Exchange Portrait Gallery: First Series* (Liverpool, 1884)

Orchard, B. G., *Liverpool's Legion of Honour* (Birkenhead, 1893)

Parrot, H., *The Mastive, or Young-Whelpe of the Olde-Dogge: Epigrams and Satyrs* (London, 1615)

Pattison, R., *Tennyson and Tradition* (Cambridge, MA, 1979)

Peacham, H., *The Compleat Gentleman* (London, 1622)

Pearsall, D., ed., *The Floure and the Lefe and the Assembly of Ladies*, TEAMS Middle English Texts (Kalamazoo, 1990)

Pegge, S., 'Memoir on the Story of Guy Earl of Warwick', *Bibliotheca Topographica Britannica*, vol. 4: *Antiquities in Bedfordshire, Berkshire, Derbyshire, Northamptonshire, Staffordshire, and Warwickshire* (London, 1790)

Phillips, H., 'Chaucer and the Nineteenth-Century City', in A. Butterfield, ed., *Chaucer and the City* (Cambridge, 2006), pp. 193–210

Phillips, H. and Havely, N., eds, *Chaucer's Dream Poetry* (Harlow, 1996)

Picton, J. A., 'On Sanskrit Roots and English Derivations', *Proceedings of the Liverpool Literary and Philosophical Society*, 18 (1864), pp. 31–64

Picton, J. A., 'On Social Life among the Teutonic Races in Early Times', *Proceedings of the Liverpool Literary and Philosophical Society*, 22 (1868), pp. 68–98

Picton, J. A., 'Our Mother Tongue and Its Convenors', *Proceedings of the Liverpool Literary and Philosophical Society*, 23 (1869), pp. 52–84

Picton, J. A., *Memorials of Liverpool*, 2 vols (London, 1875)

Picton, J. A., *Sir James A. Picton, A Biography* (London, 1891)

Pohl, W., 'Ethnicity, Theory, and Tradition: a Response', in A. Gillett, ed., *On Barbarian Identity: Critical Approaches to Ethnicity in the Early Middle Ages* (Turnhout, 2002), pp. 221–39

Ponzi, F., *Ísland á átjándu öld* (Reykjavík, 1987)

Prosser, E., *Drama and Religion in the English Mystery Plays*, Stanford Studies in Language and Literature 23 (Stanford, 1961)

Pugin, A. W. N., *The True Principles of Pointed or Christian Architecture* (Oxford, 1969)

Pugin, A. W. N., *The Collected Letters of A. W. N. Pugin*, ed. M. Belcher, 2 vols (Oxford, 2001–)

Puttenham, G., *The Arte of English Poesie* (London, 1589)

Ramsay Muir, J., *A History of Liverpool* (London, 1907)

Rask, R., *A Grammar of the Icelandic or Old Norse Tongue*, trans. G. Webbe Dasent (London and Frankfurt, 1843)

Reid, R. C., *Annals of the Tobin Family of Liverpool and the Isle of Man* (1940)

Reitlinger, G., *The Economics of Taste*, 3 vols (London, 1961–70)

Rerum britannicarum medii aevi scriptores; or Chronicles and memorials of Great Britain and Ireland during the Middle Ages. Published by the authority of the Lords Commissioners of Her Majesty's Treasury, under the direction of the Master of the Rolls, 99 vols in 253 (London, 1858–96)

Reynolds, J. H., *Poetry and Prose* (London, 1928)

Ricks, C., ed., *Poems of Tennyson*, 3 vols (Harlow, 1987)

Ridé, J., 'Un grand projet patriotique: Germania Illustrata', *L'humanisme allemand (1480–1540)*, XVIIIe colloque international de Tours (Munich, 1979), pp. 99–111

Ridé, J., *L'image du Germain dans la pensée et la littérature allemandes, de la redécouverte de Tacite à la fin du XVIe siècle* (Paris, 1977)

Rinaker, C., *Thomas Warton: a Biographical and Critical Study*, University of Illinois Studies in Language and Literature 2:1 (Urbana, IL, 1916)

Ritson, J., *Robin Hood: A Collection of all the Ancient Poems, Songs and Ballads Now Extant Relative to the Celebrated English Outlaw (To Which Are Prefixed Historical Anecdotes of His Life)*, 2 vols (London, 1795)

Robinson, D., 'The Kelmscott Chaucer', in W. Finlay and J. Rosenblum, eds, *Chaucer Illustrated: Five Hundred Years of the Canterbury Tales in Pictures* (New Castle, DE, and London, 2003), pp. 275–310

Roscoe, H., *The Life of William Roscoe*, 2 vols (London, 1833)

Roscoe, W., *An Address delivered before the Proprietors of the Botanic Garden in Liverpool, previous to the opening of the Garden, May 3rd, 1803* (Liverpool, 1802)

Roscoe, W., *On the Origin and Vicissitudes of Literature, Science and Art and their Influence on the present State of Society: A discourse delivered at the Opening of the Liverpool Royal Institution* (Liverpool, 1817)

Roscoe, W., *The Life of Lorenzo de Medici called the Magnificent*, 10th edn, (London, 1889)

Ross, M. Clunies, *The Norse Muse in England, 1750–1820* (Trieste, 1998)

Rosson, J., 'On Ecclesiastical Architecture, particularly with reference to Liverpool', *Transactions of the Liverpool Polytechnic Society for the years 1844–46* (Liverpool, 1846)

Rowlands, S., *The Famovs Historie, of Guy Earle of Warwicke* (London, 1607)

Rowlands, S., 'A Drvnkards Duello', *[A Paire of Spy-Knaues]* (London, 1613?)

Royal Institute of British Architects, *Catalogue of the Drawings Collection of the Royal Institute of British Architect: C-F* (Farnborough, 1972)

Russell-Cotes Art Gallery and Museum, Bournemouth, *Paintings from Lulworth Castle* (Bournemouth, 1967).

Said, E., *Orientalism. Western Conceptions of the Orient* (London, 1979)

Salter, F. M., *Medieval Drama in Chester* (Toronto, 1955)

Schoenbaum, S., *Shakespeare's Lives* (Oxford, 2nd edn, 1993)

Scott, G. G., *Remarks on Secular & Domestic Architecture, Present & Future* (London, 2nd edn 1858)

Scott, Sir W., ed., *The Collected Poems of Anna Seward*, 3 vols (Edinburgh, 1810)

Searby, P., 'Gladstone in West Derby Hundred: The Liberal Campaign in Southwest Lancashire in 1868', *Transactions of the Historic Society of Lancashire and Cheshire*, 111 (1960), pp. 139–65

Selincourt, E. de, ed., *William Wordsworth, Poetical Works* (Oxford, 1944)

Sellers, I., 'William Roscoe, the Roscoe Circle and Radical Politics in Liverpool 1787–1807', *Transactions of the Historic Society of Lancashire and Cheshire*, 120 (1968)

Sephton, J., *Queen's College, Liverpool. Inaugural Lecture of the Tenth Session, Delivered at the Conversazione, January 11, 1867* (Liverpool, 1867)

Sephton, J., *Thor and His Sway* (Liverpool, 1887)

Sephton, J., *The Religion of the Eddas and Sagas* (Liverpool, 1892)

Sephton, J., 'Translation of The Saga of Frithiof the Fearless', *Proceedings of the Liverpool Literary and Philosophical Society*, 48 (1894), pp. 69–87

Sephton, J., trans., *The Saga of Olaf Tryggwason* (London, 1895)

Sephton, J., trans., *Sverrissaga. The Saga of King Sverri of Norway* (London, 1899)

Sephton, J., 'Notes on the South Lancashire Place-Names in Domesday Book', *Otia Merseiana*, 4 (1904), pp. 65–74

Sephton, J., 'On the Study of Icelandic', *The Library*, 3rd series, 12.3 (1912), pp. 385–411

Severs, J. Burke, ed., *A Manual of the Writings in Middle English* 1050–1500, fascicule 1 (New Haven, 1967)

Sewter, C. A., *The Stained Glass of William Morris and his Circle* (New Haven, 1974)

Shahar, S., *Childhood in the Middle Ages* (London, 1990)

Sharples, J., 'Seel's Building, Church Street, Liverpool', *True Principles, The Journal of The Pugin Society*, 3 (2004)

Shaw, C. and Chase, M., *The Imagined Past: History and Nostalgia* (Manchester, 1989)

Shippey, T., 'A Revolution Reconsidered: Mythography and Mythology in the Nineteenth Century', in T. Shippey, ed., *The Shadow Walkers: Jacob Grimm's Mythology of the Monstrous* (Tempe, AZ, 2005), pp. 1–28

Shurley, J. (?) 'SJ', 'prefatory epistle', *The Famous and Renowned History of Sir Bevis of Hampton* (London, 1689)

Simon, R., *Un révolté du Grand Siècle: Henri de Boulainviller* (Lille, 1940)

Simons, J., 'Romance in the Eighteenth-Century Chapbook', in J. Simons, ed., *From Medieval to Medievalism* (Basingstoke, 1992), pp. 122–43

Simpson, J., 'Chaucer's Presence and Absence, 1400–1550', in P. Boitani and J. Mann, eds, *The Cambridge Companion to Chaucer* (Cambridge, 2nd edn, 2003), pp. 251–69

Smith, C., 'A Marriage of Convenience: Walter Crane and the Wallpaper Industry', in G. Smith and S. Hyde, eds, *Walter Crane: Artist, Designer, Socialist,* Catalogue, Whitworth Art Gallery (London, 1989)

Smith, R. J., *The Gothic Bequest* (Cambridge, 1987)

Southey, R., ed., *The Byrth, Lyf, and Actes of Kyng Arthur*, 2 vols (London, 1817)

Southworth, E., 'The Ince Blundell Collection', *Journal of the History of*

Collections, 3 (1991)

Spiker, S. H., *Travels through England, Wales and Scotland in* 1816 (London, 1820),

Spufford, M., *Small Books and Pleasant Histories: Popular Fiction and its Readership in Seventeenth-Century England* (London, 1981)

Spurgeon, C. F. E., *Five Hundred Years of Chaucer Criticism and Allusion, 1357–1900*, 3 vols (Cambridge, 1925)

Staab, F., 'Die Franken: Wegbereiter Europas', in *Die Franken: Wegbereiter Europas* (Mainz, 1996), pp. 10–22

Stafford, P., 'Women and the Norman Conquest', *Transactions of Royal Historical Society*, ser. 6, vol. 4 (1994), pp. 221–49

Stafford, W., '"This once happy country": nostalgia for pre-modern society', in C. Shaw and M. Chase, eds, *The Imagined Past* (Manchester, 1989), pp. 33–46

Stanley, J. T., 'An Account of the Hot Springs in Iceland with an Analysis of their Waters', *Transactions of the Royal Society of Edinburgh*, 3 (1794), pp. 127–37, 138–53

Steindór Steindórsson, trans., *Íslandslei angur Stanleys 1789: Fer abók* (Reykjavík, 1979)

Stephens, G., ed. and trans., *Frithiof's Saga: A Legend of Norway* (Stockholm and London, 1839)

Stephens, G., ed., *Ett Forn-Svenskt Legendarium*, 2 vols (Stockholm, 1847–58)

Stephens, G., '"English" or "Anglo-Saxon"', *The Gentleman's Magazine*, 36 (1852), pp. 323–27, 472–76

Stephens, G., ed., *Two Leaves of King Waldere's Lay* (London and Cheapinghaven [Copenhagen], 1860)

Stephens, G., ed., *Ghost Thanks, or the Grateful Unburied [Sir Amadace]* (London and Cheapinghaven [Copenhagen], 1860)

Stephens, G., *Handbook of the Old-Northern Runic Monuments of Scandinavia and England* (Edinburgh and Cheapinghaven [Copenhagen], 1884)

Stephens, G., *Er Engelsk et tysk Sprog?* (Copenhagen, 1890)

Stephens, G., et al., eds, *The Old-Northern Runic Monuments of Scandinavia and England*, 4 vols (London and Cheapinghaven [Copenhagen], 1866–1901)

Stobart, J., 'Culture versus Commerce: societies and spaces for elites in eighteenth-century Liverpool', *Journal of Historical Geography*, 28 (2002)

Storey, C., 'Myths of the Medici: William Roscoe and Renaissance Historiography', unpublished PhD thesis, University of Oxford (2003)

Story, R., 'Class and Culture in Boston: The Athenaeum, 1807–1860', *American Quarterly*, 27/2 (1975)

Strachan, J., ed., *Leigh Hunt, Selected Writings*, 6 vols (London, 2003)

Strong, W., *Frithiof's Saga: A Scandinavian Legend of Royal Love* (London, 1833)

Stukeley, W., *Palaeographia Britannica: or discourses on antiquities in Britain,*

Nos 1–3 (London, 1743–52)

Suhm, P. F., ed., *Kristni-Saga, sive historia religionis Christianæ in Islandiam introductæ* (Copenhagen, 1773)

Sweet, R., The Antiquaries, The Discovery of the Past in Eighteenth-century Britain (London and New York, 2004)

Thierry, A., *Narratives of the Merovingian era; or, Scenes of the sixth century: the historical essays* (London, 1845)

Thompson Yates, S. A., *Memoirs of the Family of the Reverend John Yates* (Liverpool, 1890)

Thornton, R. D., *James Currie, The Entire Stranger and Robert Burns* (Edinburgh, 1963)

Trappes-Lomax, R., 'Boys at Liège Academy 1773–91', *Catholic Record Society*, 13 (1913)

Travis, P. W., *Dramatic Design in the Chester Cycle* (Chicago, 1982)

Trevelyan, G. M., ed., 'The Poetry of Chaucer', *Poetical Works* (London, 1919)

Twycross, E., *The Mansions of England and Wales … The County Palatine of Lancaster*, Vol. III, *Southern Division, The Hundreds of West Derby and Salford* (London, 1847)

Utz, R. and Shippey, T., eds., *Medievalism in the Modern World. Essays in Honour of Leslie J. Workman* (Turnhout, 1998)

Vaughan, G., 'Henry Blundell's Sculpture Collection at Ince Hall', in *Patronage and Practice: Sculpture on Merseyside* (Tate Gallery, London, 1989)

Verduin, K., 'Preface', *Studies in Medievalism* 8 (1996), pp. 1–2

Viga-Glums saga sive Vita Viga-Glum ([Various editors] (Copenhagen, 1786)

Vincent, J., ed.,*The Diaries of Edward Henry Stanley, fifteenth Earl of Derby, between 1869 and 1878*, Camden Fifth Series, 4 (1994)

Violante, C., *La fine della 'grande illusione'. Uno storico europeo tra guerra e dopoguerra, Henri Pirenne (1914–1923): Per una rilettura della "Histoire de l'Europe"* (Bologna, 1997)

Voltaire, 'Questions sur l'Encyclopédie, s.v. Lois (Esprit des)', in idem, *Dictionnaire philosophique* (Paris, 1816)

Waagen, G., *Treasures of Art in Great Britain*, 3 vols (London, 1854)

Waagen, G., *Works of Art and Artists in England*, 3 vols (London, 1838)

Wainwright, C. and Wood, L., eds, *George Bullock: Cabinet Maker* (London, 1988)

Walker Art Gallery, Liverpool, *Merseyside – Painters, People & Places* (Liverpool, 1978)

Walker Art Gallery, Liverpool, *Pictures from Ince Blundell Hall* (Liverpool, 1960)

Wallace, J., *A General and Descriptive History of the Ancient and Present State of the Town of Liverpool* (Liverpool, 1797)

Walsh, B., *The Sequel to Catholic Emancipation*, 2 vols (London, 1915)

Ward, A.W., *History of English Dramatic Literature* (1875)

Warton, T., *The History of English Poetry from the Close of the Eleventh to the Commencement of the Eighteenth Century*, 4 vols (rev. edn, 1824)

Watt, T., *Cheap Print and Popular Piety 1550–1640* (Cambridge, 1991)

Wawn, A., 'John Thomas Stanley and Iceland: The Sense and Sensibility of an Eighteenth-Century Explorer', *Scandinavian Studies*, 53/1 (1981), pp. 52–76

Wawn, A., 'James Six and the Court of Brunswick, 1781–2. Unpublished Translations, Poems and Letters', *Archiv für das Studium der neueren Sprachen und Literaturen*, 220.135 (1983), pp. 241–67

Wawn, A., 'Hundradagadrottninginn', *Saga: Tímarit Sögufélagsins*, 23 (1985), pp. 97–133

Wawn, A., ed., *The Iceland Journal of Henry Holland 1810* (London, 1987)

Wawn, A., *The Vikings and the Victorians: Inventing the Old North in Nineteenth-Century Britain* (Cambridge, 2000)

Wawn, A., 'The Post-Medieval Reception of Old Norse and Old Icelandic Literature', in R. McTurk, ed., *A Companion to Old Norse-Icelandic Literature and Culture* (Oxford, 2005), pp. 320–37

Wedgwood, A., 'Domestic Architecture', in *Pugin: A Gothic Passion*, ed. P. Atterbury and C. Wainwright (New Haven, 1994)

Wenskus, R., *Stammesbildung und Verfassung: das Werden der frühmittelalterlichen Gentes* (Köln, 1961)

Wilkins, P., *The Church of Our Lady and the English Martyrs, Cambridge* (Cambridge, 1995)

Williams, R., *Keywords* (London, 1976)

Wilson, A., 'Culture and Commerce: Liverpool's merchant elite c.1790–1850', unpublished PhD thesis, University of Liverpool (1996)

Wilson, A., 'The Cultural Identity of Liverpool, 1790–1850: the Early Learned Societies', *Transactions of the Historic Society of Lancashire and Cheshire*, 147 (1997)

Wilson, D. M., *Vikings and Gods in European Art* (Aarhus, 1997)

Withington, R., *English Pageantry; An Historical Outline*, 2 vols (Cambridge, MA, 1918, reprinted New York, 1963)

Wood, I. N., 'Gibbon and the Merovingians', in R. McKitterick and R. Quinault, eds, *Edward Gibbon and Empire* (Cambridge, 1997), pp. 127–32

Workman, L., 'Editorial', *Studies in Medievalism*, 1.2 (1982), pp. 1–5

Workman, L., 'Medievalism and Romanticism', *Poetica*, 39/40 (1994), pp. 1–44

Wright, T., ed., *The Chester Plays. A Collection of Mysteries Founded upon Scriptural Subjects and Formerly Represented by the Trades of Chester at Whitsuntide*, 2 vols (London, 1843–47)

Wülfing, J. E., *The Laud Troy Book: A Romance of about 1400 A.D*, Pt.1, Early English Text Society 121 (Oxford, 1902)

Young, K., *The Drama of the Medieval Church*, 2 vols (Oxford, 1933)

Zosimus, *Historia Nova*, trans. J. J. Buchanan and H. T. Davis (San Antonio, TX, 1967)

Zupitza, J., *The Romance of Guy of Warwick*, Early English Text Series, es 42, 49, 59 (Oxford, 3 vols rpt. as 1, 1966)